ENVIRONMENTAL PSYCHOLOGY

.iove: Lawrence
Erlbaum Associates,
1997

0863774814

Contemporary Psychology Series

Series Editor: Professor Raymond Cochrane
School of Psychology
The University of Birmingham
Birmingham B15 2TT, UK

This series of books on contemporary psychological issues is aimed primarily at "A" Level students and those beginning their undergraduate degree. All of these volumes are introductory in the sense that they assume no, or very little, previous acquaintance with the subject, while aiming to take the reader through to the end of his or her course on the topic they cover. For this reason the series will also appeal to those who encounter psychology in the course of their professional work: nurses, social workers, police and probation officers, speech therapists and medical students. Written in a clear and jargon-free style, each book generally includes a full (and in some cases annotated) bibliography and points the way explicitly to further reading on the subject covered.

Titles in the Series:

Psychology and Social Issues:
A Tutorial Text
Edited by Raymond Cochrane,
University of Birmingham and
Douglas Carroll, *University of
Birmingham*

Families: A Context for Development
David White and Anne Woollett,
University of East London

The Psychology of Childhood
Peter Mitchell, *University of
Birmingham*

On Being Old: The Psychology of
Later Life
Graham Stokes, *Gulson Hospital,
Coventry*

Health Psychology: Stress, Behaviour,
and Disease
Douglas Carroll, *University of
Birmingham*

Food and Drink: The Psychology of
Nutrition
David Booth, *University of
Birmingham*

Criminal Behaviour: A
Psychological Approach to
Explanation and Prevention
Clive Hollin, *University of
Birmingham*

Adult Psychological Problems
L.A. Champion, *Institute of
Psychiatry, London*, and M.J.
Power, *Royal Holloway University
of London*

Psychology in Sport
John Kremer, *Queen's University of
Belfast*, and Deirdre Scully,
University of Ulster

Psychology of Addiction
Mary McMurran, *Rampton
Hospital, Retford*

Gender, Sex and Sexuality
Gerda Siann, *University of Dundee*

Contemporary Psychology
Clive Hollin, *University of
Birmingham*

Environmental Psychology:
Behaviour and Experience in
Context
Tony Cassidy, *Nene College,
Northampton*

Contemporary Psychology Series

Environmental Psychology
Behaviour and Experience in Context

Tony Cassidy
Nene College, Northampton

Psychology Press
Taylor & Francis Group
HOVE AND NEW YORK

First published 1997 by Psychology Press Ltd
27 Church Road, Hove, East Sussex, BN3 2FA

http://www.psypress.co.uk

Reprinted 2003
by Psychology Press
27 Church Road, Hove, East Sussex, BN3 2FA
29 West 35th Street, New York, NY 10001

Psychology Press is part of the Taylor & Francis Group

British Library Cataloguing in Publication Data
A catalogue record for this book is available from the British Library

ISBN 0–86377–480–6 (hbk)
ISBN 0–86377–481–4 (pbk)

ISSN: 1368–9207 (Contemporary Psychology Series)

Printed and bound in Great Britain by TJ International Ltd, Padstow, Cornwall

Contents

CHAPTER ONE

Environmental psychology: What it is and why you should know about it

The summer of 1995 was unusually hot, and lasted a longer period of time than is customary in the UK. It wasn't very long after the hot spell began that people began to complain about the heat and hints about water shortages began to appear in the media.

During the summer I was asked by local and national media to comment on stress on farmers, stress on holidaymakers, effects of commuting delays, the problem of noisy neighbours and problems in large housing estates. While on holiday in beautiful North Wales, my peace of mind was disturbed by news that a potential disaster had been narrowly averted at a nuclear powered electricity station nearby. During the same weekend I read of a father who had died as a result of an incident which had begun when his son went next door to complain about the noise being made by a neighbour. On my return I went to my office to discover that the building was being refurbished and the builders were in the process of removing all the suspended ceilings. All of these are examples of environmental factors impinging on human behaviour and experience. They are some of the subject matter of environmental psychology.

Box 1: Reflecting on the environment and you

Take a few moments to reflect on your experiences so far today. You might want to break the day down into specific experiences, such as travelling to work or college, your lunch break, etc., and to focus only on one specific period.

List all the ways in which factors external to you have influenced your thoughts, feelings and behaviours. You might include things that obstructed your progress, things that used up time you wished to use otherwise, pleasant experiences such as a pretty view (human or otherwise!), a positive interaction. In fact the list is endless.

Divide your list into factors to do with other people and factors to do with the physical environment.

Was it easy to separate the influences into social and environmental?

WHAT IS ENVIRONMENTAL PSYCHOLOGY?

In order to introduce any field of psychology it is common practice to begin with some sort of definition and, indeed, definitions are useful summaries of the basic principles of an approach. However it is also important to recognise definitions for what they are, i.e. over-simplified summaries. This poses a serious problem in a diverse area like environmental psychology since it can lead to the imposition of limitations on subject matter by setting rigid boundaries of the field. One of the lessons that applied psychologists have learned is that a narrow focus which draws only on knowledge and method in one field of psychology is likely to be ineffective. As a result you have the development of approaches which combine several fields such as the area of clinical health psychology, an amalgam of clinical psychology and health psychology. A second problem with definitions is that psychology is a living discipline which is continuously growing and changing as new research is produced. It therefore follows that definitions are likely to become outdated and need to be changed to reflect new developments. This is indeed the case with environmental psychology.

Towards a definition

Burroughs (1989) provides the following definition of environmental psychology as "the study of the interrelationships between the physical environment and human behaviour" . Gifford (1987) provides a similar definition: "environmental psychology is the study of transactions between individuals and their physical settings". An important aspect of both definitions is that they define the process as *reciprocal between the person and the environment*. In other words, not only does the environment influence the individual, but also the individual impacts on the environment. Both definitions are based on Lewin's (1951) famous equation:

$$B = f(P,E)$$

where B is behaviour, P is the person and E is environment. The equation states that behaviour is a function of the person, the environment and the interaction between the two and is referred to as a person-in-context approach to understanding behaviour. The basic perspectives in psychology tend to focus on one or other side of this equation in seeking causes for behaviour either in the person or in the environment. It is important to recognise that for Lewin it was not simply an additive effect of person and context. He argued that research should take account of the interaction, something that is accepted as the ideal by many but actually put into practice by few. An interactional perspective is a central principle of environmental psychology.

Both definitions above however focus exclusively on the physical environment in defining environmental psychology. This essentially reflects the roots of the field which had a fairly narrow focus on the effects of building design on behaviour (Ittelson, 1960; Osmond, 1957). In fact the field was initially called "architectural psychology" (Cantor, 1970). What might have been an adequate definition, reflecting the range of topics at the time, is limiting and misleading in the light of the later expansion of the field. A look at the contents page of any current text in the area reveals a much broader range of subject matter. Research into areas such as crowding, personal space, territoriality and urbanisation clearly include both the physical and social environment.

In addition, as we shall see later, understanding the influence of *physical* settings on behaviour is inextricably bound up with *social* aspects of the setting. In many cases the main effect of a physical setting on behaviour is through the meaning it has acquired from social interaction. A church in physical terms is just another building. However, people tend to behave in a particular way in a church because its function has been defined in social terms. One of the most prominent American environmental psychologists, Harold Proshansky, in the introduction to a text on environmental psychology (Proshansky, Ittelson, & Rivlin, 1976) concludes that "The physical environment that we construct is as much a social phenomenon as it is a physical one" (p.5). The French psychologist Claude Levy-Leboyer (1982) echoes this:

> The physical environment simultaneously symbolises, makes concrete, and conditions the social environment (p.15).

It would therefore seem appropriate to suggest that environmental psychology is as much concerned with the social environment as the physical environment and, although it may not be the major focus at all times it is unavoidably part of its subject matter.

Environmental psychologists have continuously identified this issue of the interdependence between the physical and social environment. As Bonnes & Secchiaroli (1995) suggest, there is currently general agreement that environmental psychology is no longer only concerned with the physical environment but rather with the socio-physical environment. They cite the work of Altman (1976) and Stokols (1978) in support of this.

Indeed this issue is partially responsible for the development of the concept of place by people like Cantor (1977) as a more holistic concept incorporating "units of experience within which activities and physical form are amalgamated".

If we were to summarise the discussion so far we could postulate a definition of environmental psychology as "the study of the transactions between individuals and their socio-physical environments".

The principles of environmental psychology

An alternative way in which we might define environmental psychology is to list its basic principles and provide a list of topics or issues to which it has directed attention. We will first turn our attention to the basic principles and in later chapters we will sample a selection of areas which have been researched by environmental psychologists. The basic principles of a field outline the *basic assumptions* or *philosophy of behaviour* of psychologists who work in the field and which determine the way in which they operate. This includes their *methodology*. The basic principles are summarised in Box 2 and will be discussed in more detail in the final chapter.

THE ROOTS OF ENVIRONMENTAL PSYCHOLOGY

A long history but a short past

The roots of environmental psychology as a separate field were put down in the 1950s although it wasn't until 1964 that the current title, environmental psychology, was introduced by William Ittelson at the Conference of the American Hospital Association in New York. In the intervening period it was variously called architectural psychology, psychological ecology, and ecological psychology, reflecting the multidisciplinary nature of its inspiration.

Box 2: The basic principles of environmental psychology

1. An interactional (or person-in-context) perspective: Behaviour is a function of the person, the environment, and the interaction between the two—(B=f(P, E).
2. An applied research focus in which there is an integration of theory and practice.
3. 'Multiple levels of analysis: All levels of analysis from individual to societal/organisational (micro/molecular to molar), are used, with a particular emphasis on the molar level.
4. A research base in the field, or natural environment. This is based on a recognition of the poor ecological validity or generalisation of laboratory research on human behaviour .
5. A multimethod approach: Qualitative and quantitative methods are used and in particular the usefulness of the full cycle model (see below) where basic and applied research can be used to complement and validate each other.
6. A model of the person as active rather than passive in interacting with the environment. This raises the issue of determinism versus freewill/autonomy. The person in environmental psychology is given some degree of autonomy.
7. An interdisciplinary perspective.
8. A holistic rather than a reductionist approach. To some extent this is contained within the societal level of analysis but goes further in recognising the limitations of breaking the environment or the person into small parts without reference to each other. A reductionist approach in this area is analogous to trying to complete a jigsaw from the individual pieces with no idea of what the complete picture looks like.
9. A systems model of the relationship between different aspects of the environment and behaviour. In other words the dynamic interrelationship between aspects of the environment is recognised and an awareness of how change in one part will affect others is part of the process.

In a more general sense psychologists have always been interested in the ways in which the environment influences behaviour and thus the history of environmental psychology is as long as the history of psychology itself.

For a variety of reasons, however, there has been a tendency to acknowledge that environmental factors play a causal role in behaviour, but not to follow this acknowledgement with serious research. In fact the environment referred to was more often than not the confines of a Skinner box or some other limited and highly controlled laboratory context. It is generally accepted that a turning point occurred with the ideas of Kurt Lewin (1890–1947) who developed some of the main principles upon which environmental psychology is based. Lewin's work is generally claimed to belong to the field of social psychology and it is within this field that we find the first serious stirrings of what was to become the separate field of environmental psychology.

The psychological roots

Lewin's legacy to environmental psychology can be subsumed under three of his major concerns: First, the interdependence of theory and application. Second, that research should be based on real world situations in terms of action research and his field theory. Third, his interactional model for explanation of behaviour and experience ensconced in his famous equation $B=f(P,E)$.

Kurt Lewin fled Germany to escape the persecution of Jews with the advent of the second World War and like many other Jewish academics, went to the USA. In just over a decade, working first at the University of Iowa and later at the Massachusetts Institute of Technology, he made some fundamental theoretical contributions to the application of psychology which provided direction for many applied psychologists and were farsighted in that they are considered up-to-date in modern psychology.

While not a prolific researcher himself, Lewin inspired many of his students who in turn became major figures in psychology. Among these were Roger Barker, Leon Festinger and Urie Bronfenbrenner. Lewin's theoretical contributions were many but three areas of focus are particularly important.

Person-in-context. Lewin was convinced that behaviour and experience can best be understood within an interactional framework. This is reflected in his famous equation $B=f(P,E)$ (see Box 2).

The interdependence of theory and practice. Lewin   was   disappointed by the way in which academic psychology was carried out, insulated from the real world, in the ivory towers of academia, while those applying psychology tended to ignore the theories of the academics. He felt that theory should be driven by social problems, and the following quote from a book published in 1951 exemplifies his position:

> The greatest handicap of applied psychology has been the fact that, without proper theoretical help, it had to follow the costly, inefficient, and limited method of trial and error. Many psychologists working today in an applied field are keenly aware of the need for close cooperation between theoretical and applied psychology. This can be accomplished

in psychology, as it has been accomplished in physics, if the theorist does not look toward applied problems with highbrow aversion or with a fear of social problems, and if the applied psychologist realises that there is nothing so practical as a good theory (Lewin, 1951, p.169).

Research located in the real world.   Lewin's concern for real world research was expressed in his field theory and his action research approach. His field theory provided a model for conceptualising research problems which incorporated person and situation variables in an ecological model of behaviour. His action research was an approach based on the assumption that the best way to understand behaviour was to try to change it.

These ideas provided a working model for applied research which, (a) was macro level and non-reductionist; (b) was problem focused; (c) utilised current theory; and (d) aimed to score high in ecological validity.

Though Lewin's ideas were not taken on board by most psychologists until the 1970s, they have tended to provide the core principles for environmental psychologists from the beginning.

Lewin introduced the term *psychological ecology* to describe his field of study and this theme was a source of inspiration to his students, Roger Barker and Urie Bronfenbrenner. It is reflected in Barker and Wright's (1955) work on ecological psychology, which is the direct forerunner of modern environmental psychology. Bronfenbrenner, though not generally described as an environmental psychologist, provided ideas on the ecology of behaviour which are increasingly being recognised as important in the practice of modern environmental psychology (Bonnes & Secchiaroli, 1995).

The architectural roots
While the direct psychological roots of environmental psychology lie in the work of Lewin and his students, there were also important influences from other fields. The use of the term architectural psychology reflects a trend which unites a number of workers who were concerned with the design of physical environments and subsequent influence on behaviour. In Canada, a psychiatrist (Osmond, 1957) contributed the initial ideas on sociofugal and sociopetal settings which describe the different ways in which seating can be arranged in large spaces and which will be covered in a later chapter (see Box 3).

His focus was on seating for patients in psychiatric hospitals and how the different arrangements encouraged or discouraged social interaction. This early work inspired the later extensive research on

---

Box 3: Sociofugal and sociopetal designs

Osmond (1957) coined the term sociopetal to describe settings that encourage interaction and sociofugal to describe situations that discourage it. Later psychologists such as Sommer (1969) restricted the terms to seating arrangements. The typical airport lounge or railway waiting room tends to be sociofugal in that seats are arranged around the perimeter or back-to-back. A sociopetal arrangement is where seating is face-to-face around small central areas such as tables (see Fig. 1). The latter tends to encourage people to talk to each other. Traditional day rooms in psychiatric institutions were sociofugal in that seating was arranged in straight rows with backs to the wall. As Sommer (1969) points out, this arrangement was preferred by; *"nurses because it made surveillance easier, by cafeteria staff because it provided a wider corridor for their food* carts, and by custodians because it left the appearance of orderliness" (Sommer, 1969). This arrangement deterred patient interaction and communication and reinforced the dependency culture which makes patient management and control easier. However, as Ayllon & Azrin (1968) demonstrate, this type of dependency inhibits rehabilitation. Experimentation using more sociopetal designs have produced major improvements in patient interaction, rehabilitation and reductions in patient violence (Luchins, 1988). Despite staff resistance improvements in staff mood and reductions in staff absenteeism have been reported; however this tends to be where staff morale was already high and the clientele were less difficult to start with (Devlin, 1992). This demonstrates the complex interdependence of factors in environmental research.

---

seating arrangements of the social psychologist, Sommer (1959, 1969). As early as the mid-1950s these ideas were being incorporated into the design of psychiatric hospitals (Izumi, 1957).

Magenau (1959) reports on attempts to draw on the physical, biological and social sciences in planning human environments, while Lynch (1960) discusses his own large-scale research on the effects of living in cities. These are just two of many examples of work in the 1950s in the USA which attempted to draw on psychology for environmental design.

In post-war Britain the social sciences became involved in architectural planning, some would suggest inspired by Churchill's famous statement, *"We give shape to our buildings and they, in turn, shape us"* (Bonnes & Secchiaroli, 1995). For a period in the 1940s government funding in the UK led to an increased psychological input to environmental design, though by the end of the decade interest had waned and funding was less forthcoming. For example Chapman and Thomas (1944) investigated the effects of lighting in homes, and

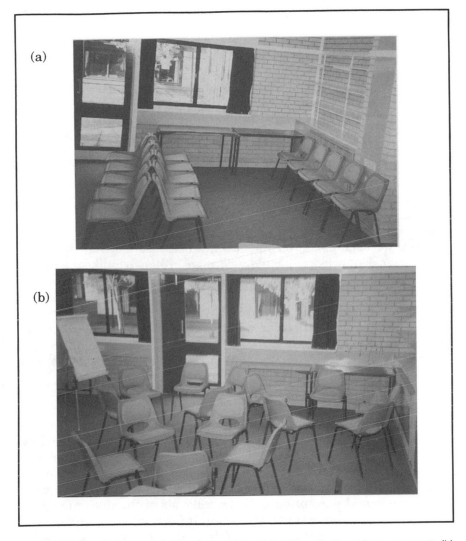

FIG. 1. Sociopetal and sociofugal arrangements of furniture. Sociopetal arrangements (b) enhance interaction while sociofugal arrangements (a) restrict social intercourse.

Hansard (1943) reports on social science involvement in the design of the new Houses of Parliament.

Interest in the area re-emerged in the 1960s and architectural psychology became popular again with one of the first European conferences on architectural psychology held in Glasgow in 1969. Several research units focusing on the evaluation of buildings and their human effectiveness were formed at British universities during the

1960s, but the two major contributors to the area were David Cantor and Terence Lee who joined forces at the University of Surrey as leaders of the environmental psychology group. The group had been formed by Lee who preferred the term environmental psychology. Cantor seems to have preferred the term architectural psychology in his early work (Cantor, 1970) and to have later adopted the terms the psychology of place (Cantor, 1977). The latter reflects his concern with the need for molar levels of analysis where environments are considered holistically. This relates to the integration of social and physical aspects discussed previously. The work of Cantor and Lee (Lee, 1976) reflects the blossoming of environmental psychology in the UK during the 1970s.

Though less well documented, the architectural theme was also emerging in Europe, generally supported by organisations such as the World Health Organisation (Baker, Davis, & Silvadon, 1960). In Sweden, for example, governmental interest also inspired the use of psychological knowledge in building design, although unlike the British experience, interest doesn't seem to have waned (Bonnes & Secchiaroli, 1995).

It is interesting that this architectural theme still continues in Britain and Europe, with the newsletter of the International Association for People–Environment Studies (IAPS), which is a European association, called the Architectural Psychology Newsletter. The term architectural seems to have been dropped in the USA.

The geographical roots

The relationship between the environment and behaviour can never be claimed as the sole domain of psychologists and, while the influence from architecture is the one most obvious in the field of environmental psychology, many other disciplines too have made a large contribution. Social geography is a case in point. Wright (1947) refers to the process of environmental perception when he talks about the role of imagination. The distinction between the physical world of cartographers and the world as perceived by individuals is the stuff of environmental perception, which is discussed later. But it was also the concern of those who would describe themselves as behavioural geographers (Gold, 1980) or those interested in perceptual geography (Downs & Meyer, 1978).

While behavioural geography does tend to oversimplify the psychological processes involved in perceiving, appraising or constructing the environment, attempts to understand the transactions between people and space bear many similarities to the work of eminent psychological theorists such as Gibson (1979) and Brunswick (1957). Behavioural geography flourished during the 1960s and 70s alongside environmental and architectural psychology, yet unlike the architectural domain there was never any real interdisciplinary work between psychologists and geographers.

Other disciplines closely associated with geography are environmental science and ecology which mainly concern themselves with environmental problems such as the use and abuse of physical resources. The rich data sources provided by research in these areas concerning trends in the use of resources and the transaction between people and their physical world generally have not really been tapped by psychologists who are also interested in these issues albeit with a difference in emphasis. The issues of pollution and environmental attitudes currently form a major area within environmental psychology. On the other hand understanding the transactions between people and environments in terms of environmental problems would seem incomplete without some psychological input.

The case of geography serves to remind us that at the level of application psychology must necessarily encroach on the territory of other disciplines. The lesson from the happy marriage between psychology and architecture should surely be drawn on in regard to other fields.

By any other name

Although research with a focus on person–environment relations only began to be gathered into a separate discipline (whether architectural or environmental psychology) in the 1960s, quite a lot of research which would now be recognised as environmental had been carried out long before. The widely known work by Roethlisberger & Dickson (1939) at the Hawthorne works of Western Electric in Chicago explored the effects of lighting and other aspects of environmental design on human behaviour. This work is generally reported in texts on work and organisational psychology, and quite a bit of early work in this field was concerned with person–environment relations.

A focus on the USA

Despite the international nature of the research discussed, the vast bulk of the research drawn directly on in environmental psychology has occurred in the USA, encouraged by political attitudes during the 1960s and 70s. However one must acknowledge the European influence on the field made by European psychologists such as Lewin who moved to the USA. It is arguably the integration of these European ideas with American pragmatism which has produced the most radical developments in applied psychology.

The international angle

In addition it is important to recognise that environmental psychology is currently alive and well in many countries throughout the world. It was only with Yamamoto's (1984) paper presented to the annual meeting of the American Psychological Association that a wider audience became aware of the work on environment–behaviour relations in Japan in the 1930s. In parallel with British and American developments, architectural psychology was developing in Japan in the 1950s and 1960s (Kobayashi, 1961). For example work on the effects of disasters has attracted quite extensive attention in Japan (Abe, 1982).

Environmental psychology is active in the former USSR, Sweden, the Netherlands, Israel, Australia, Turkey, Venezuela, Italy, and Mexico (Gifford, 1987). In Italy, for example, extensive work has been done on the effects of psychiatric institutions and has provided an example to the rest of the world in community treatment of mental illness (Orford, 1992).

The Zeitgeist

The development of any discipline is a function of a combination of many influences. The current knowledge base is only one of these factors, and perhaps one of the least influential. More important are social and political attitudes which determine the popularity of the discipline and, as a consequence, the human effort which will be exerted in its advancement. Part of this process is the funding of research and the employment of practitioners in the area. Since the early 1980s it would appear that funding for environmental research has not been a priority. Changes in political direction in the USA and Britain have led to alternative priorities. The concurrent growth in consumerism with major problems in depletion of resources in what are termed "third world countries" and increases in pollution have led to a growing concern with environmental issues. In fact as I write this in mid-February 1996, one of the main news headlines concerns another oil tanker which has been holed on rocks off the coast of Wales. Thousands of tons of crude oil are at this moment sweeping towards the coastline, threatening the wildlife and beaches.

The growth in technology has also brought with it problems of human-made disasters over the past 15 years (see Box 4). These areas form core concerns for psychological research.

THE PERSON IN THE EQUATION

Before going any further it is useful to consider some important aspects of the person in Lewin's equation. We will consider three areas of research which are important in explaining the ways people respond to

---

Box 4: A catalogue of disasters

Anyone living through the past 15 years in Europe cannot fail to be aware of the increased frequency and size of human-made disasters. While countries like the USA have experienced large-scale natural disasters in the form of earthquakes, volcanic eruptions, floods and wind storms, in Europe we have tended in the past to observe this type of suffering from a distance. Only in times of war did these events impinge on the European consciousness. However, with technological advances, particularly in transportation, we have come to experience these events on our own doorstep. Disasters such as Zeebruge, Hillsborough, the M1 plane crash, the Clapham rail disaster, the Piper Alpha oil rig disaster are some of the most prominent among a growing catalogue of events that have claimed lives and left a vast trail of human suffering in their wake. In the main these disasters have been attributed to a combination of human error and technological failure. The causes and consequences of disasters like these are discussed in a later chapter.

---

environments: *environmental perception* (how we actually perceive the context in which we live with its rich interplay of social and physical elements); *environmental appreciation* (the emotional or evaluative element in terms of how we feel about our environment); and *environmental personality* (based on the notion that there may exist stable traits reflected in our differential responses to different environments).

Interpreting the environment or environmental perception
Given that a person-in-context model is fundamental to environmental psychology, a good place to start a discussion of theory and practice is by looking at how the person sees their context, i.e. their environment. Through this we can build up a model of the person in environmental psychology. This is important because the basic assumptions that psychologists hold regarding the person in any field of psychology will set the boundaries for their theoretical perspectives and the research method they use. In turn these will determine the type of knowledge available and how that knowledge is applied.

The psychology of perception
How the person comes to understand and deal with the environment can be understood in terms of perception. The study of perception in cognitive psychology attempts to explain how we become aware of information in our environment, how we process that information and how we give meaning to that information which eventually leads us to

respond to it in one way or another. A vast amount of research has been carried out and a number of influential theories have been developed by people such as J.J. Gibson (1979), R.L. Gregory (1966) and U. Neisser (1976). Initially theories tended to be one of two types:

- Bottom-up theories, which focus on how the information itself and ultimately the environment determines our interpretation.
- Top-down theories, which focus on how our stored previous experiences influence our interpretation of new information.

It is generally accepted these days that any universal theory of perception must include both bottom-up and top-down processes (see Fig. 2 from Neisser, 1976, for an illustration).

It is difficult to conceive of a situation where the information itself and its context (the external or bottom-up aspects) will not be important in providing cues to aid our interpretation. For example let us look at the most underresearched sense modality—smell. If we were to become aware of a mix of exotic aromas while standing outside a Thai restaurant we would know the source was the Thai food being cooked inside.

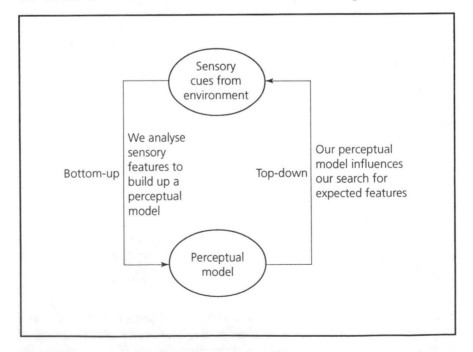

FIG. 2. The cyclical model of perception showing top-down and bottom-up processing from Neisser (1976).

However, we might be confused if we picked up the same smell in the middle of a deserted island. We require both the aroma and the context (the restaurant) in order to begin to give some meaning to the smell. But that is not the complete story. If we had never previously encountered this particular aroma we would be unable to give meaning to it. The memory of this aroma from the past is located internally and its use in helping to give meaning to the smell illustrates the top-down approach. Thus we can see both bottom-up and top-down processes interacting to give some sense of meaning to the experience. Previous experience will also be important in determining our emotional reaction to the smell.

Another example of the interaction of bottom-up and top-down processing can be seen in the area of vision. Although the light reflections that hit our retina are essential to seeing, it is true that ultimately we see with our mind. We can demonstrate this very simply by the visual illusion shown in Fig. 3. In this illusion, we see an overlaid triangle which in fact is not there because we add the information from our experience which leads us to expect a complete picture. This principle of *closure* (completing the picture) is central to Gestalt approaches to psychology. The Gestalt approach is based on the assumption that "the whole is greater than the sum of its parts". What makes the whole greater than the sum of its parts in psychology is generally the meaning given to the experience by the individual.

FIG. 3. The invisible triangle illusion.

From the vast store of research on the area, it can be concluded that, as we grow and develop, we encounter a wide range of information which increases in complexity with the complexity of encountered environments. We develop *cognitive schemata*, *blueprints*, or *cognitive maps* of our world, which guide our perceptual processes. The essential aspects of this guidance are *filtering of*, and *giving meaning to* incoming information from the environment. Filtering occurs at all stages in the process and determines what aspects we attend to, what aspects we store in memory, and ultimately the aspects to which we respond. Bottom-up aspects are also active in this filtering process, for example, attention will be influenced by aspects of the stimulus such as novelty, intensity, and movement. Any consistency over time within an individual's behaviour can be partly explained in terms of similarity or continuity between situations (the *environment* factor) and partly in terms of the development of particular *cognitive styles* reflecting stability in cognitive schemata—in other words, an enduring cognitive map of the world (the *individual* factor).

Perception of the spatio-physical environment

The process of research in cognitive psychology tends to be experimental, reductionist and focused on individual-level explanations. Environmental perception (a central area of environmental psychology), on the other hand, adopts a holistic approach which focuses on perception as a total process in the natural environment. The aim is to bring together the pieces gleaned from the reductionist, laboratory-based research in order to understand how we perceive the real world and from this understanding to devise ways in which we can improve it. It uses a multimethod approach with the ideal being the *full-cycle model* proposed by Cialdini (1980), where research begins with an initial analysis of the behaviour in its natural setting. The model devised from this initial analysis is then tested experimentally, and the results from the experimentation are then tested again in the natural setting. Modification of the model occurs at all stages as appropriate, particularly in adapting experimental explanations to the real world.

In making the transition from laboratory to the real world, the psychology of perception went through several phases. In the beginning there were the Gestalt theorists who focused on the phenomenological world rather than the objective world of the individual. This was challenged by the ecological theorists who focused on the physical environ- ment. Meanwhile the constructivist approach had evolved from the Gestalt roots. Eventually came the interactionists who tried to incorporate the phenomenological and the physical under the theme of transaction.

The Gestalt approach

The Gestalt school originated in Germany and was a very strong force in European psychology during the 1920s and 30s. Originating in the work of Köhler (1929, 1940), Koffka (1935) and Wertheimer (1944), it focused on the world that exists within the mind as opposed to the external physical and social environment. They talked of the 'phenomic' world which was what determined behaviour. The Gestalt school argues that studying aspects of the external environment is irrelevant since it is the picture of that external world that people have inside their heads which motivates and directs them. In other words, if I believe an overhanging rock is going to fall I will quickly get out of its way even if an expert on rock structures assures me that it won't fall. This discrepancy between what is and what we believe is what Allport (1955) described as the inside–outside problem in psychology. For the Gestaltists the solution to the problem was to see the inside as being dominant over the outside. Koffka (1935) described this internal or phenomic world as the behavioural *environment*, because it was here that we would find the causes for behaviour. One of their major pieces of evidence rested on the principle of closure which is demonstrated by the illusion in Fig. 3. We see the overlaid triangle, yet there is no physical evidence of it in the real world. In other words no matter how we measure the drawing we could never predict from it alone that the overlaid triangle would be perceived. Clearly what we see is often more than the sum of the physical or social elements that make up the external environment. An essential ingredient in the equation is the role of meaning.

The significance of meaning

Since the meaning given by the individual to experiences is central to the process of perception, any analysis must pay particular attention to the personal meaning. All too often research ignores the very simple rule embodied in the first principle of George Kelly (1955), who suggested, "If you really want to find out what is wrong with a client, ask them, they may tell you".

As the theorist who developed a true cognitive theory of the person 20 years before the "cognitive revolution", Kelly's ideas are important and we will return to his work later. It was in the Gestalt tradition that the roots of constructivism developed.

The ecological response

While we accept a role for the phenomic world it seems rather naive to suggest that the external environment doesn't matter. After all in the case of the illusory triangle, if the physical elements in the drawing didn't exist we wouldn't see the overlaid triangle at all. Someone who had a fear of flying once made a comment upon seeing an aeroplane fly overhead, "I wouldn't like to be up there in one of those". His companion responded, "I would much rather be up there in one of those than be up there without one".

Clearly the inside and outside in the perceptual dilemma both exist.

The ecological approach to perception developed in response to the Gestalt school, and is reflected in the work of Brunswick (1947, 1957) and Gibson (1950, 1979).

Brunswick's ecological validity

Brunswick's theory of perception is referred to as the lens model and is based on the probabilistic nature of the perceptual process. He was concerned with the ecological validity of perceptual cues and with the need to understand the outside or environmental aspect in perception.

> This preoccupation of the psychologist with the organism at the expense of the environment is somewhat reminiscent of the position taken by those inflatedly masculine mediaeval theologians who granted a soul to men but denied it to women (Brunswick, 1957, p.6).

Brunswick seems to have been particularly critical of Lewin's field theory concept of life space which he saw as a psychological rather than a physical environment. Lewin in return from his phenomenological position was critical of Brunswick's approach. Brunswick argued that environmental cues contain information which is more or less accurate in terms of representations of the external world. The perceptual processes sample these environmental cues and make probabilistic judgments about them which lead to the perceptual representation. Essentially he sees the process being driven from the bottom up, with the person reacting as a physiological organism. Elements of Brunswick's theory are similar to the more directly environmental approach of Gibson.

Gibson's affordances

Gibson's ecological theory is very much a bottom-up theory, with a focus on the fundamental properties of the external world in generating a perceptual repertoire. Gibson argued that all stimuli in the environment contain information and posed the central problem of perception research as determining how stimuli provide this information, what he called the "laws of stimulus information" (Gibson, 1950, p.702).

He rejected the simple single stimulus approach of much laboratory research and defined stimuli in a molar sense whereby persons perceive total environments and not just an accumulation of parts. Perception can then best be understood by analysing the information provided by the ecological environment. He argued that it was important to describe the process of perception but the process in question is to be found in "the invariants from the flow of stimuli" (Gibson, 1979, p.2), not in the sensory system. The organism is equipped with the physiological means to perceive, and this equipment responds to the information contained in the external world by producing a perceptual image. He saw this as being a physiological response to a physical stimulus which did not involve any construction on the part of the person. He saw meaning as existing in the physical environment in terms of affordances. As he says, "The affordances of the environment are what it offers the animal, what it provides or furnishes, either for good or evil" (Gibson, 1979, p.127).

Different environments offer different things to different species. A rigid, reasonably flat surface tends to offer (or afford) support. Gibson describes the qualities of a supportive surface as being stand-on-able, and not sink-into-able. These affordances exist irrespective of the presence of the person or animal. According to Gibson it is these affordances which determine perception.

There are numerous studies which support the Gibsonian model, perhaps the best known of which is the *visual cliff* (Gibson & Walk, 1960). As shown in the photograph (Fig. 4), this is an experimental situation which gives the illusion of a cliff edge, but in fact no cliff exists since the total surface is covered in a perspex sheet which affords support. Animals that walk from birth, such as sheep, will not venture beyond the edge from the first. Children will not venture beyond this as soon as they learn to walk. This is interpreted as evidence of an innate ability to respond to external stimuli. It is assumed that the young animals or children see the cliff edge before they have any store of experience in memory to use in constructing images. The *physical realism* propounded and demonstrated by the Gibson school is a challenge to those who argue that we construct a psychological reality which is what determines our behaviour. However, while it demonstrates the existence of bottom-up processes in perception, it doesn't preclude the existence of top-down processes.

The constructivist contribution

The constructivist strand in psychology originated in the Gestalt school and its earlier tendrils sprout from the phenomenological and existential strands in philosophy. It deals with Allport's inside–outside problem by according a central role to the phenomic world of the

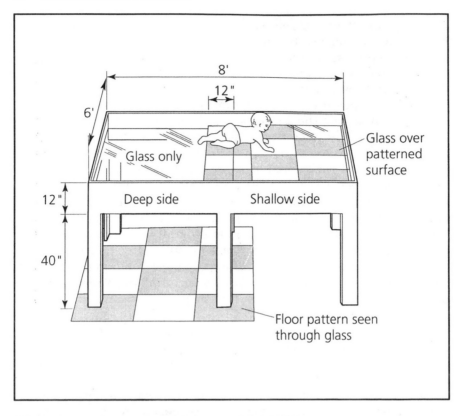

FIG. 4. The visual cliff as used by Gibson and Walk (1960).

individual. In the area of perception two well-known theorists have adopted a constructivist position, Neisser (1976, 1987) and Gregory (1966, 1973). Neisser's book, *Cognition and reality*, published in 1986 is a fairly definitive statement of the constructivist approach, although his model of the perceptual process attempts to integrate inside and outside (or bottom-up and top-down) processes.

Seeing and thinking

Neisser distinguishes between two aspects of perception. The first he refers to as seeing a process which he assumes is fairly passive and driven by the information contained in the environmental stimuli. This accords with Gibson's model of perception. However the other part of the process of perception involves thinking and this is where top-down or constructivist aspects intrude. Neisser proposes a perceptual cycle which involves attention, motivation and perceptual processes in a dynamic process being stimulated by and acting upon information from all sense modalities. Whereas Gibson saw the person as reacting to the information in the natural environment, Neisser sees the person as actively exploring their world. They are guided by the cognitive schema they have developed, which are in turn continually being modified in the light of new information. This higher level cognitive processing is actively seeking meaning in the information available in the environment and in the case of illusions, where information is sketchy, information is drawn from previous experience. When we come to look at the work of George Kelly you will see the similarities between Neisser's model of the person and Kelly's analogy of the person as scientist. In fact one can see the philosophy of Kelly in many of the cognitive theories of the 1970s.

From illusion to perception

Gregory (1966, 1973) suggested that the perceptual process is analogous to the scientific process of generating and testing hypothesis. He suggests that the individual's previous experience, stored in memory, is all important in the process and his theory is therefore top down. Much of his evidence is drawn from visual illusions, which he sees as the result of perceptual hypothesis going wrong because of insufficient information. For Gregory too, perception involves the higher level cognitive elements involved in thinking. From this level hypothesis are generated and then attempts are made to match them with the environmental information. Through this process perceptual images are generated that guide behaviour.

An alternative construction

The theorist who best expresses the constructivist position in psychology is George Kelly who in 1955 proposed a theory of personal constructs based on his experience as a clinician. Central to the theory is constructive alternativism which is embodied in the proposition that there are as many different forms of reality as the individual is capable of construing. Constructions of reality for any individual will be limited by the range of their experience. In its extreme the approach holds that the world of the schizophrenic is as real as the world of the scientist. As Koestler says "Einstein's space is no closer to reality than Van Gogh's sky". Kelly's ideas are elaborated upon in Chapter 9.

In the theories of Brunswick and Gibson we see evidence that the external physical reality plays an important role in providing the information in the perceptual process. Thus we could argue a role for *physical realism*. On the other hand in the theories of Gregory, Neisser, and Kelly we have a strong case for constructivism and the importance of the psychological or phenomic world. While none of these theories argue totally for an inside or an outside solution, they do not present an equitable role for person and environment in the process. In addition they imply that person and environment can be meaningfully studied as separate entities. An alternative view is found in the transactional approach.

Transactionalism

The transactional approach considers the person and the environment (subject and object) as interdependent parts of one transactional process. The focus of study is switched from analysis of subject or object to a focus on the process of interaction between the two. Its main theme is the indivisibility of subject and object in the research exercise.

The term transaction seems to have been introduced by Dewey and Bentley (1949) and is reflected in the work of Ames (1955), Cantril (1950), Kilpatrick (1961), Ittelson (1961) and more recently in the work of Altman and Stokols (1987).

In many ways the transactionalists come to the same conclusion as the constructivist perspective, that the outcome of the perceptual process is a phenomic or psychological environment.

> Taken altogether, our assumptions form our "assumptive world" which we bring to every occasion and on which our perceptions are based; therefore the only world we know is determined by our assumptions (Kilpatrick, 1961, p.4).

The transactional process is based on a model of the person having autonomy or freewill in choosing among the stimuli available in producing a perceptual image. In addition, the major driving force in the process is the function it serves.

> ... perception is of functional probabilities, of constructs which emerge from the consequences of past action and serve as directives for furthering the purposes of the organism through action (Kilpatrick, 1961, p.4).

Ames' work centred around designing experimental conditions wherein the external environment was distorted in some way. As a result the person has to work to interpret the information. In the famous Ames' room (Fig. 5) floor height and the distance of walls are manipulated to produce distorted views of the relative size of people. Using this room researchers have shown that when participants have time to perform actions such as throwing a ball or touching the walls with a stick, they come to see the room as distorted (Kilpatrick, 1954). In other words,

FIG. 5. The Ames room, where distortions of physical shape fool our perceptual processes.

action in the environment changes the perception, and perceptual processes are no longer fooled. This demonstrates the interactive nature of subject and object in perception.

The outcome of the transaction between person and environment is the production of a phenomic environment which is ultimately unique to the individual. As Ittelson (1973) says, "The environment we know is the product, not the cause of perception" (p.105).

The fact that a perceptual image is at least partially the product of an individual's experience suggests that individuals whose experiences differ markedly will have different perceptual images of the same physical environment.

From shape perception to shaping perception

The way in which cultural differences influence perceptual processes was explored by psychologists within the transactional school. For example Allport and Pettigrew (1957) found differences between 'angular' cultures and 'non-angular' cultures in response to visual illusions based on angles. Zulus whose culture tends to be dominated by circular shapes (e.g. round houses) were less likely to be fooled by the trapezoidal window illusion. Cultural differences in the ability to see depth in two-dimensional pictures have been observed (Deregowski, 1980). Perceptual differences have also been demonstrated between city dwellers and their rural neighbours which reflect the effects of both the more 'angular' city environment, and the restricted distances over which one can see in the city (Coren, Porac, & Ward, 1984; Segall, Campbell, & Herskovits, 1966).

The carpentered world hypothesis

A proposed explanation of how different environmental experiences can lead to differences in perception between cultures is the carpentered world hypothesis demonstrated by Turnbull (1961). Turnbull was a social anthropologist who worked with the Bambuti pygmies who inhabit the rain forest of the Congo region in central Africa. These people live most, if not all, of their life in a forest environment and hence never develop distance perception, i.e. the ability to relate size to distance over longer distances and to understand that objects appear smaller the further away they are in the natural environment. Our reliance on a variety of learned cues in distance perception is demonstrated by a currently popular advertisement for a particular beer. In the advertisement a man appears to walk off into the distance across a desert, leaving a beer bottle in the foreground. However after walking for some time the man turns to his left and walks into a giant beer bottle. The illusion is based on our expectations about the relationship between distance and size. Meanwhile, back in Africa, Turnbull took his pygmy guide onto the plains and showed him the plains buffalo. As they walked towards the buffalo, the guide grew fearful and wanted to run away in terror. He couldn't understand how objects (the buffalo), which appeared tiny insects at a distance, grew larger as they approached. The phenomenon is explained in terms of our cognitive schemata (view of the world) becoming shaped to fit the physical environment within which we live.

Environmental illusions

Just as our perceptual processes can be demonstrated to be vulnerable to deception in the form of visual illusions in the laboratory, so also can we (like Turnbull's pygmy) be deceived by the physical environment. An example of this is the terrestrial saucer effect discussed by Gifford (1987). This is an illusion created by the juxtaposition of mountains in a natural landscape which can lead to rivers appearing to run uphill or to roads which actually incline upwards appearing to be sloped downwards. I know of a road (in the north of Ireland) where if you stop your car with the handbrake off, it will appear to roll uphill. You may have experienced the phenomenon whilst driving, when your car engine indicates that you are travelling uphill while what you see seems to be a level or downward sloping road. If you are a cyclist you will have perhaps experienced this even more closely (and more emotionally!).

In terms of environmental perception the evidence presented allows us to draw three conclusions.

1. The environment provides information (affordances) which are necessary and important in the perceptual process.
2. The environment shapes our perceptual processes by determining the content of our perceptual memory, in the developmental process.
3. The person selects, interprets, and gives meaning to the information received and constructs a phenomic environment which then overrides the objective environment in determining behaviour.

While we may separate out these different aspects of the process for the sake of explanatory simplicity, the process operates as a transaction in terms of an interdependent dynamic systemic process between person and environment, between inside and outside in Allport's problem, or between subject and object in the perceptual process. In constructing the phenomic world the person reflects and makes choices, and insomuch acts as a free agent.

Because of the overriding role of the phenomic environment, each of us will see the environment we look at in different ways. For example a developer, a farmer, and a tourist looking at the same piece of countryside will have quite different perceptions of it. Though they receive much the same physical stimuli, the tourist might have an overall view (a gestalt) of "a pretty scene", the farmer may see the fields in terms of current crops, who they belong to and so on, whereas the developer may superimpose a new bypass or superstore complex. The different ways in which we appraise the environment influences our attitudes towards it. Attitudes to the environment are important on two counts. First, they influence our likes and dislikes—how we appreciate our world; and second, they are related to how we use and abuse our environment.

Environmental appreciation

The work of Kaplan and Kaplan (1982) in the USA is the most prolific in the area. They have conducted a great deal of research into the factors that influence our likes and dislikes and hence preferences for different types of environment.

The major contributor to research on environmental evaluation and meaning in Britain was David Cantor (Cantor, 1968, 1969, 1983). His work demonstrates the ways in which our evaluation of the environment and meaning we give to it influence our behaviour in that environment and this can be usefully applied in the planning of physical environments such as new housing projects (Cantor & Thorne, 1972). We will return to this work when we look at environmental design.

The fact that individual differences in preferences for different environments exist is obvious to any observer. Some people prefer beach holidays, some prefer to get away from the beaten track. Apart from the obvious restrictions of time and money, the question to be answered is why such preferences occur. Kaplan and Kaplan (1978) and Kaplan (1973, 1975, 1979, 1987) have helped to enlighten us by linking environmental cognition with environmental evaluation. Here too the person–environment process is an interactional or transactional one. We react emotionally in different ways to different environments, but our feeling about our world is also coloured by our previous experiences. A good example of this is the way in which professional training engenders different world views. Architects see form and light where most of us see buildings, and developers see buildings where most of us see hills and valleys. The differences between perceptions of different professionals has been demonstrated by studies such as Hershberger's (1968)

The empirical evidence from perception and social cognition research raises important questions about our definition of reality. It would appear that, in fact, the real world of our experience is more a subjective than an objective reality—the notion that "beauty" really does partially "lie in the eye of the beholder". However to ignore aspects of the environment would be to provide an incomplete picture. Four aspects of environments which are important in relation to our emotional response are coherence, legibility, complexity and mystery (Kaplan & Kaplan, 1978). Coherence refers to the organisation of parts and how well the whole fits together, and will be closely related to legibility, which reflects how easily the observer can "read" the environment—i.e. how they can process the information available and understand what they see. Complexity and mystery are elements which attract attention and hold our interest with more complex environments and those with some degree of mystery providing most interest. Another aspect that is important is the novelty of the environment. Numerous animal and human studies in psychology have shown that novelty attracts attention and arouses interest, whether explained at the very basic physiological level of initiating the *alarm reaction*, the initial reflexive stage in the fight/flight response, or at a higher cognitive level. The general conclusion from research in the area is that these different dimensions of the environment operate on the individual through the interaction of physiological and psychological processes. In terms of the arousal level or adaptation level theories covered in this chapter, aspects of the environment which instigate physiological arousal will generate an emotional or affective response. While there are debates about the order of events between biology and psychology in generating emotions (Plutchik, 1995), there is strong evidence that cognitive processes intercede between external events, biological responses and the emotion experienced (see Box 5).

It would appear that a "happy medium" rule applies in that an optimum level of environmental elements exists which produces satisfaction and appreciation in the person. In other words a highly coherent, easily legible, simple, well-known environment will be dissatisfying, as will be an environment which lacks coherence, is confusing, overly complex, mysterious and strange. Mehrabrian and Russell (1974) focus on the amount and intensity of information contained in the environment and suggest that levels of environmental

---

Box 5: She's smiling so I must be happy

In a classic study Schachter and Singer (1962) explored the relationship between cognitive, social, and physiological aspects in determining emotion and as a result generated what is sometimes referred to as the *lability theory* of emotion. Three-quarters of the participants in the study were given injections of adrenalin which has the effect of increasing physiological arousal, and the remaining quarter given an injection of saline solution, a placebo. There were four conditions in that some participants were told what to expect, others were misinformed about what to expect, a third group were not told anything and the placebo group were also left ignorant. Each individual was then left for some time in the waiting room with either an angry or a euphoric stooge. Participants' emotions were then assessed both by observing them when with the stooge (through a one-way mirror), and by self-report measures of mood. The placebo group and those told exactly what to expect showed no effect, but the groups that were left ignorant or misinformed reported feeling euphoric when with the euphoric stooge, and angry when with the angry stooge. The interpretation of all this is that the emotion experienced is a consequence of the cognitive appraisal of external cues. The ignorant and misinformed participants experienced physiological arousal in the absence of an immediate explanation. They resorted to the external cues, either the angry or euphoric stooge, to provide an explanation in terms of a corresponding emotion—a process which would follow the sequence, "I feel aroused, he is angry—so I must be feeling angry".

elements have their effect through information underload or overload. The optimum level of arousal and information load is very much determined by the person's previous experience. One person may like cities because they contain high levels of novelty, mystery and complexity, another may dislike cities for exactly the same reasons. What is clear is that we can identify a range of important dimensions of the environment which will influence the person's affective response, but this will not allow us to predict the person's evaluation of the environment unless we know something about their phenomic world which is made up of the internalised store of their life experiences.

Environmental personality

The traditional approach to understanding the person aspect in determining behaviour was to identify personality traits. In the area of environmental appreciation this involves categorising people in terms of their typical reaction to the environment. In a broad sense we are probably all aware of individual differences in this area. For example, some people like cities while some prefer rural life. Some people enjoy sandy beaches while others prefer rugged mountain terrain. In considering these examples we have identified one of the problems with personality approaches, i.e. they provide a *description* of behaviour or experience, not an *explanation*. We describe a person as being a "city lover" as opposed to a "country lover", but doing this does not provide us with an explanation as to *why* this is the case. In order to explain their preference we would need to consider their life experiences or their particular biological or psychological needs and motivations. On the other hand it can be argued that any scientific approach begins with some sort of classification or description of subject matter. There is a strong case to be made that personality theory has always been based on the environment since the traits that have been produced are based on the person's reaction to their environment. From observing how people behave we infer a level of need for stimulation from the environment which is the basis of Jung's extraversion–introversion concept. Indeed many of the early personality theorists did adopt a person-in-context model. Henry Murray's needs–press theory of personality explained behaviour in terms of the interaction between the needs of the person and the influence of the environment which he called "press" (Murray, 1938). A number of environmental psychologists have attempted to describe the environmental personality using traditional questionnaire methods. An example is the work of McKechnie (1974) who developed the Environmental Response Inventory. This 184-item questionnaire measures eight dispositions towards the environment which are outlined in Box 6.

Box 6: The eight environmental personality traits from the ERI

Pastoralism: The tendency to oppose land development, preserve open space, accept natural forces as influences and prefer self-sufficiency.

Urbanism: The tendency to enjoy high density living, and appreciate the varied interpersonal and cultural stimulation found in city life.

Environmental adaptation: The tendency to favour the alteration of the environment to suit human needs and desires, oppose developmental controls, and prefer highly refined settings and objects.

Stimulus seeking: The tendency to be interested in travel and exploration, enjoy complex or intense physical sensations, and have very broad interests.

Environmental trust: The tendency to be secure in the environment, be competent in finding your way around, and be unafraid of new places or of being alone.

Antiquarianism: The tendency to enjoy historical places and things, prefer traditional designs, collect more treasured possessions than most other people, and appreciate the products of earlier eras.

Need for privacy: The tendency to need isolation, not appreciate neighbours, avoid distraction and seek solitude.

Mechanical orientation: The tendency to enjoy technological and mechanical processes, enjoy working with your hands, and care about how things work (from Gifford, 1987, p.85).

The personality approach has obvious utility in environmental design and trying to fit people to places—for example in designing rehousing projects where people are being moved from their original homes for some reason (Lee, 1976). The utility of traditional personality perspectives which assume stable traits is however questionable in the light of work showing that situations produce similar behaviour patterns irrespective of any individual personality differences. Many theorists these days tend to prefer a more interactional model with personality traits being seen as *relatively* stable patterns of behaviour which change as a consequence of experience across situations and time. I would argue that the term cognitive style is more useful because it is a more accurate reflection of what occurs. For example this assumes that the dimensions of environmental personality in McKechnie's model are not fixed. Rather a person may score high on urbanism at one point in time, but score low on the same dimension at another.

The cognitive style approach to individual differences tends to be exemplified in theories such as the attributional style theory discussed in regard to stress in the next chapter.

A major challenge to stable personality trait theories comes from those who focus on environmental control of behaviour. An example is the work of Barker and Wright (1955) on behaviour settings, which is considered in Chapter 2.

PLAN OF THE TEXT

In Chapter 2 we will consider theoretical and methodological issues in environmental psychology before going on in Chapter 3 to look at some more specific work on the ways in which the context within which behaviour occurs, influences the behaviour and experience of the person. Chapter 4 looks at the ways in which the environment impinges on our senses through noise, smell, light, colour and the effects of weather, air quality and climate. These are often referred to as the classic environmental stressors. In Chapter 5 we reverse the process and look at how we as human beings impact on the environment through chemical pollution of one sort or another, and through technological development and its unfortunate consequence in human-made disasters. In Chapter 6 we turn to the social environment and look at how living in cities, travelling and controlling access to the space we inhabit affects our behaviour and experience. We will consider the social stressors, crowding, personal space, territoriality and privacy and the growing problem of commuting. Having considered a range of effects of both the social and physical environment, we turn in Chapter 7 to the area of environmental design, to consider how we might make our environments more satisfying, healthy, and safe. The next stop on our tour will be to consider how we use and abuse our world in Chapter 8. We consider there the problems caused as a result of human demands on the earth as a resource, and the major fears for the future that our excessive demands and environmentally destructive behaviours have instigated. We look at why such behaviours occur and what might be done to reverse the process. Finally in Chapter 9 we take a look forward, by reviewing the basic principles that need to be our guides in research and practice if environmental psychology is to grow and develop, and by considering a range of factors that seem to be indicated by current research as productive areas for the future.

CHAPTER TWO

Theory and method in environmental psychology

Environmental psychology is interdisciplinary in nature, therefore perhaps even more than some other fields of applied psychology it relies on a diverse range of theory. In any area of applied psychology there is no single or unified theory. Rather, applied psychologists have access to the total range of theoretical perspectives in psychology. Indeed this is as it should be because it allows greater scope and flexibility in application and there is little reason to expect that the complex subject matter of psychology, human experience and behaviour, should lend itself to a simple or single theoretical explanation.

In terms of the basic perspectives in psychology, environmental psychology adopts an interactional framework both in terms of person–situation interaction and nature–nurture interaction. Explanations incorporate all the psychological perspectives and, since environmental psychology is an applied area, it is not a matter of any one theory being the correct one, rather it is a case of which one provides the most useful explanation and enhances a practical intervention.

While no unifying theory exists, some themes can be identified which reflect a number of different ways of conceptualising the person–environment transaction. Veitch and Arkkelin (1995) identify four major historical trends and six current theoretical themes. The historical trends are geographical determinism, ecological biology, behaviourism and Gestalt psychology (p.17).

Geographical determinism

The basic premise of geographical determinism is that the geographical environment directly influences behaviour and experience in that it provides challenge. Extremely low levels of challenge fail to provide the stimulation necessary to motivate. Extremely high levels of challenge are damaging. This effect is akin to the arousal level theories to be discussed later, and reflects the Yerkes–Dodson law (see Fig. 6).

An intermediate level of challenge leads to the development of appropriate coping responses and hence particular types of behaviour and experience which enhance survival within the specific geographical environment. This is essentially a macro-level explanation in that it purports to explain common behaviours and experiences within total cultures. From this it is argued that each culture develops particular child rearing practices, characteristics, attitudes and values which reflect the geographical world they inhabit. Thus nomadic cultures emphasise independence whereas non-nomadic agricultural cultures emphasise responsibility and obedience.

This theme of the environment setting the scene for behaviour pervades many different approaches within environmental psychology, from Barker's behaviour settings, to the effects of buildings on behaviour which will be covered in later chapters.

The theme of environmental challenge can be elaborated by extrapolating from Warr's (1987) vitamin model of the relationship

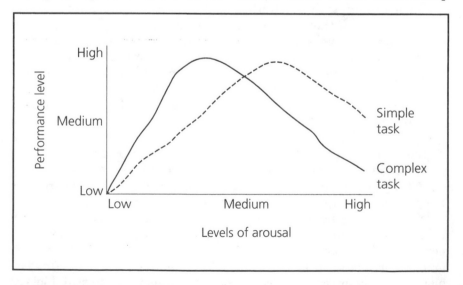

FIG. 6. The Yerkes–Dodson law which reflects a curvilinear relationship between arousal and performance.

between environmental pressures and mental health. Warr suggests that environmental demands can be usefully considered in terms of two major types. The first he calls constant effect which is where environmental demands are analogous to the effect of vitamins C and E on the physical body. Too little of these vitamins has a detrimental effect on health, but we can't really have too much of them. Some aspects of the environment work like this and can perhaps be seen as environmental resources. Having an unpolluted environment works like this, in that air can never be too clean, for example.

On the other hand we have what Warr calls additional decrement effects where, like vitamins A and D, both too little and too much are damaging. This is like the environmental challenge described in geographical determinism (see Fig. 7, an adaptation of Warr's model). Stressors in the environment operate like this and when we come to consider the effects of noise, weather, and crowding, for example, you will again encounter this theme.

Ecological biology
The idea of interdependence between biological and social factors in the person–environment transaction is another traditional theme which is expressed in many areas of research in environmental psychology.

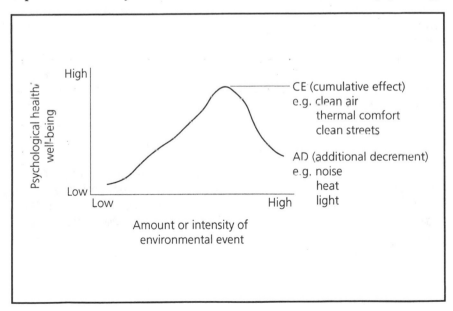

FIG. 7. The vitamin model of the relationship between environmental events and mental health from Warr (1987).

Essentially the approach views the initial human response to external factors as instinctual with the child being born with a set of instinctual responses that help it to survive. The work of the ethologists Lorenz (1958) and Tinbergen (1951) demonstrates how young animals instinctually attach themselves to protective figures (Box 7). It was from this perspective that Ardrey (1966) developed his ideas on the territorial imperative. Theories about people living together in a spatial environment (territoriality, personal space, crowding) all echo this theme of ecological biology.

The behavioural perspective

There are at least two very important contributions from the behavioural tradition which lie at the heart of environmental psychology theory. These are the development of interactionism and the analysis of the ways in which physical environments enhance or constrain behaviour. It was the behavioural (or situationist) challenge to traditional personality approaches to psychological explanation which brought the person–situation debate into the public arena and as a result set the wheels in motion for the development of the interactionist perspective in the 1970s (Mischel, 1968). Although Lewin had advocated an interactional approach (B=f(P,E)) in the 1940s and in fact many earlier theorists such as James (1890) had begun by assuming interactionism, it was only as a result of the experimentally based arguments from behaviourism that the issue was taken seriously.

In addition, the extreme insistence on objectivity and an external perspective in behavioural research provided both a language and technique with which to articulate more clearly the behavioural control exerted by the physical and social environment. Skinner's

---

Box 7: The imprint of survival

Lorenz (1958) reported on studies which demonstrated an innate instinct of the young to become attached to a caretaker immediately after birth, an instinct he named imprinting. Lorenz was an ethologist, studying behaviour in the natural environment. While studying geese, he noticed that the young goslings who were hatched when he was present would follow him around and become agitated when he was out of sight. His research showed that the goslings tend to imprint on the first moving object they see. He explained this imprinting as an instinctual response which is important for the survival of the young. Work like this has led to a generally accepted belief that all living things are endowed at birth with a set of instinctual reflexes which are important in immediate survival. After all the organism needs to survive in order to begin learning.

discriminative stimuli provided a model for Barker's work on behaviour settings (see Box 8).

Gestalt psychology

The Gestalt principle that the whole is greater than the sum of its parts is the basis for the more important theories of environmental perception. The Gestalt approach began in Germany and found its origins in the writings of Wertheimer (1944), Koffka (1935) and Köhler (1940). A central principle of Gestalt psychology is closure, which refers to the way in which our cognitive processes complete the picture in an attempt to see a whole. The visual illusion in Fig. 3 illustrates the principle. We see a triangle which isn't there because of the bits presented by the cut-out segments of the three black circles.

Box 8: From the Skinner box to the real world— the case of behaviour settings

Skinner's (1953) concept of a discriminative stimulus can be used to explain why we behave in different ways in different situations. We have learned to associate certain cues in the environment with particular types of behaviour and consequent reinforcements. The extreme example is a church where a wide range of cues such as an altar, pews, and stained glass windows immediately indicate what type of behaviour is expected (and will be socially rewarded). The process operates at a much more subtle level than this very obvious example, and is inextricably bound up with social and cultural factors. Buildings and other environmental objects cue different types of behaviour as a function of our culture and our social experience. In another study Skinner (1938) demonstrated how superstitious behaviour develops. While training pigeons to peck a disc for food, he noticed that the birds often associated food delivery with whatever they were doing just before reinforcement was delivered. This eventually produced some quite bizarre and irrelevant behaviour which Skinner termed "superstitious behaviours". For example one bird turned around three times before pecking, while another moved its head up and down vigorously. The explanation was that it was not only the pecking which was being reinforced, but a sequence of behaviours which all became associated with the acquisition of food. Do you ever "knock on wood", or press the button for a pedestrian crossing even if someone else has just pressed it? If you do you are behaving just like Skinner's pigeon. These are all unnecessary behaviours and have no connection with outcomes, but they are controlled, according to Skinner, by association with other behaviours or experiences. You can probably think of a large number of places in your everyday experience which exert a control over your behaviour. These are what Barker and Wright call behaviour settings.

The Gestalt influence led to non-reductionist approaches to explanations of person–environment transactions and to a constructivist perspective generally. The approach is concerned not so much with the stimuli as with the ways in which the person perceives and appraises the stimuli, something that is central to an understanding of environmental stress.

Commonalities across themes

Although each of these four themes stems from a distinctive background, there are commonalities which are often not drawn out in discussion. The geographical determinism, which holds that the geography places demands on the person to adapt and survive or not adapt and perish, echoes the ecological biology perspective which sees the newborn emitting instinctual responses to environmental stimuli in order to survive. It is a matter of emphasis. The former considers the person subservient to the environment, whereas the latter places the role of biological instincts in a central position.

As we shall see geographical determinism is more closely reflective of the more modern ecological perspective of Bronfenbrenner (1979) and Barker (1968) who reduce the biological emphasis.

In addition geographical determinism reflects the environmental determinism of the behaviourists, except on the macro- rather than the micro-scale. Indeed many of the apparent differences between theorists rest on the issue of levels of analysis or explanation.

Grand theories and themes

Veitch and Arkkelin (1995) suggest four reasons why no grand theory exists in environmental psychology: (1) There is not enough data available regarding environment–behaviour relationships to lead to the kind of confidence needed for a unifying theory; (2) the relationships that researchers have looked at are highly varied; (3) the methods used are inconsistent; and (4) the ways in which variables have been measured have not always been compatible from one research setting to the next (p.18).

These may be problems which create difficulty in drawing general conclusions, but there are much more fundamental reasons why no unified theory exists. Given the complexity of human behaviour and experience it could be argued that pursuit of a unifying theory is both naïve and futile.

However it is true that theorists have tended to favour particular approaches and a number of general frameworks are used in attempting to explain the person–environment relationship. These may be categorised in a number of ways, but I have chosen to look at them in terms of four categories,

- Theories that look inward.
- Theories that look outward.
- The role of cognition and appraisal.
- Theories that assume interaction.

THEORIES LOOKING INWARD

Theories that adopt an internal perspective tend to treat the person as a biological organism and produce explanations which are essentially based on biological determinism. These include arousal-level theories (Berlyne, 1960) and adaptation-level theories (Helsen, 1964).

One of the themes which runs through explanations in environmental psychology is that of homeostasis, or optimum levels. This approach in psychology originated in the work of Yerkes and Dodson (1908) on the relationship between anxiety and performance, from which they produced what is known as the Yerkes–Dodson Law. This is illustrated in Fig. 6.

Yerkes and Dodson found that in general people performed best under medium levels of anxiety. In other words a certain amount of anxiety was necessary and enhanced performance, but excess amounts of anxiety reduced performance producing the inverted U shape in Fig. 6. Anxiety reflects physiological arousal in that high levels of anxiety correlate with high levels of arousal and vice versa. People differ on the optimum level of arousal required to perform a task and aspects of the task also influence the optimum level. In general simple tasks can be performed well under higher levels of arousal while more complex tasks are very sensitive to levels of arousal.

Optimum levels of arousal reflect the homeostatic state of the organism and both the physical body and the person will be motivated to maintain this state or to return to it if external factors cause a reduction or increase above or below the optimum level. These theories explain the person–behaviour relationship in terms of discomfort resulting from external pressures which increase or decrease arousal levels with responses being dictated by attempts to return to homeostasis.

Adaptation-level theories are really an extension, or special case, of arousal-level theories based on a similar biological process. The focus here is on the biological organism's ability to adapt to external stimulation. Two factors are considered: first, individual differences in adaptation-levels; and second, the human capacity to adapt or habituate to new environments (Box 9).

The adaptation-level perspective explains the person–environment relationship in terms of the optimum adaptation-level for the person and the range of adaptation possible. Thus some people find the extra stimulation of city life a tonic while others become overwhelmed. However some people moving to the city for the first time may find it threatening to begin with, but after adapting they may begin to actually thrive on the hustle and bustle. Research comparing physiological homeostatic states have shown that city dwellers have on average a higher operating level than their rural counterparts. In addition after moving to the city the rural individual's operating level of physiological arousal adjusts to a comparable level to the long-term city dweller. Just as, for example, many people find their walking speed adjusting to city or rural norms, so too our internal physiological states adjust.

A close relative of the arousal- and adaptation-level perspectives is the stimulus load approach. This approach has two different perspectives: the stimulus overload theories (Cohen, 1978) which focus on the upper range of physiological arousal and explore the consequences of arousal levels above the optimum; and the restricted environmental stimulation approach (Suedfeld, 1980) which considers the effects of stimulus underload. Using Warr's vitamin analogy we can see that many environmental factors, such as temperature and crowding, operate in terms of stimulus load, in that low levels and high levels can both have detrimental effects. However a major problem with this approach, as we shall see, is that there are no objective stimulus load levels which operate for every individual. As already suggested from arousal- and adaptation-levels perspectives, individuals differ in

---

Box 9: Things that go bump in the night

In a residential area of New York during the early 1970s the overhead tram system which had been part of the environment for many years was removed. While it had been running it had passed quite close to many blocks of flats at periodic intervals throughout the day and night. After it ceased to run there was a massive increase in the number of residents reporting to their local medical centres complaining of sleep disturbances. It took the medics some time to make the connection, but eventually the only plausible explanation was in terms of habituation. The residents had habituated to the sound of the trams over the years and now that they were no longer there, they were aware of something missing. They were being disturbed by the sound of silence, to quote the Simon and Garfunkel song.

their optimum levels. In addition, and perhaps the most important factor, is that individuals differ in the ways in which events are appraised (Lazarus & Folkman, 1984). The most obvious example relates to noise. For some noise levels at a rock concert are enjoyable, for others they are sheer hell. In addition those who enjoyed the rock concert would probably not enjoy the same level of noise in a work setting.

The biology of stress

Another theory looking inward is the biological approach to stress exemplified by Seyle (1956). This approach considers what happens when environmental factors pose a threat to the individual with an emphasis on biological adaptation. Seyle devised his general adaptation syndrome explanation, a three stage process, in 1956 and it has stood the test of time.

His approach echoes the ecological biology theme in that it assumes individuals have an automatic, instinctual reaction to threat, in terms of the fight/flight response. This is the first stage in Seyle's proposed process known as the alarm stage. The alarm stage involves the reflexive preparation of the body to fight or flee in response to a novel stimulus. Heart rate increases, pupils dilate, digestion ceases, muscles tense in readiness to fight or flee, the whole process serving to raise the body's arousal level above the level of homeostasis. Unfortunately in the stressful situations encountered by humans fight or flight is often neither possible or appropriate.

The second stage of the process, the resistance stage, reflects the stage of actual fight or flight in that the body draws on its resources in order to optimise performance. In the human condition these resources are used in attempting to restore homeostasis. The main physiological process at this stage is the production of adrenalin and noradrenalin. In this process, resources needed for normal bodily functions such as digestion, are depleted—which in the short term has no major consequence—and would under fight/flight conditions last for the duration of the fight or the flight.

Where no fight or flight is possible, a third stage, the exhaustion stage, ensues. In this stage, organs may collapse leading to death or the prolonged draining of resources may produce ulcers, hypertension, cardiovascular disorders or other physical symptoms. More recent work in the field of psychoneuroimmunology has extended Seyle's work. They have focused on specific cells which mediate the processes outlined in Seyle's general adaptation syndrome. These are cells that operate to produce the physical consequences of long-term stress. Two types of cells have been identified. Th (T helper) cells increase resistance to disease and are absent in AIDS' victims. NK (natural killer) cells destroy tumors and infections. These cells are thought to be suppressed by the stress process and lead to "immune deficiency" (Laudenslager & Reite, 1984). As we shall see this biological response depends also on appraisal of external events.

THEORIES LOOKING OUTWARD

Theories that take an external perspective tend to fit within the behavioural tradition and explain behaviour in terms of the ways in which the environment controls behaviour. They take two main forms: the behavioural constraints approach and the ecological perspective. What unites them is their emphasis on environmental determinism.

Central to behavioural theories is the notion that the environment is a source of reward or punishment and sets the scene for behaviour. Behavioural constraints theories focus on the ways in which the environment prevents or limits behaviour. Stimulus control was studied on the micro-level by Skinner (1938, 1953), where the environment was the Skinner box. The physical environment can constrain behaviour by making it impossible for the behaviour to occur. For example the person in prison cannot engage in a wide range of behaviours associated with freedom. The concept of impedance in the study of travel environments (Novaco, Stokols, & Milanesi, 1990) is a good example of how the stress of commuting is a function of how the environment (rush hour traffic, etc.) impedes travel. However environments can constrain behaviour in much more subtle and wide-ranging ways. One way of describing this process is through the discriminative stimuli described in Box 8. Our behaviour is constantly under stimulus control in terms of the cues which control behaviour in different settings. We tend to whisper in a library and a church even when other people are not present. As we shall see aspects of the physical environment lead to different ways of perceiving the world. This will be discussed in more detail in the next chapter.

Another way in which behavioural theories contribute to environmental psychology is in the application of operant principles to modify behaviours and attitudes in the context of environmental issues such as recycling and waste disposal. In a review of behavioural programmes in the area (Dwyer et al., 1993) reviewed 54 studies between 1980 and 1990 and concluded that many potential benefits were lost due to lack of follow-up evaluation, and uninventive interventions. However a range of approaches including gaining participant commitment, modelling, and setting realistic goals were effective in improving environmentally related behaviours.

The ecological perspective sees behaviour as the function of its physical and social setting. A direct descendant of geographical determinism this perspective is exemplified in the work of Barker and Wright (1955) on behaviour settings. Though not often considered in the context of environmental psychology, the work of Bronfenbrenner (1977, 1979), also fits within this perspective. Bronfenbrenner's work extends beyond the focus on the physical environment imposed by earlier definitions of environmental psychology, because it considers the totality of physical and social environments in determining human behaviour and experience. Barker and Bronfenbrenner were both students of Lewin, and were united in their reaction against the preoccupation with person focused, individual-level explanations for behaviour. Both were concerned with the lack of research on environmental factors.

> What we find in practice, is a marked asymmetry, a hypertrophy of theory and research focusing on the properties of the person and only the most rudimentary conception and characterisation of the environment in which the person is found (Bronfenbrenner, 1979, p.16).

The work of both Barker and Bronfenbrenner has an interactional flavour although they did tend to focus more on the E element in Lewin's $B=f(P,E)$.

Another theorist within this ecological perspective is Gibson (1950, 1979) who conceptualised perception in terms of the direct result of external stimuli. He was concerned with the information provided by stimuli and how the stimuli provides this information. His approach strongly emphasises the external perspective, but in his concept of affordances he incorporates a view of the interdependence of person and environment.

> I mean by it something that refers to both the environment and the animal in a way that no existing term does. It implies the complementarity of the animal and the environment (Gibson, 1979, p.127).

The it referred to in the above quote is the concept of affordances. Like Barker and Bronfebrenner, Gibson was concerned with a focus on external world in a total or holistic sense, very much in the tradition of

Gestalt psychology. His stimuli were not the narrow range of simple stimuli used in traditional studies of perception carried out in laboratories. He insisted that we perceive total environments, not just an addition of single snapshots.

> The single, frozen field of view provides only impoverished information about the world. The visual system did not evolve for this (Gibson, 1979, p.2).

What unites the ecological perspective is this molar level of analysis which can be said to be a more accurate reflection of the purpose of evolution both in terms of humans and environments.

The role of cognition and appraisal

I have singled out cognition and appraisal for special attention in this grouping of theoretical themes because while traditionally they have not been a major focus, the growing evidence is that they play a central role in understanding the person–environment relationship. In a later chapter we will consider how we perceive the environment and will see that the ways in which we think about and give meaning to our context are central to responding to, acting on, and appreciating our external world. Within this cognitive theme we encounter the philosophy of constructivism which is rooted in phenomenology and expressed in Kelly's (1955) theory of personal constructs. According to this perspective the person is a rational processor of information, being active rather than reactive, and engaging in the exercise of free will through the ability to be reflexive. In many ways this perspective challenges the traditional model of personality with its emphasis on stability over time and situations. Instead it poses a model of an adapting, changing person, who operates within an external world which is at least partially constructed by the individual. Essentially the person selects from the mass of information available in the environment, processes that information in the context of their previous experience and comes up with a map or blueprint which guides their behaviour. The central factor in the process is meaningfulness or the search for meaning. In environmental psychology this perspective transcends the laboratory-based experimental and reductionist cognitive psychology by merging it with the phenomenological and existential principles of humanistic psychology and within the Gestalt framework. We will return to this in the next chapter. I raise it here to redress what I feel is often a glaring omission in previous texts in the area.

THEORIES THAT ASSUME INTERACTION

Although the core ideas in environmental psychology stem from Lewin who was an ardent interactionist, as we have seen many of the theoretical themes that followed, even from his own students, did tend to focus more on either the person or the environment and ignored the interaction part of his famous equation. In the wake of Mischel's (1968) text, *Personality and assessment*, psychologists again became interested in person–environment interaction within psychology generally. The success of interactionism seems to be undecided as yet, with two reviews by the same author coming to slightly conflicting conclusions. Endler (1982) claimed with confidence that interactionism had come of age, but a year later he (1983) argued that interactionsism had some way to go before becoming a fully fledged theory. The main reason for this pessimism was that the vast majority of research did not reflect a truly interactional methodology. Often what appears as interactional is no more than an addition of person and environmental variables. However the attempt to include both person and environment in the analysis must be applauded as a development, and the difficulty in devising interactional methods acknowledged.

In environmental psychology at least three different forms of integral theoretical themes focusing on variations of Lewin's B=*f*(P,E) can be identified. Gifford (1987) describes these as interactionism, transactionalism, and organismic theories.

Interactionism refers to a model where persons and environments are seen as separate entities, which engage with each other in various forms of interaction. To some extent it would appear that the rejection of this term in favour of transactional is partially based on the way in which interaction has been operationalised by many as the additive effect of person and environment. However interactionism does tend to suggest that individual, isolated interactions are the focus of study.

Transactional emphasises the interdependence of person and environment in the process thus ensuring that additive effects are not acceptable as explanatory models. In addition it includes the notion of sequences or chains of interactions in a developmental process. As such it extends the interactional framework and is usefully applied, for example, in models of stress.

The organismic approach emphasises the person–environment relationship as an interdependent system in which social, societal and individual factors operate in a complex process. This approach unites the system perspective with multiple levels of explanation.

These themes of interaction reflect both a move forward from the person or environment focus, and a return to basics in terms of the early theorists such as Lewin who began with an interactional focus. They recognise the complexity of person–environment relations and their interdependence. It is here that we find the basic principles outlined in Chapter 1 more fully endorsed in research and practice.

CHAPTER THREE

The context of behaviour and experience

With some basic ideas about the person in the environment in mind, we now turn to the context within which the person operates, the environment. The way in which the environment impacts upon the person could be considered in a number of ways. One way is to consider two categories of impact: the environment as a setting for behaviour, the ecological perspective; and the environment as a source of demand on the person. The former begins with the seminal work of Barker and Wright (1955) on behaviour settings, and leads to the work of Cantor in the UK and Stokols in the USA on place, while the latter tends to be subsumed under the area of stress, particularly the stimulus model of stress (Cassidy, 1994b).

Reward and punishment

In very basic terms, our encounters with both physical and social aspects of the environment will impact on us in a number of ways. This may be by restricting or facilitating our behaviour, providing resources which improve the quality of our life, or making demands which over-stretch our coping resources and lead to negative health consequences.

In other words, the environment is a source of either reward or punishment. In many cases, in fact for the greater part of our lives, our encounters with the environment will appear to be neutral, but appearances are deceptive. It will be the case that strength of reward or punishment present is low, or that some aspects are rewarding and others punishing. In any situation, the variety of stimuli impinging on us is numerically great, interrelated and complex. However, as we know from perception research, only some of these stimuli will actually be attended to or come to have any significant meaning for us. It will be those with greater reward or punishment strength that become most significant.

BEHAVIOUR SETTINGS—SETTING THE SCENE

One focus has been to recognise that in any interaction the environment provides a behaviour setting. The term behaviour setting is associated with the work of Roger Barker and Herbert Wright whose fieldwork in the 1950s was a radical departure from accepted mainstream practice in psychological research. Barker was a student of Lewin, and his approach was inspired by his respect for Lewin's ideas. However, while Barker's methodology is an example of interactionism, his explanations for behaviour focused on the environment rather than the person. This was in reaction to the predominance of person-focused theory in the 1940s and 50s. Barker called his approach ecological psychology to distinguish his emphasis and indeed he found himself being ostracised by the American Psychological Association as a result. Ecological psychology was denounced by the APA in the 1970s because of a mistaken belief that Barker's approach was totally opposed to person variables being considered in explaining behaviour. In fact Barker simply felt that environmental factors were more important and tended to ignore personality in the process. This lack of inclusion of person variables in ecological psychology sits uncomfortably with Barker's admiration of Lewin, who is regarded as the epitome of the interactional approach. Barker's special interest lay in developmental psychology and his aim in setting up the famous Midwest Psychological field station in Oskaloosa, Kansas, in 1947 was to explore the ecology of child development. The work at Midwest is jointly accredited to Barker and his colleague Herbert Wright. The town had 715 inhabitants of which 100 were children. In a meticulous study which lasted 25 years the effect of the context on behaviour was monitored. At a time when video equipment was not available the detailed observations carried out were remarkable. The group began by identifying behaviour settings, using the inductive methodology so important to Barker. He distinguished between the experimental laboratory approach which involved the researcher manipulating or operating on the variables under study and the model of the researcher as a transducer, meticulously collating observational data and devising explanations from that data, much in the same spirit as the grounded theory perspective in modern qualitative approaches.

In the work of Barker and Wright, the behaviour setting provided information which allowed explanations for the behaviour observed. Individuals move through a wide range of behaviour settings each day, and it is these, not personality traits, which control their behaviour.

For example, in Midwest the main street, the post office, a classroom, the school yard, and the hairdressing salon were all behaviour settings. Each is defined in terms of interdependent environmental features which make it homogeneous. Each was evaluated in terms of how well it fitted the behaviour which took place there and essentially how well it served its function. Barker concluded that behaviour cannot be separated from its setting and there tends to be a fit between the behaviour and the characteristics of the setting. In essence, the setting provides clues as to the roles to be played by the person in the setting and determines the range of behaviours that are possible in that setting. A micro-analysis might lead us to the behavioural concepts of discriminative stimuli (Skinner, 1953)

Situational control of behavioural consistency

In a behavioural setting, the discriminative stimuli will include aspects of the physical environment and aspects of the social environment, but will also extend to non-visible aspects in terms of the behavioural rules which we have learned through our socialisation. We can all recognise how rearranging the physical objects in a setting can change the behaviour in that setting. For example, if we are at a party where the tables are arranged around the room and laid out with buffet food, we feel reasonably comfortable about moving around the room and talking to lots of different people. Now picture the same room set up for a sit down meal. We no longer feel comfortable about walking around the room and moving from group to group. However the restriction on our behaviour is not simply a function of the physical structure of the setting, but is a relationship between the structure and the social norms which prevail.

One of the most important conclusions from the ecological psychology of Barker was that knowledge about the behaviour setting is more useful in predicting behaviour than knowledge about the characteristics of the individuals in the setting. In other words, there is much more consistency *between* individuals in the same behaviour setting than there is *within* the same individual in different behaviour settings. For example there is often very little variation in the behaviour of a large group of students in a lecture theatre. The same group of students in the university bar would again tend to behave in fairly similar ways.

However if I were to take any one student and compare their behaviour in the lecture theatre to their behaviour in the bar I would probably find quite a difference.

Of course if I were to know about both the person and the situation I could predict behaviour with an even greater degree of accuracy. It is clear that behaviour in the real world cannot be understood from one or other perspective alone, but requires a person-in-context or interactionist approach.

People in settings

In assessing the behavioural fit of the setting, Barker introduced the concept of undermanning and overmanning. We will use the terms understaffed and overstaffed to avoid the sexist bias of the original terms. The theory of staffing relates to the number of people in a behaviour setting and introduces the notion of optimum levels. In other words each behaviour setting has an optimum number of people. When there are more than the optimum number the setting becomes crowded or congested and solutions would include: increasing the physical size of the setting, controlling admission into the setting, or controlling the amount of time each person can spend in the setting. This overstaffing issue will be considered in more detail when we consider the research on crowding. Alternatively a setting may be understaffed which makes different demands on behaviour. For one thing it means that each person may be required to take on extra responsibilities and roles.

More than simply settings

The work on behaviour settings provides us with a great deal of insight into the impact of the environment and indicates the need to incorporate this approach in environmental planning and design.

However in some ways it is reductionist since it reduces the environment to discrete behaviour settings. Another perspective which also emphasises the ecology of behaviour, but which considers different levels of both physical and social environments, and their interaction, is to be found in the work of Bronfenbrenner (1977, 1979). This work is not generally cited in environmental psychology because of its inclusion of social environments, but with current directions which integrate social and physical aspects it provides a useful model. Bronfenbrenner was also a student of Lewin's and, like Barker, interested in developmental psychology. However, while he shared Barker's critical view of controlled laboratory research, he was also critical of ecological psychology because of its external perspective. His approach was much more truly interactional and emphasised the active, interpretative role of the person, with behaviour settings being defined by both their objective elements and the person's experience in them and appraisal of them.

Nested systems

Bronfenbrenner used the term micro-system rather than behaviour setting, arguing that the setting was defined by its objective elements, while a micro-system includes the person's experience of the setting. Bronfenbrenner's theory envisaged a world made up of nested systems, at a range of levels from individual to societal, and ranging from direct to indirect impact on the person's experience and behaviour. Micro-systems reflect the immediate setting and its experience, within which the person is directly located. So the family home, or the school class would be a micro-system directly impacting upon and being acted upon by the person. At the next level there is the meso-system which comprises the relationships and interactions between two or more micro-systems. So the interactions between home and school would form a meso-system for a child. The exo-system consists of settings which are influenced by and influence the micro-systems or meso-systems, but with which the person is not directly in contact. So for a child the board of governors of the school would be an exo-system. At the very highest level there is the macro-system which consists of the broader social and cultural values, norms and attitudes which impose consistency upon all the other systems. While much of Bronfenbrenner's work is a departure from the focus on physical environments it provides a very useful model for modern environmental psychology. The work of Novaco et al. (1990) on commuter stress adopts an ecological model which reflects the multi-system perspective of Bronfenbrenner (see Fig. 8). In addition we can see how issues such as attitudes to recycling and environmental protection are best understood in terms of the interdependence of physical and social aspects across the different systems within a society.

Settings, systems and place

In the 1970s another term was introduced and developed by Cantor (1977, 1986) and by others such as Russell and Ward (1982), Stokols and Shumaker (1981) and Altman (1986). This was the concept of place which also extends the behaviour setting of Barker to include the phenomic world of the individual.

> The central postulate is that people always situate their actions in a specifiable place and that the nature of the place, so specified, is an important ingredient in understanding human action and experience (Cantor, 1986, p.8).

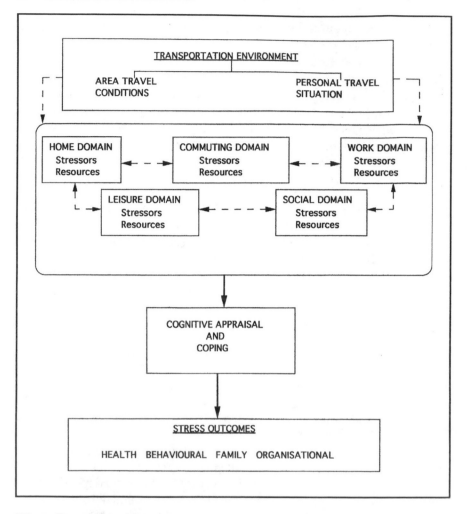

FIG. 8. The ecology of commuting stress (adapted from Novaco et al., 1990).

The argument is that behaviour is place specific in the sense that while one behaviour is appropriate in one place, the same behaviour would be inappropriate in another place. One can see the importance of understanding the place specificity of behaviour in the planning and design of environments.

While ecological psychology as exemplified by Barker has had a major impact on environmental psychology, many researchers including those whose background was within ecological psychology, such as Wicker (1987), have become critical of the concept of behaviour setting. As with the radical behaviourist perspective in psychology generally, the rigid focus on external factors generated some useful data but is ultimately limited and incomplete without some consideration of the cognitions, emotions and motivations of persons. The objections of modern environmental psychologists to behaviour settings as defined by Barker tend to reflect the criticisms offered by Bronfenbrenner. In other words they argue that behaviour settings provide incomplete explanations because they do not include the person's experience and appraisals of the context, and because they appear as isolated settings which do not consider the interdependence of parts within an individual's world. The concept of place includes these aspects and is offered as a way of building upon the ideas generated by the behaviour-setting perspective. Cantor (1986) defines place as "a unit of environmental experience". As for Barker behaviour cannot be separated from its setting; for Cantor, places cannot "be specified independently of the people who are experiencing them" (Cantor, 1986). Cantor's perspective is very much in tune with social psychological theories of social representations (Moscovici, 1984) (see Box 10).

The relationship between behaviour setting and place is captured very nicely by Stokols and Shumaker (1981):

> Places are viewed not only as composite of behaviour-shaping forces, but also as the material and symbolic product of human action (p.442).

In this quote behaviour shaping forces reflect the behaviour setting which is combined with the material and symbolic product of human action to produce the concept of place. Stokols' addition to the concept is to consider the element of commonality, by proposing that place involves shared meanings. In other words the social representation of place involves important aspects which are shared by those who inhabit the place. In addition he emphasises the architectural elements which transcend the more immediate functional and social aspects of Barker's behaviour setting. Between Cantor and Stokols a holistic model of the context of behaviour is presented in terms of place incorporating the ways in which the environment serves a function, motivates the person and is evaluated by the person all at the same time. It is this total experience of the environment which is important in determining the behaviour that occurs within it, not just the cues and constraints provided by Barker's behaviour setting. The shared meanings or social representation of place unite groups in their preference or attraction to a specific place. Different terms are used to describe this link between people and environments. Stokols talks of place dependence, while others talk of place attachment (Shumaker & Taylor, 1983) and place

---

Box 10: Sharing thoughts and feelings

When Kluckholn and Murray (1953) stated, "In some ways we are like all other men, in some ways we are like some other men, and in some other ways we are like no other men" they identified a basic division between theorists and a basic truth about human behaviour and experience. Traditionally psychologists have focused on individuals in seeking explanations for behaviour and experience, and have tried to explain similarities and differences in terms of stable personality traits. However this has been challenged by psychologists who hold a constructivist view of human nature. Moscovici (1984) for example holds that knowledge about the world is socially constructed in that we come to know through social interaction and discourse. Thus the similarities between people are the result of shared meanings acquired through interaction within specific groups, cultures or societies. The basic idea of shared meanings is very similar to Kelly's (1955) commonality corollary which was one of the basic premises of his personal construct theory:

"To the extent that one person employs a construction of experience which is similar to that employed by another, their processes are psychologically similar to those of the other person". Because of the interdependence between social and physical environments we can see how both play an important role in establishing and maintaining shared meanings, and in reflecting those meanings. The most obvious example are religious buildings. Closely related to the work of Moscovici, and those who share his social representation view of behaviour and experience, is the work of Tajfel and those who share his social identity theory perspective. An essential part of social identity is the sharing of meaning or a common construction of experience. Thus we can see how theorists working in different areas, often at different times, share ideas which can be integrated to provide more comprehensive explanations of real-world behaviour. Kelly, Moscovici, and Tajfel provide us with a way to understand how we come to think and feel like many others around us.

---

identity (Proshansky, Fabian, & Kaminoff, 1983). The social representation of place or the sharing of dependence, attachment or identity to place is analogous to the development of social identity (Tajfel & Turner, 1979). The relationship between social identity and physical environments has not been investigated, although it is clear that social groups are located within physical and geographically defined contexts.

The concept of behaviour setting has evolved into a more holistic concept of place, reflecting the interactional model of person–environment relations. In doing so it has raised the issue of motivational and evaluative aspects, which leads to the issue of how the environment impacts upon the emotional life of the individual, something that is contained within the area of stress.

THREAT AND CHALLENGE—ENVIRONMENTAL STRESS

The area of stress has attracted more attention than anything else within psychology over the past 10–15 years. Almost every newspaper or magazine in the UK has carried an article on stress in the recent past, and many of them feature stress several times per year. I have myself been interviewed about a range of stress issues, from commuter stress to stress in farmers. A growing literature suggests that an ever increasing list of environmental factors are sources of stress, and that stress has become a major factor in increased illness. As with any area of social science that becomes widely known, there are the critics who suggest that stress is a myth created by social scientists and a media thirsty for sensationalism. While it is a reasonable criticism that the term has been rather loosely used, to dismiss it is to ignore the evidence of the human suffering generated by the pressures of living for those who adopt ineffective coping strategies. It seems clear that, rather than treating the concept as trivial, we need to clarify what we mean when we talk of stress. One problem has been that workers in the area have used the term to describe the demands made by environmental factors on the person, and also to describe the person's response to those demands. It is important to recognise that the former refers to sources of stress and the latter refers to the consequences of stress. More recently workers have begun to view stress as the transaction between the person and the environment, or the process between the demands and the consequences.

The literature tends to categorise these areas under three main headings: stress as stimulus, stress as response, and stress as a process.

Stress as a response

The literature attests to a vast and ever increasing list of consequences attributed to ineffective coping with the stress of living. Stress has been causally implicated in the whole range of affective disorders, the range of problems that can be grouped under substance abuse, or addictive disorders, a wide range of dysfunctional behaviours— including sexual and negative health behaviours and an ever growing list of physical illnesses (Fisher & Reason, 1988). It is difficult to come up with a physical illness which has not been linked to stress either as a cause or as a factor in its maintenance.

In the recent past we have had the first worker in the UK to win a legal case against his employer for stress-related ill health induced through work overload. To some this is a rather too general use of the concept of stress, but work in the area of the biology of stress tends to support the broader view. The work of Seyle (1956) provides the link between biology and stress. The evidence is that the biological response is a generalised physiological arousal. The emotional response generated by this generalised arousal depends on the person's appraisal of the physical and social cues in the environment (Schachter & Singer, 1962). The outcome will also depend on appraisal of the coping resources available (Lazarus & Folkman, 1984). In addition the level of physiological arousal will depend on the person's appraisal of the situation as either a threat or a challenge as we shall see when we consider the transactional model of stress below.

Stress as stimulus

The focus of the stimulus approach has been to identify potential sources of stress for the individual in the physical and social environment. A vast literature has accumulated, providing evidence of the stressful effects of a vast range of stimuli, which at first seems to provide the reader with an impossible task in trying to produce any general conclusions. However, some general statements can be made. First of all, a system which allows categorisation is useful, and the one used by Rotton (1990) seems to be appropriate. This gives us four categories:

- ambient stressors
- cataclysmic stressors
- life stressors
- micro-stressors

It is important to be aware from the outset that any categorisation such as this is a working tool which does not preclude alternative categorisations, and acknowledges the overlap and interaction between categories and the coexistence of events in the life experience of the individual which appear under different categories. In order to place events in particular categories, one must have dimensions, which allow evaluation of events, and for this system the dimensions are: severity, scope, and duration.

The severity of an event is assessed on a dimension from high to low, the scope in terms of the numbers of people affected ranging from individual to community, and the duration in terms of how long it lasts, which can range from acute (of temporary duration) to chronic (always present).

Ambient stressors such as noise, temperature, climate, pollution and crowding are low to moderate severity, affect from large groups to whole communities in scope and are chronic in duration.

Cataclysmic stressors such as war and major disasters are high in severity, affect whole communities and are generally acute in duration.

It is important to point out the changing nature of stressful events at this point in noting that the immediate impact of war or disaster is severe, widespread and acute, but that effects of disaster or war for survivors and families become less severe, more individual and chronic in the long term. Thus the immediate impact fits the cataclysmic label, but the long-term effect fits the life stressor category.

Life stressors are those generally listed under the label "major life events", such as bereavement, divorce, unemployment and moving house. They tend to be high in severity, individually focused and towards the acute end on the duration dimension. The classic studies of life events are those of Holmes and Rahe (1967) which produced the well-known Social Readjustment Scale listing 43 major life events with their stress weightings, and Brown and Harris (1978) which produced the Life Events Directory, a structured interview technique for assessing life events.

Daily hassles and uplifts. It is not always the major events which cause most stress however, and it is often said that the accumulation of little irritations can be much more stressful. These micro-stressors such as losing your keys, sleeping in and being late for work, dealing with an awkward or pushy salesperson and concerns about weight, are everyday events which have a cumulative effect.

In any day a large number of micro-stressors will occur. Today already, and it is only 10 a.m., I have had an unexpectedly high telephone bill, my cat knocked over a glass of water which almost spilled onto my computer keyboard, and my printer cartridge ran out leaving me without a printer since I don't have a spare. None of these were major life events, but together they did have an emotional effect. These types of events tend to be low in severity, mainly affecting the individual, but chronic in that they are always around. Kanner et al. (1981) label these daily hassles. This perspective provides an important addition to the other perspectives in that the effects of positive as well as negative events are considered. The positive alternative to daily hassles are called daily uplifts (Kanner et al., 1981). It is the balance between daily hassles and the lack of daily uplifts which determines their effect. For example I still remain cheerful because the micro-stressors above were offset by receiving an unexpected advance on a chapter I had just written, and a phone call from my daughter—both uplifts.

Stress or challenge?—Warr's vitamin model

These four categories of stressors each covering a very large number of events give us some idea of the vast number of events that have been empirically linked with the experience of stress. In fact research supports the conclusion that any event in the physical or social environment has the potential to be a stressor (Lazarus & Folkman, 1984). Alternatively the same events have the potential to be challenges which stimulate individuals to greater efforts in problem solving and coping, and ultimately produce a sense of growth and development as a person. Even the most distressing events can have a positive side if dealt with successfully. Peter Warr's (1987) vitamin model of the relationship between the work environment and mental health can help in understanding the notion of threat and challenge (see Fig. 7). Warr's model was derived from research on the positive and negative effects of work and unemployment. Warr suggests that the analogy of the effect of vitamins on physical health can be applied. Some vitamins such as C and E have a detrimental effect if we don't have them in sufficient quantities, but more than the required amount has no ill effect. This type of influence Warr calls cumulative effect. On the other hand, vitamins such as A and D have a negative effect if we have too little or too much and need to be sustained at an optimal level for good health. This effect is referred to as additional decrement. Events which are positive such as good health, or daily uplifts, tend to operate in terms of cumulative effect, in other words, we cannot really have too much good health. However, events that have the potential to be stressful operate within the additional decrement model in that an optimal level of stress acts as a motivator while too much becomes detrimental. Stress that motivates is a challenge, while stress which has negative consequences is a threat, and it is true that the same objective level of external demand may be a threat to one person and a challenge for another.

Appraising demand

Turning to the psychological process involved in the stress experience, it is clear from research that negative consequences are not simply a function of the physical stimulus involved. If this were the case then we should be able to identify the physical threshold where noise, for example, becomes a stressor. However, this is not the case since a noise level in a factory may be experienced as stressful while an even greater noise level of music may be experienced as pleasurable. Alternatively the same loudness of music may be pleasurable to one person and a source of stress to another. There is strong evidence in the literature on stress that the relationship between a physical stimulus and a physiological reaction is not direct but is mediated by cognitive appraisal. In other words, the individual must process the information received from the stimulus and interpret it and it is only if the person perceives the stimulus as threatening that it becomes stressful. Lazarus and his colleagues (1984) conclude after what was probably the most extensive research programme on stress in the literature that "no environmental event can be identified as a stressor independently of its appraisal by the person". In the words of Shakespeare, "there is nothing good or bad, but thinking makes it so".

In other words stress actually occurs in the phenomic world of the individual.

Appraisal in the stress process operates in at least three different ways. Lazarus and Folkman (1984) identify primary appraisal and secondary appraisal. Primary appraisal is essentially the first stages in the process described above, where the individual decides whether or not a problem exists. In other words the primary appraisal process decides whether external events contain information which could pose a threat. The secondary appraisal process involves choosing a response, and involves evaluating the external information in the context of the person's coping resources. At this stage the person decides if the external demand is a threat or a challenge and selects a response. Other workers draw on the lability model of emotion demonstrated so effectively by Schachter and Singer (1962), and suggest that an important component of the appraisal process is the attribution of cause (Halpern, 1995), or whether a cause can be readily identified or not. According to this perspective where a cause can be clearly identified, the person can easily label their emotion and take appropriate action. Where a cause is not available, the person is more likely to feel out of control and helpless. You have probably experienced this yourself at some time when you are caught in a traffic jam, or a flight is delayed. Where you know the cause you tend to feel more in control, even if objectively you still cannot do anything about it. The process then seems to be something like that outlined in Fig. 9.

Stress in a vacuum

Cognitive appraisal refers to the perceptual process discussed in the previous chapter involving attending to, processing and giving meaning to experiences. Accepting that the person's appraisal of the event is central in determining whether or not stress is experienced or the level of stress experienced does not mean that the role of the external environment is reduced in any way. The stress experience begins in the external environment. It is important to deal with the issue of "stress in a vacuum" here, since we tend generally to think of stimuli as the occurrence or presence of an event. However, the absence of events in our environment becomes an event in itself and is also a source of stress. We can refer here to Warr's vitamin model and to the notion of homeostasis and optimum levels. A typical example is the boring job which becomes stressful because of the lack of events and stimulation from the external environment.

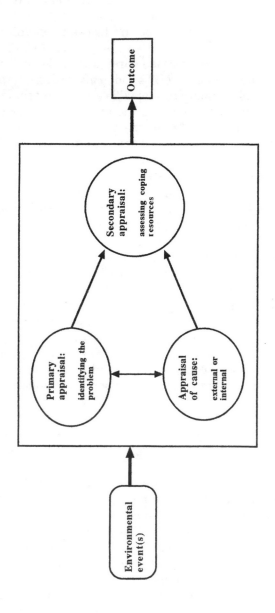

FIG. 9. Appraisal of events in terms of the stress model.

Characteristics of demand

In trying to understand the role of the environment in the stress process, one useful approach is to try to identify aspects or characteristics of events or stimuli which increase their probability of being perceived as stressful. We know that any event has the potential to be stressful but what are the distinguishing features of the event where stress occurs? Four dimensions have been identified in the literature and these are controllability, predictability, threat, and loss, with control being central. Control is both an aspect of the environment and part of the person's appraisal process. The classic studies are the learned helplessness studies of Seligman and his colleagues carried out in 1966–67 and reported in Seligman (1975). Using animals, they demonstrated the stressful consequences of being in an environment where escape was blocked while being given electric shocks. These studies were later modified to demonstrate that when the animals were given an escape route and therefore some control over the environment, the stressful consequences were modified. The evidence for the central role of controllability in the stress process is very strong (Skinner, 1995).

If an event is unpredictable, it will also present problems of control in that we can never be totally sure of our effectiveness in coping with the unpredictable. On the other hand, events that are totally predictable may also be stressful. It is not surprising that studies have shown that stressful events tend to rate on one or other of the extremes of predictability.

The literature also shows that stressful events contain elements of threat or loss. For example, being told one is to become unemployed involves both a loss of job and a threat to social identity (Branthwaite & Trueman, 1989). In essence, if one looks at the range of events that have been shown to be stressful, one can see elements of threat and loss and of predictability. Threat, loss and predictability influence control and it is likely that it is through their effect on control that they determine appraisal. What is suggested is that where an event removes or reduces the opportunity for control, it is more likely to be perceived and experienced as stressful.

In summary, we can say that any event has the potential to be stressful, but will only be experienced as stressful if so perceived by the person. Events are more likely to be perceived as stressful if they involve threat, loss or are unpredictable, therefore reducing or removing opportunities to exercise power or control over them. The controllability of external demands and of the environment generally is central to whether any situation is seen as a stressor. However the reverse is also true, that is environments which offer opportunities for control will enhance the stress resistance of the person. In other words, as well as providing sources of stress, environments provide resources which enhance coping.

Environments as resources in coping

Coping with demands is not simply a matter of personal characteristics but is more a transaction between person and environment. In that process however the phenomic world of the person is often given precedence over the environment. The area of control is a good example of this, with research tending to focus on person variables such as locus of control (Rotter, 1966) and self-efficacy (Bandura, 1977). However as Orford (1992) argues, perceptions of control are unlikely to exist in the absence of some objective degree of control. In research on commuting for example, environmental psychologists have shown that perceived control is important in determining whether or not stress is experienced (Cassidy, 1992; Novaco et al., 1990). However it is very clear also from this research that actual disruption of travel or impedance is a necessary precondition to lowered perceptions of control.

POWER, CONTROL, AND AUTONOMY
WITHIN THE ENVIRONMENT

As stated above there is consensus in the literature on the role of control in the stress process and in the psychosocial causality of health and illness in general. It is central to the major theories and has been looked at as a variable in its own right (Skinner, 1995; Steptoe & Appels, 1989). The exercise of control involves autonomy and power, and it is in understanding power that we can understand the potential for and constraints on the individual's ability to be autonomous. As argued in the previous chapter individuals are to some extent active participants in constructing their phenomic world and exercise some degree of free will in the process.

Distribution of power in society has never been equal whatever society we wish to consider and at whatever level we wish to look, be it at the interpersonal, group or organisational level. Some would argue that engaging in power play is a throwback to our evolutionary history when it was essential to our survival to dominate in a hostile world (Lorenz, 1966; Wilson, 1975). Ethologists such as Lorenz draw their conclusions from the study of animal behaviour in their natural setting, and comparative psychologists such as Wilson (1975) argue that a legitimate comparison can be made with human behaviour. One could scarcely deny that threat and hostility still exist in our environment albeit of a less direct and physical nature and that competition is still part of the process of human survival. Pecking orders or hierarchies exist in all human groups, from families to work groups and we tend to build them into many of our institutions as a means of control or behaviour modification. Children in school are given higher status as a reward in the same way that patients in a psychiatric hospital or workers in an organisation are rewarded. The sociological literature abounds with studies of power differentials in families, organisations and societies (Dahl, 1957; Wrong, 1979). Ng (1980) provides a social psychological analysis of power. The debate about the dimensions of power has never been completely settled but we all tend to recognise concepts such as force, authority, persuasion, manipulation, and categories such as coercive, induced, legitimate, competent, and personal authority (Orford, 1992). We are also familiar with responses to power such as conformity, compliance, identification, obedience, resistance, and conflict. We tend to base our response to power from others on our perceptions of its legitimacy or illegitimacy. It is important to acknowledge that as with any psychological concept we cannot understand the influence of power on the individual without an understanding of the individual's perception and interpretation of the power. Legitimacy or illegitimacy will be conferred as a result of giving meaning to the experience and will be based on a functional analysis of the power source. For example those who perceive police power as providing a safe environment will accept the legitimacy of that power while those who see it as suppressing freedom will not see it as legitimate.

The social and physical location of power

Power resides in all social structures and organisations and will most often be involved in decision making. In other words in our society it is those who have decision-making authority who are seen as powerful and vice versa.

In essence the literature on leadership supports the consensus–conflict distinctions drawn by Dahrendorf (1959). Two views of power in society have been proposed. On one hand there is the functional differentiation of power associated with the work of Talcott Parsons, which argues that power is distributed in ways which ultimately serve the good of all. This is the notion of consensus. On the other hand the conflict analysis views power as a function of competition. Power resides in the dominant groups who will wield it to serve their own ends and hence is likely to disadvantage others. The extreme situation is where all power resides in the hands of a small power elite (Mills, 1956). As with most competing theories they turn out not to be competing at all. In fact both types of power exist. Without getting into any heated debates about the inequalities of power, it is fair to say that individuals will differ in their perceptions of power as a function of their previous experience and current situation and these differences in perception will determine their behaviour. An example to demonstrate this was the study by Hopkins (1992) on "young people's perceptions of police power". The study shows how young people are able to maintain different perceptions of the police in two different behaviour settings, i.e. in the school and on the street. The police in school were seen as different, less powerful, members who were unsuitable for street duty, while those on the street were seen as powerful and motivated to use their power in suppressing freedom. Furthermore the school was seen as the young people's territory where through knowledge they had control. Hence the balance of power was different. Power and control were central to their analysis of their relationship with the police and it would appear that these are the concepts to be focused on in changing that relationship. Power differentials were seen as a function of the behaviour setting, or place, with police power being reduced when taken out of place.

Social identity and power
The place specificity of power is a function of both physical and social aspects of the environment, just as a school is both a physical location and a social environment. The physical environment is an important component of the identity of groups ranging from the graffiti covered derelict blocks which provide a place identity for street gangs, through to impressive buildings which provide a place identity for religious groups. The social representation of place discussed above will form an important part of the social identity of the person and group. Social identity theory hasn't yet been applied to the role of the physical environment in group processes, though the evidence would suggest that such an application is warranted. Social identity theory provides a model within which we can explain the interaction between groups who stand in power and status differences to each other in society.

Place and powerlessness
The way in which power is place specific is not the only way in which power and control is important for environmental psychology.

In the wider social context every individual will find themselves in a power relationship with others at different levels in the social structure: for example, workers and managers, clients and professionals, prisoners and wardens, patients and doctors, and children and parents. The power differential will be located in the role each plays in the decision-making process. For the most part one group will find themselves in a dependent relationship where they exercise little or no control over decision making. The effects of being institutionalised are pertinent here. Work by people like Goffman has shown how the social aspects of institutions create dependency. Similarly work organisations, hospitals, schools, universities and other large organisations exert effects on individual power and autonomy. Research in institutions has also shown that the physical environment influences dependency and powerlessness (Olsen, 1978) although the evidence is not as extensive. The way in which seating is organised (Sommer, 1969) enhances or reduces interaction and hence dependency. As we shall see in a later chapter the physical design of all sorts of buildings has an effect on the powerlessness experienced.

SOCIAL SUPPORT

Another aspect of the external world which has been clearly identified as important in the stress process and in the development of problems is the quantity and quality of social support available.

We tend to apply a developmental analogy to society in that we see later societies as developing from previous ones and improving with this development. However there is also a view which argues that we pay a price for development in that although advances in technology and material aspects of society have benefits there may be sacrifices in other areas. One such area is social support. A classic series of studies by the sociologists Young and Willmott (1957) in the East End of London demonstrated how social development led to the demise of the extended family and generally to a reduction in the size of kinship networks. With the advent of the nuclear family and indeed with single parent families and same sex couples, social units become smaller and sources of support are reduced. There is an argument that many of the needs for counselling in modern societies were in the past provided by sources within the kinship network and are a function of the increasing isolation of the person. An example is the natural "counselling" support provided for the bereaved by the "waking" system in some cultures. This involves friends and neighbours gathering around the bereaved for two or three days after the bereavement and providing social and emotional support.

A sense of isolation
The sense of isolation experienced by many in modern communities is often only visible when the community is under some form of threat. The ways in which communities rally around at times of tragedy is an example. The week in which I write this has seen a terrible tragedy in Scotland   where   a   gunman   entered   a   primary   school   and

indiscriminately murdered many of the children. The way in which the community came together in response demonstrates something that is not usually the practice. In the area where I myself live, I rarely have opportunity to talk to neighbours. However this week we have also had a situation where a gunman barricaded himself in the local cathedral. During the two-day siege neighbours have been out on the street talking to each other, and people I have never known before have spoken to me.

The breakdown of traditional communities is not simply a social change. In fact it is more to do with changes in the physical environment, brought about by social mobility and the design of new work and living environments to meet the new demands. An example is the new towns process in Britain during the 1960s and 1970s. This social isolation is exacerbated by technology in work places which mean that people more often communicate indirectly rather than face-to-face. The increasingly competitive world where emotions are a sign of weakness not only increases isolation but reduces the likelihood that individuals might admit to being lonely. The influence of the technological environment on behaviour and experience has not really been considered in the psychological literature, but the way in which it is an influence on the shape of our world needs to be investigated.

The nature of social support

The first question which we need to address is what is social support? In essence it is support from other people and research has identified five main types. These are material, emotional, esteem, informational, and companionship support (Orford, 1992). Material support is simply tangible aid. Emotional support involves caring and counselling. Esteem support involves affirmation or reflection of the individual as valued. Informational support involves advice and clarification, and companionship support provides positive social interaction.

The literature is confusing on the effects of these different factors of support since most studies have focused on social support as a unitary concept or on a limited number of factors. However a strong link between social support and a range of psychological and physical health problems has been established and the process involved seems to be twofold in that social support can buffer the effects of stress or support may provide resources which enable more effective coping.

Sources of support

Given the importance of social support to the individual and its multidimensional nature we can now turn to the sources of support. Considering the five dimensions outlined above it is clear that sources can exist at various levels in the community. For example material support may be provided by a close friend, or by family, or by work, or at the organisational level by the social services. This at once illustrates the limitations of focusing on one level in understanding social support and suggests that support networks may vary in complexity. For most people different dimensions of support will have different sources. Emotional, esteem and companionship support are likely to be focused on at lower levels in terms of immediate partner, close friends and family, while material and informational support may be imbedded in the larger scale social systems such as social services or the legal system.

Social networks

Studies of social networks have looked at both the structure and function of such networks. The structural approach measures networks in terms of size, types of relationship, and density. An individual will generally have a finite number of people in his/her network. These will be people at the personal level, group level and organisational level. The types of relationship will vary from simple dyadic to complex multiple interactions and will vary also in terms of formal/informal processes. Density in this sense refers to connectedness of the network which can vary from very loose knit to very closely interwoven and interdependent parts. In simple terms most individuals will have relationships at the interpersonal level with friends and family members, group level relationships at work, leisure or in social activities, and relationships at the organistaional level with the representatives of institutions and social systems. This sort of structure can be represented by a concentric circle model such as that by Kahn and Antonucci (1980) reproduced in Orford (1992, p.64), where closeness of relationship decreases with outer circles. It is important to recognise that although close relationships are represented within the inner circle an individual may be dependent on people represented in outer circles for some aspects of support. For example a schizophrenic patient in the community may have close family but may be very dependent on professionals for essential support. Which brings us neatly to the functional approach to networks. In essence this approach looks at the dimensions of social support in terms of their source of provision in the network. Using the concentric circle (or onion) model emotional, esteem and companionship support is likely to be embedded in inner layers of the network while material and informational support may be more diffuse with roots in the outer circles or layers of the network. This is not always the case, of course, since there are cases which differ. For example an individual whose relationship has broken down may need and prefer emotional support from a professional source. Social support networks are place dependent in that the physical world will enhance or constrain both size and ease of access within the network. The development of new towns has been associated with the breakup of social support networks. Early developments in the 1960s tended not to deal with the issue of community. Families were provided with housing which enhanced privacy, but there were little or no attempts to recreate the sort of free and easy communication channels that had existed in traditional communities such as that of the East End of London reported by Young and Willmott (1957). In addition other physical factors such as the building of new motorways which dissected towns had a major impact on social support networks (Lee, 1984).

Using social support

It is important to bear in mind the distinction between availabilty of social support and the individual's perception of its quality. For example a common finding among depressed children is their sense of lack of social support despite the fact that support is available. However it is also true that it is unlikely that an individual will perceive social support which is actually not there. Furthermore intervention must begin with the provision of adequate support networks.

The multiple-level approach of environmental psychology allows us to begin to understand the support resources required at different levels in the community. Related to this is the identification of groups with special support needs and the types of support which are most effective in improving their quality of life. The old will differ in needs from the young and individuals who are disadvantaged physically will differ not only from those not disadvantaged but also as a function of the way in which they are disadvantaged. A wide range of groups can be visibly identified, but there also exist groups whose special support needs may be less visible. One area for example is the area of specific stress associated with particular occupations.

Recent developments in disaster research (Hodgkinson & Stewart, 1991) demonstrate the long-term effects of disasters on both the survivors and disaster workers (paramedics, fire service, etc.) in terms of post traumatic stress disorder (PTSD). This led to research into the consequences for individuals such as police and paramedics who deal with accidents on a smaller scale such as road traffic accidents. These events are similar to large-scale disasters in most ways except for their scope. Research shows that a large percentage of such persons do experience PTSD or other long-term health consequences (Thompson, 1990). Because the effects are at the level of the individual, individual-level explanations have been invoked in terms of personal characteristics such as oversensitivity. The result has been to blame individuals for their own incapacity. Taking the larger view leads one to the conclusion that individuals who deal with such situations should be prepared for the consequences in training and should have available the support services necessary to help them cope with it.

A great deal needs to be done in understanding social support as a resource in the external world. It is clear that social isolation is on the increase. Today the society section of the *Guardian* carries a two-page article (Porter, 27th March, 1996) which considers why so many people feel isolated and lonely to the point of despair. Certainly social scientists such as Sennet consider that increased material wealth and advanced technology have undermined the need and the environments for people to interact on a frequent basis. There exists a clear need to understand the effect on health and emotion and to consider these factors in designing new environments.

Box 11: Fear of crime: Control and support

There is a widely accepted view, propagated by the media, that crime is on the increase. There are also arguments that there is no real increase, rather crime has become more visible, due to more media coverage. One can find figures which appear alarming on the numbers of robberies, burglaries, violent assaults, and other forms of crime which involve loss or suffering for individuals or groups within society. Associated with this are the stereotypes of the typical criminal and his/her typical habitation. These stereotypes engender fear. A news programme called *Crimebeat* is currently running on TV and as I write this Martin Lewis is talking about the spreading fear of crime. It is just one of the many programmes that bombard us with information, which may have some positive uses, but certainly has the negative one of spreading the message of fear. Who can deny experiencing some fear while walking in a strange area, which is run down and graffiti strewn, where groups of young males congregate, as darkness begins to fall?

Some suggest that the fear of crime has become almost more of a problem than crime itself. Clearly environmental factors are important. Lighting at night, providing a brighter and more open design in cities, and so on, will have an effect not only on reducing crime, but reducing the fear. One of the concerns of modern city living is the threat experienced by females travelling alone. It is a rather sad aspect of our advanced society that the best advice offered is often to avoid travelling alone, avoid some areas, and carry personal alarms. This is a reactive approach to a problem which would appear to need a proactive intervention. Consider for yourself whether you want a world where freedom to travel is restricted in this way. The evidence suggests that in more closely knit communities, in past times, in rural areas and in more primitive societies, crime and its accompanying fear is less prevalent. Perhaps we have something to learn from this.

CHAPTER FOUR

The environment through the senses

We have seen how the environmental impact upon the person's emotional life can be understood in terms of the interplay between demands and resources provided by the external world. We now turn to a more detailed look at specific aspects of the environment that have been explored in this context. There are several possible ways in which this research could be categorised. For example we could use traditional categories such as noise, atmosphere, and urbanisation. However there are different problems with each classification. For example to focus on noise is to ignore stress imposed through other sense modalities—which has in fact been the case traditionally in environmental psychology. However more recently it is recognised that environments are experienced holistically and we do need to consider other aspects such as smell and visual impact. To talk of atmosphere generally invokes a vision of the natural atmosphere involving temperature, weather, and so on. What this ignores is the increasing importance of the human-made atmosphere involving chemical pollution. Urbanisation tends to invoke issues such as crowding, personal space, territoriality, and privacy. Again recent research shows that these variables are all part of one complete process and to understand their impact requires an understanding of their interdependence. In addition urbanisation generates other issues such as commuting, break-up of communities and social isolation, as well as influences upon perception. In this chapter we will first look at how the environment impacts upon the senses, in terms of noise, smell, colour, light and then consider the effects of weather and climate. The next chapter will look at the human role in self-damage through chemical pollution and technological disasters. Issues related to urbanisation will be reserved for Chapter 7.

SENSING THE ENVIRONMENT

We experience the environment through all our available senses at the same time, and it is this accumulation of experiences that produces a physiological and psychological effect. However research has tended to focus on one sense modality at a time. Most researched has been the impact on our auditory modality, the effect of noise.

Noise

Our environment is subject to permanent and continuous noise pollution. It is impossible to find places even in the most isolated rural areas of Britain where our peace is not broken by the distant hum of traffic, the sound of passing aeroplanes or the sound of farm or building machinery. We are often unaware of the noise that fills our world and we do habituate to it to some extent. Have you ever listened to music which has been so loud you are unable to talk above it? Have you ever stood beside a railway track as the express sped by, or tried to work while workmen dug up the road outside? What is common to all these situations is the high level of sound. In fact the level of sound of music is probably much the highest. You probably enjoyed the music, but the other noise caused some annoyance. In fact the latter was unwanted sound, which provides us with a useful and simple definition of noise.

Sound is generally described on three dimensions, the most obvious of which is loudness. This is technically defined in terms of the amplitude of the sound waves. In addition there is timbre, or tonal quality and pitch, which describes the frequency of wavelengths but is experienced as "high" or "low" sound, as in musical scales. The human ear can only detect sounds within a range of pitch and above a minimum level of loudness. In addition the combined effect of loudness, timbre and pitch vary in the way they are perceived.

Sound may be unwanted for two main reasons. It may be of a loudness, timbre or pitch which causes us physical discomfort or it may be unwanted because of the situation. For example a lawn mower is not normally uncomfortable but is unwanted outside the window while you are in the middle of an examination! Listening to music is generally enjoyable, but sitting next to someone listening to a Walkman playing loudly on a long flight is not generally appreciated.

Physical damage by noise

The physical damage to hearing caused by noise in the work place has attracted both extensive research and legislation. Research has shown that large numbers of workers develop hearing problems because of noise. One estimate based on a survey carried out in 1972 by the Environmental Protection Agency in the USA, suggests that three million Americans had suffered noise induced hearing loss. This figure had grown to nearly 10 million by 1991 (Veitch & Arkkelin, 1995). This is despite extensive health and safety legislation which both controls noise levels at work and makes it a legal necessity to wear protective ear devices. The sorts of alarming statistics produced are of the type which compare hearing acuity of people experiencing different levels of noise. For example 70-year-old individuals living in the Middle East were shown to have comparable acuity to Americans in their 20s (Rosen et al., 1962). Note that this finding was produced over 30 years ago and noise levels have increased in the Western world since then. In fact estimates of an increase of one decibel per year in our major cities lead to predictions that unless interventions occur most city dwellers will eventually become deaf.

Psychological effects of noise

In addition to physical damage it is also clear that, as a stressor, noise contributes to many mental health effects (Dubos, 1965), and to both acute and chronic physical illness (Cameron, Robertson, & Zaks, 1972). A link between noise at work and reduced performance has also been suggested, though the evidence is not conclusive (Kovrigin & Mikheyev, 1965; Kryter, 1970). One explanation for this lack of agreement in results may lie in the fact that humans adapt to sound, a process known as habituation (see Box 9).

While the potential to habituate to ambient stressors such as noise means that people may not be aware of these stressors, the question that psychologists need to address is whether habituation removes the harmful effects. The correlational evidence would suggest that whether or not we are aware of noise, over long periods it is still a chronic stressor (Levy-Leboyer, 1982). Noise is part of our general environment and has effects other than those observed at work. For example, noise in the home has been shown to have a detrimental effect on child development in areas such as language acquisition and attention (Wachs, Uzgiris, & McHunt, 1971) and reading ability (Cohen, Glass, & Singer, 1973). Given the evidence for recent massive increases in noise levels in all areas of life, this developmental effect is rather worrying.

Noise and health

Noise levels have also been shown to correlate with admission rates to psychiatric hospitals. For example Herridge (1974) and Abey-Wickerama et al. (1969) compared admission rates between high and low noise areas around Heathrow airport in London and found significantly higher rates of admission in higher noise areas. This effect remains after other contributory factors have been controlled. Kryter (1970) identifies aircraft noise as a significant contributing factor in health disorders requiring psychiatric attention. More recently Halpern (1995) explored the relationship between symptoms such as nervousness, depression, sleeplessness, undue irritability, and asthma, and road traffic noise and found a consistent increase in symptoms as a function of increased noise levels. Nevertheless Halpern's conclusion is that the direct link between noise and mental health is rather weak. First of all the effect is subject to vast individual differences, and second Halpern argues, noise is a stressor which generally has an identifiable source. Thus it allows individuals to attribute causality and thereby establish some sense of control.

Barnes (1992) studied the effects of various work place stressors on railway personnel and found noise to be one major contributory factor in increased anxiety, lower self-concept and general reductions in morale. Morin (1989) found the effects of noise in supermarkets and cafeterias to be mediated by work involvement, family situation, and aspects of identity.

Noise has also been linked with miscarriages and birth defects (Veitch & Arkkelin, 1995). It is important to recognise the wide range of environmental variables which may contribute to these sorts of problems and the difficulty in isolating the effect of any one variable. Hence the best that can be said is that noise is one of the possible contributory factors.

Other studies have looked at the relationship between noise and social behaviours such as aggression, attraction and altruism. The evidence suggests that noise can facilitate aggressive behaviour (Geen & O'Neal, 1969; Konecni, 1975), and can reduce altruism or helping behaviour (Page, 1977). The effect of noise on aggression has attracted a lot of public attention in the UK recently with numerous court cases, at least one suicide, and one murder charge being attributed to noisy neighbours. Noise tends also to exacerbate fear of crime in that loud people are seen as more threatening and raised voices are associated with fighting and violence. The effects of noise on helping behaviour are worrying in that most violent crime occurs in cities where noise levels are high and hence would suggest that altruism is less likely to occur. Of course noise is only one factor associated with lack of helping

---

Box 12: Noise in shopping malls

Hopkins (1994) investigated ambient sound levels in a shopping mall in an attempt to identify effects on those using the mall. He assessed responses from 748 participants and concluded that the physical intensity of noise had a detrimental effect on shopper well being. Given the variety of sound from different sources which tend to accumulate in large shopping malls, he suggests that managers need to rethink their policy on noise and to attempt some more coordinated control of sound levels in the interest of their clients. It is worth pausing the next time you are in a shopping mall to consider the level of sound, and whether you would consider it sound or noise. Visiting a mall when shops are closed provides a contrast which might surprise you.

---

behaviour and as we shall see other factors such as the number of people around tend also to be associated with urbanisation.

The findings for interpersonal attraction are ambiguous and tend to suggest a gender effect with noise reducing attraction for males but not for females (Bull et al., 1972). The best conclusion from the research on noise and social behaviour seems to be that noise disrupts the harmony of interpersonal relations and under particular conditions may have negative consequences. These conditions are not well understood and require more investigation.

Noise and communication

One fairly easily observed effect of high levels of noise is the disruption of communication. Have you ever tried to hold a sensible conversation in a noisy bar or on a noisy city sidewalk? Apart from the fact that some city dwellers seem to have acquired an ability to talk much louder, most ordinary mortals find that the effort isn't worth the outcome. Research from the social psychology of organisational behaviour has clearly shown how important the informal functions of groups are in maintaining performance and satisfaction in monotonous or difficult jobs. One important informal function is to provide opportunities for social intercourse. Noise levels at work make communication difficult, and legislation now makes it necessary to wear ear plugs or ear muffs where noise levels are high. Thus one effect of noise on communication would appear to be a reduction in performance and satisfaction in some jobs (Kryter, 1970).

Noise effects on communication in schools are indicated from two sources. On the one hand hearing-impaired children have difficulty coping with the school environment (May & Brackett, 1987). On the other hand it is seems that noisy classrooms reduce clarity regarding tasks and therefore reduce pupil performance (Biassoni-de-Serra, 1990; DeJoy, 1984; Grosjean, Lodi, & Rabinowitz, 1976). Marascuilo and Penfield (1972) report on an intervention programme designed to teach pupils how to focus on oral communication thereby screening out unwanted sound. The programme had some success in improving pupil performance and motivation. Noise has also been shown to have some effect on the performance of university students at lectures in terms of motivation and attention (Grobe, Pettibone, & Martin, 1973). This study produced an inverted U-shaped relationship between noise and performance similar to the Yerkes–Dodson arousal–performance relationship.

In a study of communication between astronauts in space, Kelly and Kanas (1992) show that ambient noise was one of the factors judged to hinder communication.

Cohen & Weinstein (1981) suggest from their review of noise effects on behaviour and health that the effect is mediated by noise effects on communication. In the development of a general measure of the effects of environmental noise Guski et al. (1981) identify disruption of communication as one of the main dimensions.

The direct effect of noise on communication has not attracted as much research as one might expect given the important role played by communication in human interaction. Of course noise is only one factor that influences communication, but its effect may often be ignored.

Noise and accidents

Given the evidence of effects of noise on emotions and performance, one might be forgiven for wondering if noise might have an effect on accidents. Noise and confusion in the home was identified as one of three major factors in the prediction of accidental injury among children (Matheny, 1986, 1987). In a review of the traffic accident literature in Japan, Nakajima (1986) identified noise as one of nine contributory factors. Noise levels on school buses have been implicated in bus accidents (Greene, Bailey, & Barber, 1981). Stave (1977) suggests that noise may be one factor leading to lapses of attention and hence pilot error in helicopter pilots. In a study of 6000 city dwellers, Tarnopolsky, Watkin, and Hand (1980) found an increase in minor accidents in the home as a function of higher levels of aircraft noise. Noweir (1984) compared noise levels in three textile mills with 2458 workers and found that both frequency and severity of accidents were greater in noisier environments. It is important to remind ourselves that noise will coexist with many other factors and it is the cumulative effect of these that will be important. For example it is likely that factories which do not take action to reduce noise levels will also be less concerned with other aspects of the work environment such as health and safety regulations. From a rather brief literature, there would seem to be indications that the role of noise in accidents needs to be investigated more fully.

Individual differences in noise perception

As with any external factor, not everyone has the same experience. For example some people are much more sensitive to noise levels and have difficulty in habituating to noise generally (Glass & Singer, 1972). This supersensitivity tends not to be the result of more sensitive hearing in terms of auditory thresholds (Stansfeld et al., 1985). One factor associated with sensitivity to noise is current psychological health. Neurotic individuals and those diagnosed as hysteric tend to have difficulty in habituating to noise and react more violently to it (Halpern, 1995). This might lead one to the optimum levels of physiological arousal as an explanation. Highly anxious individuals tend to be already physiologically aroused to a level of discomfort and one could postulate that any additional stimulation would have a more noticeable effect. Not surprisingly attitudes and expectation play an important role in reactions to noise. Where we have a positive attitude to the source of the noise we are less likely to be disturbed by it. In a way this belies the definition of noise as unwanted sound, since having a positive attitude towards the source implies that it is not necessarily unwanted. However a particular special case is that of work. If a job provides us with a much needed income and if we actually enjoy other aspects of it we are more willing to tolerate high levels of noise. In addition there is some evidence that noise toleration is affected by social class, with middle- and upper-class individuals being more sensitive to noise (Tarnopolsky & Morton-Williams, 1980). The evidence for this class effect is however based on incidence of noise complaints. An alternative explanation is that being intolerant of noise is a luxury the financially challenged cannot afford.

Personality traits have also been implicated in the noise sensitivity debate. Neuroticism, introversion–extraversion, locus of control, and TypeA/Type B personality have all been studied. The evidence is that individuals who score high on neuroticism as a personality trait tend to be more sensitive to noise (Ohrstrom, Bjorkman, & Rylander, 1988). The relationship between noise sensitivity and extroversion–introversion is equivocal with some studies suggesting that introverts are more sensitive and others that extraverts are sensitive (Geen, McCown, & Broyles, 1985). Both Type As and those with a high internal locus of control seem to be able to shut out noise better and therefore perform better on cognitive tasks in noisy conditions, than their Type B or external locus of control colleagues (Collins-Eiland et al., 1986; Moch, 1984).

Gender differences in response to noise do not produce consistent effects, but seem to vary depending on factors such as noise level and time of day (Smith, 1985).

On the face of it individual difference evidence suggests a need to match individuals to environments in order to reduce stress and improve performance, which is of particular interest in the workplace. However one recurrent problem with this research is that it doesn't really clarify whether those who appear less sensitive to noise are in the long term unaffected by it. For example the Type A person may be more able to focus on the task, but at what cost? It is well established that Type A behaviour patterns correlate with high stress levels and poorer health.

In summary, research supports the conclusion that noise in the environment is associated with negative consequences in terms of both physical and mental health. However not everyone suffers these negative consequences. On the other hand the evidence has been sufficient to lead to legislation. It would seem appropriate that environmental psychologists should be involved in preventing these negative consequences. The question is what can be suggested from the evidence. One problem with this area is that much of the noise in our environment has been the result of developments in industry and

---

Box 13: What sounds do you detest?

People often have weird and wonderful likes and dislikes as a result of experience. Most people seem to hate the noise made by foam packing material rubbed on glass. In one study a group of researchers in Japan played 138 pleasant sounds and 150 unpleasant sounds to 596 male and 136 female college students. They found that males preferred louder sounds such as rock music and racing cars, while females preferred melodious sounds such as rain or harp music. It seems that natural sounds and musical sounds were most likely to be rated positively. In addition it seems there was more similarity than difference between males and females in choosing unpleasant sounds. They found that sounds of alarm, excretion, and scratching were rated negatively by most participants. You might wish to think about the sounds that you like and dislike, and how your world could be improved by changes in the sound (or noise) you are exposed to each day. For example how do you feel about the explosion in technical sound, from computers, games machines, and the computer-generated voices that instruct us every where we go these days? Nosulenko (1991) argues that our acoustical environment has undergone qualitative changes that require more and different approaches in research including international cooperation.

technology. With the major economic contribution involved it is not surprising that the attempt to reduce noise levels is a somewhat uphill struggle. The most obvious intervention must be through changing attitudes of governments and those who wield the reins of power. However one alternative is to utilise the potential positive side of sound (see Box 14).

In addition a positive outcome of technological advance is the development of sound-absorbing materials and computer-generated noise cancellation techniques. Increasingly we see sound-absorbing walls or fences being erected between housing areas and motorways, and similar techniques are being applied to soundproofing buildings. Furthermore, it appears that where sound waves are predictable, it is possible to generate mirror image sound waves which have a cancelling effect (Veitch & Arkkelin, 1995). We do seem to have the means for combating noise, what we really need is the will to use these means.

One of the side effects of writing this chapter on noise has been that I have become more observant of the noise in my own environment, and as a result more frustrated by it. Even as I sit here now in my office, early in the morning with no students around, I am aware of the hum

---

BOX 14: If music be the food of love ...

While unwanted sound in the form of noise can be both physically and psychologically damaging, sound that is desired (e.g. music) can have a healing effect. It is widely recognised that music, and other sounds such as the sound of the sea, birdsong or whale communication can be relaxing and can be used effectively in stress reduction. Research on memory and recall in cognitive psychology has shown that noise interferes with the ability to recall in serial recall tasks (Salame & Baddeley, 1989). Initially it was thought that any type of noise had a disruptive effect on attention and rehearsal. However recent research has begun to distinguish between background music and other forms of noise and there is some evidence that background music can enhance perform-ance on some types of tasks (Davies, Lang, & Shackleton, 1973). It is worth speculating that the subjective distinction between unwanted sound (noise) and wanted sound plays an important role in the process. Given the potential positive effects of some forms of sound on both emotions and performance it may be worth looking at the possibility of modifying noise in situations where it cannot be eliminated. No doubt the idea of 10-ton trucks with exhausts blasting out the 1812 Overture, the current number one, or sounding like a nightingale singing in Berkeley Square, are pipe dreams. However, a basis for future research might be the notion that if we cannot eliminate noise we could make it more pleasant.

of my computer, the sound of the cleaner's vacuum somewhere along the corridor, and the roar of a plane overhead. It seems impossible to escape noise in our world and it is surprising to find that I probably never consciously noticed these sounds before. This in many ways is the problem with noise, we do become accustomed to it.

Smell—the undervalued sense

Smell is one of the most underresearched sense modalities despite the fact that it is seen as one of the most sensitive senses. The importance of smell in the environment cannot go unnoticed, since we experience such a wide variety of smells during our waking, and sleeping, hours. Recently I read of a court case between a celebrity who had bought a large house in the country and a local pig farmer over the smell caused by the pigs. I never did discover the outcome, but the essence of the case was that the celebrity was suing the farmer. In the past year I have also read of at least one American company having made it a disciplinary offence to exude excessive body odour whether natural or artificial. Smells can make us feel ill, hungry, happy, sad, and they can trigger memories of past experiences. Many vegetarians find it difficult to resist the smell of bacon cooking, and people brew up fresh coffee so that the smell can create a good impression when showing potential buyers around their house. We bathe our bodies in exotic fragrances and splash on expensive perfumes to make us more attractive to others. Such a widespread recognition of the potent effects of smell on experience and behaviour surely justify a more structured understanding of the effects. Research in the area has not been extensive but some evidence does exist.

Smell and health

One study by Steinheider and Winneke (1993) assessed the degree of annoyance caused by industrial odours on almost 1600 participants in four German cities. Those exposed to highest levels of industrial odours reported more dissatisfaction with health, and poorer coping strategies. Several studies have demonstrated that individuals with anorexia nervosa and bulimia exhibit deficits in sensitivity to smell (Fedoroff et al., 1995; Kopala et al., 1995). In the Fedoroff et al. study it was the very low weight participants who showed the deficit. Kopala et al. argue that the deficit cannot be explained by metabolic or nutritional disturbances alone. Anxiety has also been related to reduced sensitivity to smell (Rodrigo & Williams, 1986). Odours can be a particularly potent stimuli in the evocation of flashbacks in post-traumatic stress disorder (PTSD) (Kline & Rausch, 1985). The recalled smell of mutilated bodies at disaster sites is also an important variable in reported helplessness among rescue personnel at one month and one year after a disaster (Raphael et al., 1984). While the literature is rather sparse and the studies often have small numbers of participants, there is sufficient evidence to warrant further investigation of the link between smell and health.

Smell and memory
Smell acts as a trigger to recall as demonstrated by the studies on flashbacks in PTSD patients and in experimental studies of the associative power of odour (Engen, 1987; Schab, 1990; Zhong & Gao, 1992). The latter studies involve pairing odour with other stimuli such as words and testing the effect on recall.

Smell and communication
Smell can be categorised as a dimension of non-verbal communication. For example in animals smell plays a very important part in mating rituals. While natural smells seem to play a less important role in human sexual transactions, they have to some extent been replaced by artificial smells. This doesn't mean that natural smells are no longer important aspects of the communication process in humans. Research has suggested that mothers have a significantly greater than chance ability to identify their babies by odour alone (Russell, Mendelson, & Peeke, 1983), an ability apparently not shared by fathers. A study by Kaitz and Eidelman (1992) suggests that this ability is common to females, whether mothers or not. In the study both the natural mothers and females who were not mothers, but who had spent some time interacting with the babies, were equally effective in later identifying the babies by smell alone. McKenna (1990) in an investigation of sudden infant death syndrome (SIDS) suggests that access to parental sensory cues including smell can help to regulate breathing and therefore prevent breathing control errors which have been implicated in the syndrome.

Doty (1981) reviewed the evidence on human ability to communicate and detect information about gender and reproductive state and on the claim that odours are involved in producing menstrual synchrony. He concluded that while further research is needed, there is strong support for the existence of a human ability to communicate through biological channels including odour. In another interesting study he and colleagues (1982) demonstrated that both males and females were able to identify breath odours as either male or female at a level greater than chance.

While the evidence cited above needs replication, it highlights the sensitivity of the olfactory sense in picking up information often below the level of conscious awareness. Each day we are bombarded with smells in our environment which form an important part of the environmental information which we process in producing our constructions of the external world, and hence are influential in determining our response to it.

Individual differences in smell perception

Because the area has not been extensively researched there is not a lot of evidence on individual differences in the area of olfaction. However there is some evidence of gender and age differences. As discussed above females seem to share an ability to identify a child by smell, an ability which is less well developed in males. In a review Velle (1987) concluded that females show superiority to males in olfactory sensitivity. Doty et al. (1985) compared white Americans, black Americans, Korean-Americans and native Japanese participants and found that females demonstrated more sensitivity to smell than males across all four groups. In another study Doty et al. (1984) produced evidence that this female superiority transcends age in a sample of almost 2000 participants ranging in age from 5–99 years old. However Koelega (1994) argues that sex differences are odour specific. He compared male and female responses to five different odours and found that sex differences only occurred on some odours.

Age differences have also been reported with a general finding that olfactory sensitivity decreases with age after a peak somewhere between 30 and 50 years old (Doty et al., 1984). This age deterioration is particularly important for older age categories when it coincides with a general reduction in sensory acuity linked to lowered psychological well being (Winogrond, 1984). The age effect is supported by other studies (Ship & Weiffenbach, 1993; Stevens, Bartoshuk, & Cain, 1984). However it can be moderated by other factors such as physical fitness (Wysocki & Gilbert, 1989) and exposure to smoking (Hepper, 1992). In the latter study Hepper shows that the smoking effects apply to passive smoking as well, with an effect lasting up to one hour before an advantage over smokers in smell detection is restored. While the Doty et al. (1985) study did not produce evidence of cultural differences, there is some evidence of cultural differences in smell from other sources. In a comparison of people from the central Andean highlands with Amazonian participants, Classen (1990) noted that Amazonians place much more emphasis on the sense of smell.

Factors affecting the sense of smell

As noted from the Hepper (1992) study, smoking and passive smoking have adverse effects on olfactory acuity. In an analysis of 712,850 participants who responded to the National Geographic Smell Survey, Corwin, Loury, and Gilbert (1995) conclude that both male and female factory workers consistently reported poorer sense of smell than other workers. The effect was greater for males than for females. They conclude that exposure to noxious events damages the olfactory sense. While the number of studies is limited, there is reason to believe that exposure to invasive substances generally, such as chemical pollution in the atmosphere, is likely to affect the sense of smell.

Effects of smell on attitudes and behaviour
We have seen that smell has some effect on health and in communication, but what about direct effects on our attitudes and behaviour? Breckler & Fried (1993) found that smell played a role in elicitation of attitudes among college students. In a consideration of the role of smell in interaction Synnott (1991) concluded that we associate pleasant smells with goodness and bad smells with evil, and vice versa, in evaluating people. In other words someone who smells good is good, and so on. Birley (1987) identifies smell as one reason why many practitioners are disinclined to enter the field of psychogeriatrics, and personal experience would tend to confirm this. In fact when asked what they dislike about hospitals, many people identify smell as a major factor. People talk about the "smell of death" and so forth. Smell doesn't seem to have been investigated as a factor in patient recovery, but the evidence would suggest that it needs to be considered. Smell also pervades the world of job selection as demonstrated in a study by Baron (1983). In a mock interview situation confederates of the experimenter posed as job applicants and either wore or did not wear a popular

---

Box 15: Believing is smelling

We are aware that our visual and auditory senses are subject to illusions, but what of our sense of smell? Some evidence that smell illusions exist was demonstrated in a study carried out by O'Mahony (1978). Viewers of a television show about chemical senses were told that particular tones played during the show were of the same frequency as the vibration of molecules of particular odorous substances. The particular odour, they were told, was a pleasant country smell. One hundred and thirty people responded with reports of experiencing the smell of hay or grass and some reported having sneezing fits and attacks of hay fever symptoms. The experiment was repeated on the radio with similar effects. Have you ever experienced a continued association between a place or object and a smell, even when the smell has been removed? Or smelled cooking when you were hungry and nowhere near a kitchen? It does seem that we have some ability to recreate smell from memory.

perfume. The two factors that affected ratings of applicants were their sex and whether or not they wore perfume. Females tended to rate perfume wearers higher, while males rated the same participants lower. It appears that the effect was greater for male interviewers, who appeared to have greater difficulty in ignoring such extraneous variables. In addition odour has been causally linked to aggression (Rotton & Frey, 1985).

Again the evidence is sparse, but it confirms our everyday experience. Smell is another factor in appraising others. We may feel more inhibited about admitting it, but we are influenced by body odour. We are much less likely to tell someone else that they smell, than we would be to tell them they had a crumb of food on their face. But which will have the greater impact on our attitude towards the person?

Colour in our experience

The way in which different colours in the environment impinge on behaviour and experience has not been widely researched either, although there is a popular belief that bright colours are cheerful and pastels relaxing. People talk of warm colours and cold colours in interior decorating and we all have favourite colours for particular objects such as toys, cars, and clothing.

Colour and performance

Gifford (1987) cites a study reported in the popular press in 1973 which suggests that IQ measured in blue, orange, or yellow rooms was on average 26 points higher than when measured in white, brown, or black rooms. Seidler (1995) tested volunteers on treadmills in red, blue, or white environments, but found no difference in performance. However 80% reported feeling more negative in the red environment. Alington, Leaf, and Monaghan (1992) did find that using colours instead of black and white improved performance significantly on mental rotation tasks. In a study of crane drivers depth perception (something that is of practical importance in the accuracy of driving cranes) Zhang & Pan (1994) showed that increasing colour contrast in markings on the shank of the crane hook improved driver performance. Colour has also been suggested as important in cognition and language. There is some evidence that the use of coloured lens improves the performance of those with dyslexia (Irlen, 1983; Stanley, 1990). The lack of extensive evidence prevents any real conclusions, but the studies reported do indicate sufficient effect of colour on performance to warrant further study.

Colour, health, and emotion

A slightly more productive area has been that of the relationship between colour and emotion. As noted the Seidler (1995) study, although finding no effect on performance, did find a strong effect on emotion with red inducing more negative feelings than blue or white. Meerum-Terwogt and Hoeksma (1995) found consistent matching of colours with emotions within three groups, but differences across groups. The groups were age cohorts, children 6–8 years old and 10–12 years old and adults 20–56 years old. The differences between groups in preference for colour–emotion pairs suggests a developmental effect. In a study of children aged between 4–7 years old, Boyatzis and Varghese (1994) found that children tended to produce distinct colour–emotion associations, and on average were more positive towards bright colours. This positive association with bright and negative association with dark colours was more consistent among the girls. Among those reacting positively to dark colour boys tended to predominate. Valdez and Mehrabian (1994) looked at three different emotional reactions, pleasure, arousal and dominance, to a range of colours in an adult sample. They found that blue, blue-green, green, red-purple, purple and purple-blue were most pleasant with yellow and green-yellow being least pleasant. Green-yellow, blue-green and green were most arousing and purple-blue and yellow-red least arousing. Dominance was increased most by green-yellow and least by red-purple. In another study Jacobs and Blandino (1992) varied the colour on which the Profile of Mood States was printed to test for any colour effect. The colours used were yellow, red, green, blue and white. The only difference found was on the fatigue dimension where lowest scores occurred on the red paper and the highest scores on green paper.

Box 16: You prefer blue, you must be feeling better!

Given the apparent effect of colour on emotions, one might expect some relationship between colour and health. Fleming, Holmes, and Barton (1988) studied 72 children aged between 7–12 years old. The children fitted into one of two categories, physically ill, or physically healthy but experiencing adjustment problems. By using the Luscher Colour Test, they found that blue was most frequently the first or second choice of those who were physically well, while red was generally first or second choice of those who were physically ill. The consistency of the findings lead the researchers to suggest that colour might be used to distinguish the physically ill from others. While one can see many difficulties with this it is another piece of evidence relating colour to emotions and potentially to health.

The case of Baker–Miller pink

The identification of a new colour referred to as Baker–Miller pink, which appeared to have an effect on aggression attracted applied research in the 1980s. In a review Schauss (1985) concludes that the use of this colour in juvenile correctional centres, psychiatric hospitals and its testing under laboratory conditions with students confirms its effect in suppressing violent and aggressive behaviour. Profusek and Rainey (1987) compared students on a range of measure in either a red or a Baker–Miller pink room and found significantly lower anxiety levels in the pink room. Gilliam and Unruh (1988) compared white and Baker–Miller pink offices and measured blood pressure, pulse rate, grip strength and performance on the Digit Symbol subtest of the Wechsler Adult Intelligence Scale. They found differences on the Digit Symbol test in favour of the pink office, but suggest that this might have been due to practice effects. A case study on the use of a Baker–Miller pink time out room found no effect (Thompson & Gerhardt, 1985). More recently Gilliam (1991) explored the use of Baker–Miller pink with emotionally disturbed participants. Compared to a white condition the pink room seemed to reduce both systolic and diastolic blood pressure, but Gilliam recommends caution in using Baker–Miller pink to control aggression. Also in 1991 Bennet, Hague, and Perkins investigated the use of Baker–Miller pink in police cells. They found that prisoners allocated to a Baker–Miller pink cell were less abusive and violent than those allocated to the normal magnolia coloured cells. In a second part to the study a mock prison cell was constructed in a university building and male university students took part as the prisoners. As well as varying the colour between Baker–Miller pink and magnolia, they also introduced pink, green and blue light filters at different times. Overall the study confirmed the pink effect with both the Baker–Miller coloured cell and the filtered pink light reducing arousal and time to return to calm. Overall the studies do seem to support an effect of Baker–Miller pink on physiological arousal and emotion, but the lack of more recent evaluation of its effect would indicate caution is required. It is being used in psychiatric hospitals and police cells around the UK, indicating a practical faith in the effect of colour on emotion.

Colouring the environment

Most people tend to agree that the colour scheme used in decorating a room has an effect on the overall experience of the room. Some studies have looked at the effect of colour schemes in other settings. Kwallek and Lewis (1990) set up mock offices which were painted either red, green, or white and measured the performance of students on a proofreading task in each condition and their mood after completing the task. They found that participants made fewer errors in the red office and most errors in the white. The only mood difference was on the confusion dimension of the Profile of Mood States, with those in the red office reporting least confusion and those in the green office most. However in another study also using mock offices and students Ainsworth, Simpson, and Cassell (1993) found no effect of colour on performance or emotion. They used what they describe as warm red, cool green-blue and neutral white, again demonstrating the lay belief in colour–mood interactions.

Gutkowski and Guttman (1992) report on the design of a day hospital for psychiatric patients in Israel, where colour was specifically one of the foci in improving the quality of life for patients and staff. It would seem to be important to understand the effects of colour on patients in hospital given the widely accepted link between colour and emotion.

Children and colour

To revisit the effect of pink in another context, Hamid and Newport (1989) observed the effects of pink, blue and grey environments on six New Zealand preschool children aged 50–55 months, over a period of eight weeks. Over the eight weeks the children varied their time between the different coloured environments, spending up to seven days in each one. There was a clear overall effect of colour with pink generating greater physical strength and more positive mood paintings. Blue had lowest effect and grey an intermediate effect. Again the researchers describe the colours as warm pink, cool blue and used grey as a control presuming its neutrality. There is also some evidence for the early development of gender differences in colour preference. Cohen and Trostle (1990) studied environmental preference in 78 kindergarten or first grade children and found that girls consistently demonstrated a preference for more diverse, dramatic and complex stimuli involving more light, brighter colours and more complex shapes than did the boys. Perhaps this is not surprising given the way colour is used in distinguishing boys and girls as babies. (See Box 17)

Culture and colour

One cannot remain unaware of the differences in the use of colour in clothing around around the world. In fact nations are colour coded by their flags. However more obviously we have cultures where people wear multicoloured clothing, others where white is most commonly worn and yet others which seem to prefer the more sombre greys, browns and darker colours. Cultural differences in colour are not widely researched but again some evidence exists which supports observed differences. Saito (1994) compared student preferences in three Asian cities, Tokyo,

---

Box 17: If it's blue it must be a boy

Of course colour is one way in which gender stereotypes are perpetuated, blue for a boy and pink for a girl. Although many parents these days tend to try to avoid this, how many times do gifts of clothes from relatives and friends actually conform to the traditional colour coding of babies. Pomerleau, Bolduc, Malcuit, and Cossette (1990) compared the environments of 120 boys and girls all under 2 years old, in Quebec, Canada. Boys and girls were given different toys, reflecting traditional stereotypes. In addition girls were most frequently dressed in pink or multicoloured clothes, had pink pacifiers and jewellry. Boys most often wore blue, red or white, and had blue pacifiers. Recently trying to buy a present for a little boy I decided on clothing. I had great difficulty in finding something which wasn't colour coded along traditional lines. You might wish to investigate if your local baby clothes shop is perpetuating gender stereotypes.

Taipei, and Tianjin. Significant differences in colour choices were found between the cities indicating that people from each city share a common preference at a level above chance. However there did seem to be a strong consensus between cities in choosing white. Saito suggests that while each region has a particular colour preference, there is an underlying preference for white across Asian cultures. Huang, Huang, and Li (1991) studied colour–emotion pairings among almost 7000 participants and concluded that colour–emotion links reflect the significance of colour in Chinese culture.

Tosca (1994) assessed 900 inhabitants of Thessaloniki, Greece, on their choice of colour for the facades of three city buildings. The result showed an overwhelming majority in favour of using multiple colours. Tosca attributes this to a longing for "polychromacy in their environment in order to enjoy liveliness, aesthetic quality, and space–time continuity with their roots".

Light in our lives
Another environmental factor which impinges most obviously on our visual sense, and is related to colour, is light. Evidence of the effect of light comes from two angles, natural light effects (sunlight), and artificial lighting in buildings.

Night and day
It has been recognised that the absence of sunlight may have a negative effect on mental health. A small number of individuals exhibit behaviours such as social withdrawal, loss of motivation and general unhappiness during winter months to such a degree that they are

considered clinically depressed. In the summer they tend to move to the other extreme and appear almost manic. This effect has been linked to the amount of sunlight available and is recognised as a clinical disorder called Seasonal Affective Disorder (SAD). SAD is believed to be more frequent in high latitude countries which have longer nights and shorter days, or where winter is almost all darkness such as in Finland (Nayh, Vaisanen, & Hassi, 1994). A study of effects on men living in polar conditions where it is continuous night during the winter seasons showed increases in emotional tension, neuroticism, and introversion as well as poor social adaptation during the polar night (Panin & Sokolov, 1988). However a study by Partonen, Partinen, and Lonnqvist (1993) found only four cases of SAD in a sample of 486 Finnish adults, a finding which would contradict such a generalisation concerning seasonality. A study of 82 meteorological technicians working in Artic conditions involving prolonged periods of night time found some increased sleep disturbance, irritability, and apathy, but it did not find any evidence of clinical depression or anxiety (Cochrane & Freeman, 1989). The existence of SAD seems no longer in dispute, but there is no consensus on its cause and whether it is seasonally dependent or simply related to light from whatever source.. Some researchers suggest that it is due to disruption of circadian rhythms (Lewy et al., 1987; Sack et al., 1990). The argument is that in SAD patients circadian phases are abnormally delayed and light therapy functions to advance these phases to the normal rhythm. However psychological factors have not really been investigated and in essence it must be subject to the same debate as is evident in the literature concerning the causes for other types of affective disorder.

Treating SAD

The use of "light therapy", which is exposure to bright light for about two hours per day, appears to alleviate SAD (Byerley, Brown, & Lebeque, 1987). The use of light therapy is supported in a number of clinical studies.

Partonen (1994) compared 13 patients with SAD and 13 non-depressed controls on a two-week treatment programme of one hour light therapy per day, and found a significant reduction in SAD.

Other studies however are not always so clear. For example Bushnell and Deforge (1994) describe the case of a nurse with SAD and suggest that nurses may be more susceptible to SAD because of their shift work, suggesting that it is not just a seasonal effect.

Paptheodorou and Kutcher (1995) used light therapy successfully with seven bipolar depressives, whose depression was not seasonal, thus confounding the issue even more. It would appear that light has an effect on emotions in a much more general way than in terms of seasonal changes. Lam et al. (1994) demonstrate the effectiveness of light therapy for bulimia nervosa in a crossover control study of 17 female patients.

Other studies have linked light, through seasonal variations, to a range of physical and psychological illnesses. Gallagher et al. (1995) show that patients with myofascial face pain suffer more during the darker months. Levine, Duffy, and Bowyer (1994) link SAD with alcohol dependence through their common relationship with melatonin, a neurochemical which tends to show variation that correlates with variations in mood.

Genhart et al. (1993) hypothesised that elderly people who spend a lot of time indoors might benefit from light therapy. However the outcome was an increase in irritability and anxiety. All of this evidence points to an effect of light deprivation on mood and emotion, and a positive effect of light therapy on individuals with depressed mood. The term "seasonal" in the labelling of the disorder may be misleading, although one would expect it to be more prevalent during winter.

The confusion over causality

Most attempts to provide an explanation for the effect of light on affect have postulated a direct link between sunlight and physiological processes underpinning emotions, whether in terms of disrupted biological rhythms or neurochemical depletion. However such explanations tend to ignore more psychosocial possibilities. Most people experience some depressing of mood during winter and some elevation of mood during summer which raises questions about the best explanation. One such alternative explanation is based on the observation that there are more positive experiences associated with summer in most people's lives. Summer is associated with holidays, more freedom to engage in outdoor leisure activities, and the opportunity to wear a greater variety of bright, comfortable, and attractive clothing. Similarly there are many negative associations with darkness, and we do go to great lengths to light up the darkness. There is a need to investigate the relationship between light and dark and cognitive processes associated with depressed mood before any real causal conclusions can be drawn.

The effects of artificial lighting

One of the earliest studies on behaviour at work involved an investigation of the effects of lighting on worker performance (Mayo, 1933; Roethlisberger & Dickson, 1939). What they discovered was that simply being aware of being studied increased worker performance regardless of the changes in lighting, something that has become known as the Hawthorne effect. This serves to remind us that expecting to find a simple effect of lighting on performance is naïve given the number of stimuli that will impinge on a worker at any one time. The alternative is also true, that is we shouldn't ignore light as a factor in the process.

Researchers in the work place have tended to be more concerned with establishing adequate levels of lighting and not concerned with direct effects of light on mood or motivation. In many ways this hasn't really changed. For example Bhattacharya, Tripathi, and Kashyap (1989) studied the effects of lighting on performance in a weaving mill and concluded that workers desired better illumination for comfort and safety. While the direct effects of light at work on the feelings of workers have not been investigated some work has looked at the effects of light on mood in other settings.

In the Gutkowski and Guttman (1992) study reported in the section on colour, they also explored lighting as an important consideration in the design of the day hospital. In combination with other factors of colour and design, brighter lighting seemed to improve the quality of life for patients.

Also in the Cohen and Trostle (1990) study, the children showed preferences for brighter lighting. Hathaway (1995) carried out a two-year longitudinal study of 327 fourth grade students under four lighting conditions. Students under the full spectrum fluorescent lamps with ultraviolet supplements showed fewer dental cavities, better attendance, higher achievement, and better overall growth and development. Students in the high pressure sodium vapour lighting condition did worst on all measures. Kuller and Lindsten (1992) assessed children in classroom conditions of no direct access to windows and sunlight, with windows and direct access to daylight, fluorescent lighting which mimics the effect of daylight, and normal white fluorescent lighting. They found that access to direct daylight and daylight fluorescent lighting had a positive effect on stress hormones compared to the other two conditions. Zamkova and Krivitskaya (1990) investigated the effects of different levels of ultraviolet lighting on children in Leningrad schools. They found that low level mid-range ultraviolet light decreased fatigue, and lowered absence rates due to illness.

Noise, smell, colour and light

While it would be rather naïve to expect to find a simple direct effect between noise, smell, colour, or light and human behaviour and experience, it is reasonable to conclude that variations in the stimuli that impinge upon our sense modalities are related to changes in our experience of the external world and our response to it. In addition it

---

Box 18: Smelling sounds and hearing colours

In 1993, Richard Cytowic, a neurologist in Washington DC, wrote a book called *The man who tasted shapes*. It was based on his encounters with a man who tasted shapes and a woman who heard and smelled colours. He discovered 40 other cases over a period of 10 or so years and it led him to conclude that we all have the ability to perceive the world by accessing any type of information through any sense modality. In other words we could potentially hear smells, smell colours, taste sounds, etc. This ability is called synesthesia, and the individuals described by Cytowic are synesthetics. His argument is that this ability lies dormant below the level of our conscious awareness. An alternative view would be that as our brain and nervous system develop we differentiate between sense modalities and that synesthesia is maladaptive development. For current purposes it serves to remind us that we sense with our minds. In other words seeing, hearing, smelling, etc. occur within the brain, not at the eye, ear, or nose. In experiencing the world we may begin with different messages (smell, sound, etc), but we end up with one experience. One area where integration of the senses is easily demonstrated is between taste and smell. Part of the culinary delight of food is a combination of smell and taste. Individuals with damaged or lost sense of smell have more difficulty in discriminating between different tastes. It seems useful to consider how all sense modalities are affected in designing the world in which we live.

---

seems clear that noise, smell, light, and colour operate in a cumulative and interdependent way in the real world and it would be unrealistic to expect to be able to disentangle their effect. All our sense modalities receive information from the environment and noise, smell, colour, and light are important dimensions of that information. Through perceptual processes they become transformed into a phenomic world also inhabited by light, colour, noise and smell. They are important aspects of the environmental demands in the stress model outlined in Fig. 9. Thus they are all potential sources of stress and as such affect emotions and health. However it is also important to recognise their alternative effect, in that they have positive consequences. Colour, sound, light, and smell are important determinants of environmental appreciation and will determine the coherence, legibility, complexity, and mystery of the environment that we perceive which in turn determine how we evaluate it aesthetically (Kaplan & Kaplan, 1978). Pleasant smells, comfortable lighting, relaxing colours, and music for example, all contribute to our positive well-being. The lesson for environmental planners and designers is not to forget to enhance the positive aspects when trying to remove or modify the negative ones.

WEATHER AND CLIMATE

Weather is somewhat of a preoccupation for many people in our society and is often used as a non-controversial topic when making polite conversation. When I was growing up in a farming community I remember how boring it was to listen to the many predictions and speculations about current and future weather. Of course weather is of particular concern for the farming community since its livelihood depends on the predictability of seasons. Weather and climate cover a wide range of atmospheric conditions including wind, rainfall, sunshine, heat, humidity, and storms. Like it or not, much of our behaviour is controlled by these aspects of our environment, determining things like the clothes we wear, whether we can go outside or are confined indoors, the types of leisure activities we can pursue and how comfortable or uncomfortable we feel physically. These are the obvious effects. Research in psychology has shown that there are many more subtle and far reaching effects of weather and climate. As with many other areas of real-life research there are many problems involved (see Box 19)

Weather, climate and health

One health effect of weather that has been explored is the relationship between sunlight and health, in seasonal affective disorder. Recently, with the recognition of the deterioration of our upper atmosphere as a result of pollution, and the fact that this has led to people being exposed to more harmful rays, there has been an increase in concern for direct effects of sunlight on health. It is recognised that while sunlight is necessary for the survival of our planet, direct exposure to some forms of ultraviolet radiation can cause illnesses such as skin cancer. This has impinged on the field of environmental psychology in terms of attempting to understand environmental behaviour and how it might be changed to reduce pollution.

There is clear evidence that weather and climate are implicated in a wide range of effects. For example, Rosen (1985) suggests that there are correlations between weather factors and 44 conditions including blood pressure, migraine headaches and mood shifts. Some of the claims seem a little premature given the research problems involved in trying to disentangle the effects of weather from the many other variables with which it coexists. For example Rim (1975) found increases in neuroticism and extroversion and decreases in IQ during periods of hot desert wind in Israel. Given the effects of temperature on performance (discussed shortly), one might query whether these effects might be better explained in terms of interference with cognitive functioning or motivation.

Box 19: Heat or just opportunity

One major problem is that weather and climate coexist with a wide range of other environmental factors and hence it is difficult to distinguish between the direct causal effects of weather and the effects of confounding variables. An example will illustrate this. One effect of weather and climate that has been widely researched is the effect of heat on aggression. The best known work on this is the work of Baron (1972, 1978). Baron used his theory of the causal relationship between heat and aggression to explain the American university campus riots of 1976. He suggested that the most intense rioting took place after the hottest periods. However there are other possible confounding variables. For example there were a range of student issues which were being opposed at the time. There is also the fact that the warm dry weather facilitated large open air meetings and correlates with an increase in all sorts of behaviours. As Carlsmith and Anderson (1979) point out the same graphical relationship can be identified between changes in temperature and number of baseball games, as between temperature and the number of urban riots. Consumption of beer and lager tend to increase during periods of hot weather in an obvious response to heat-induced thirst. These are only three from a range of possible factors which could have contributed to the violence. You can begin to see the difficulty in identifying which factor was most influential. In fact some would argue that this type of thinking is essentially the problem because it leads to attempts to establish simple explanations based on single variables. Real life does not operate like this and perhaps a more fruitful approach would be to try to identify the combination of factors which contribute to behaviours such as aggression. This multivariate approach reflects many of the principles of environmental psychology outlined in Chapter 1.

A wide range of factors have been looked at, of which heat, sunshine, and wind are examples. One of the most productive in terms of research has been heat, or ambient temperature.

Temperature and emotion

One of the most prolific workers in this area is Robert Baron (1972, 1978), who argues that hot weather increases the potential for aggression up to an optimum temperature. In fact the relationship between heat and aggression tends to produce the inverted U pattern indicated in the Yerkes–Dodson law and underlying the relationship between physiological arousal and a wide range of effects including performance, aggression, and emotional responses generally. The finding is robust indicating that as ambient temperature rises aggression levels increase up to an optimum level above which increases in temperature reduce aggression. This is called the negative affect escape model by Baron (1978a). It describes a process which can be generalised to any noxious stimuli and holds that as levels of the stimuli increase, so too does negative affect and aggression until fatigue and escape responses become preferred and thus a reduction in aggression. Bell and Fusco (1989) found that the number of assaults per day increased up to a peak between 95–99 degrees Fahrenheit and there after decreased. Other studies have shown the inverted U-shaped relationship between increases in temperature and behaviours such as car horn honking among drivers in traffic jams (Kendrick & McFarlane, 1986), and number of police call outs to violent incidents (Cohn, 1993). These are just a sample of findings which seem to confirm the results of experimental studies by Baron (1972), Baron and Bell (1975) and Bell and Baron (1976) among others. One problem however with all the findings supporting the negative affect escape model is that ambient temperatures are moderated by other factors such as air conditioning indoors, shade, and cool drinks. As Anderson (1989) shows, sometimes there is no turning point. In this study the incidence of murder, rape, assault, and wife-beating were found to continue to increase with increasing temperature with no ceiling effect. In fact he argues that the reason for this is that there are not that many days when the ambient temperature exceeds the ceiling level identified by Baron and colleagues, and when it does we do try to take measures to moderate it.

This doesn't negate the effect of heat on aggression. While critical of the applicability of the negative affect escape model in real-life situations, Anderson and Anderson (1984) monitored daily occurrence of violent crimes including murder and rape and ambient temperature over a two-year period and found a high level of correlation between the two. In the UK Field (1992) used regression models to explore relationships between crime rates and weather. He compared annual figures over a 40-year period, quarterly figures over 20 years and monthly figures over 10 years. His conclusion was that temperature was positively correlated with most types of property and violent crimes with no effect of rainfall or sunshine.

Towards an explanation

Research on aggression shows that the best explanation involves psychological, social, and biological factors within the lability model of emotion (Schachter, 1964), as reflected in the excitation–transfer model (Zillman, 1979) and the cognitive-neoassociationist analysis (Berkowitz, 1993) (see Fig. 10). It would appear that heat acts as one environmental factor which increases physiological arousal which may be directed into

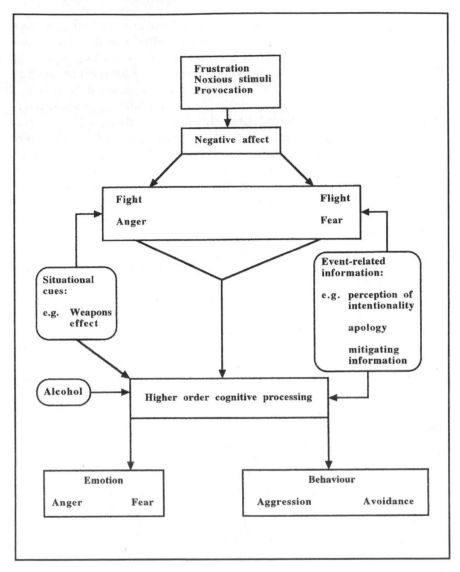

FIG. 10. Berkowitz's (1993) model of aggression.

aggressive behaviour in the presence of appropriate social cues and the appraisal of the situation. For example in inner cities where deprivation is experienced and a target group causally linked to the deprivation is present, the hot weather may trigger aggressive behaviour towards that target group.

Box 20: Triggers and fingers

In Berkowitz's model (Fig. 10), he identified the importance of situational (or environmental) cues. One aspect of this he calls the weapons effect. We generally assume that when someone uses a gun, which is becoming only too common, that they are responsible, not the gun. In other words we generally assume that the finger pulls the trigger. However, in a study carried out by Berkowitz and LePage (1967) this was questioned. Participants in the study believed they were taking part in a learning experiment and they were placed in a cubicle with a machine which could deliver different strengths of electric shocks to a learner who was wired to the machine in another room. In fact there was no learner and the machine was bogus. The strength of aggression of the participant could be measured by which button they pressed which indicated the level of shock they were willing to give. Participants in the experimental conditions were given negative feed-back, supposedly from the learner, which the researchers assumed would increase arousal and anger and hence the potential to aggress. For some participants a revolver and a rifle were left lying in the room, and for others it was a badminton racquet and shuttlecock. The results showed that participants gave stronger electric shocks in the presence of the guns. Thus it appears in this study, the presence of weapons increased the potential for aggression, a weapons effect. Berkowitz argues that this is evidence that the trigger may actually pull the finger, and it has been used as evidence in arguments against the arming of police officers.

Temperature and performance

Quite a number of studies have demonstrated a link between ambient temperature and performance. Experimental studies of the effects of increased ambient temperatures have produced findings such as reduced visual acuity (Hohnsbein et al., 1984), a reduction in attentional perseverance (Hancock, 1986), and an impairment of cognitive functioning generally (Curley & Hawkins, 1983). These effects have been replicated in field studies in the work place (Crockford, 1967; Kobrick & Sleeper, 1986; Meese et al., 1984).

It is not only increased temperature that has an effect; decreased temperatures affect performance on tasks involving dexterity (Riley & Cochran, 1984).

An effect of temperature changes on safety and accident risk in the work place has also been demonstrated (Ramsey et al., 1983), and on children's performance in schools (Aucliems, 1972).

As with aggression, effects on performance will tend to be in combination with other variables such as noise, and subject to individual differences and task-related factors. Individuals who live in hotter countries will tend to be able to cope with higher temperatures generally and vice versa for people from colder countries. In regard to task variables, an important factor will be the complexity or difficulty of the task and the person's experience with it. Hancock (1986) concludes that people skilled at the task perform better than those not skilled under adverse temperature conditions. These factors fit well with the literature on arousal, anxiety, and performance first explored by Yerkes and Dodson (1908) and the work of Zajonc (1965) on the performance of the dominant response (see Box 21).

Studies of the effect of ambient temperature have shown that it is a factor of importance in understanding human behaviour and experience in the environment. Studies have considered natural effects of seasonal or daily variations in temperature in regard to crime statistics and behaviour in the real world. Other studies have looked at ambient temperature indoors, often in experimental laboratories, where heat can be controlled. In understanding the effects of heat on aggression, researchers have employed both types of study. For example the effects of heat on riots have been considered as variations in climatic temperature. Aggression has also been looked at in laboratory conditions. This reflects the full cycle model of research. We can be more

---

Box 21: Arousal, dominant responses, and task complexity

The Yerkes–Dodson law refers to an inverted U-shaped relationship found between physiological arousal and performance on a variety of tasks. In general people perform better at a medium (or optimum) level of arousal, with both low and high arousal reducing performance. One factor that influences the optimum level is the complexity of the task with complex tasks showing a decrement in performance at a lower level of arousal than simple tasks.

Arousal is associated with anxiety in a linear fashion. Essentially if the task is simple we can still perform it well even at higher levels of anxiety and arousal. Another finding which usefully combines with this comes from the work of Zajonc (1965) on the effects of having an audience on our performance of tasks. Zajonc found that when people are being watched by others while performing a task, they experience increased levels of arousal and their performance on the task conforms to the Yerkes–Dodson curve. This audience effect is moderated by the person's experience with the task. If the task involves the use of well-practised skills the person's performance is less impaired by the presence of an audience. Well-practised skills are referred to as dominant responses. In regard to factors like temperature and other environmental stressors which increase arousal levels, their effect will be moderated by the complexity of the task and whether it requires dominant responses.

confident of our conclusions when they are consistently produced in different settings using different methodologies. However, while temperature must be an important factor to consider in planning environments, and in building design, we must not lose sight of the fact that it does not act in isolation.

The effect of wind on behaviour and experience has been less well researched, and its effect is particularly difficult to disentangle from effects of heat with which it coexists. The winds that seasonally occur in hot countries, the Bora, Chinook, Foehn, etc. are hot and dry themselves, and while they have been associated with effects ranging from depression to increased numbers of traffic accidents (Sommers & Moos, 1976), it is impossible to decide whether it is wind or heat which has the effect. In the UK we are more familiar with the cooling effects of wind, where winter days are often made unbearable by the wind chill factor. In fact one important effect of wind is that it may combine with other weather conditions such as rain to force people to stay indoors. For example studies have shown that inmates of prisons are less likely to try to escape during high winds, and burglaries are less likely.

Laboratory studies have attempted to disentangle the effects of wind and other weather conditions by using wind tunnels, but findings tend to be rather more related to increased difficulty in performing various tasks such as donning clothing, and to reported discomfort (Poulton et al., 1975), than to any effects on emotions, health, or behaviour.

Ion concentration effects

An aspect of weather and atmosphere which has attracted growing attention in the recent past is ion concentration, essentially the amount of electricity in the atmosphere. Generally the atmosphere contains approximately equal amounts of negative and positive ions, which balance each other out. However, changes in weather conditions often involve a disturbance in this balance. Warm dry winds such as the Chinook are associated with excessive positive ions, while rain storms tend to produce an imbalance in favour of negative ions. This has led some researchers to focus on the balance of ions in explaining weather effects (Baron, 1987).

It has been demonstrated that air electricity has an effect on plant growth (Soyka & Edmonds, 1978) and on the behaviour of rats (Lambert & Olivereau, 1980). Early findings of a relationship between ion concentration and a range of cognitive and emotional outcomes have not always been replicated, which has led to opposing views. However studies like that by San-Gil-Martin, Gonzalez-de-Rivera, and Gonzalez-Gonzalez (1988) found that variation in ion concentration was one of the two most frequently implicated meteorological factors in psychopathology. The other factor was displacement of great masses of air. Baron's work (1987; Baron, Russell, & Arms, 1985), has attempted to vary ion concentration under experimental conditions to study their effects more closely, but the evidence remains inconclusive.

An integration of weather conditions

While it is useful to identify individual aspects of weather and their effect, research shows that disentangling effects is practically impossible. This has recently led many more researchers to look at combined effects of different weather conditions on behaviour and experience. For example negative weather conditions generally involve a combination of wind, rain (or snow), poor visibility, and lowered temperatures. Extremely hot weather is also generally seen as negative, and will involve variations in humidity, and ion concentration as well as heat. Warm, dry, calm weather is generally seen as positive.

I have just listened to a news bulletin reporting the crash of an American air force plane in Bosnia. All 33 passengers, including an American Government official, have died. Currently the crash is being blamed on poor weather conditions, which is also hampering the rescue. The enhancing or limiting effects on behaviour of weather conditions may actually be more important than direct effects of individual factors. For example patients are less likely to elope from psychiatric hospitals during winter months and during adverse weather conditions (Molnar & Pinchoff, 1993). Essa, Hilton, and Murray (1990) found that preschool children tend to interact more with adults and peers during cold, windy, rainy and low pressure weather conditions, and to spend more time interacting with objects (e.g. toys) during pleasant, stable weather conditions. Sinclair, Mark, and Clore (1994) found that students reported more positive moods during pleasant weather conditions than during unpleasant conditions. However the negative effect of weather on mood was less apparent in conditions where students were cued to the effect of weather on mood. In addition the unpleasant weather conditions produced more negative attitudes towards a hypothetical proposal to introduce comprehensive examinations for graduating students. A study by Lester (1991) suggests that regional variation in suicide and homicide rates in the USA could also be explained by variation in weather conditions between the regions. Children with Down's syndrome appear to be particularly intolerant of variations in weather conditions as was shown by Cocchi (1989) in a study of 432 Italian children. Individuals with a range of psychiatric disorders also show this sensitivity with a general increase in psychiatric emergencies coinciding with variations in weather (Garcia-Carretero et al., 1989).

Box 22: Driving under the weather

A major causal factor in road traffic accidents is the consumption of alcohol. Drink–driving campaigns attempt to educate and change attitudes, and it is generally accepted that driving while under the influence of alcohol is a very serious offence. While it is widely recognised that perceptions of own abilities are distorted by alcohol, it is also useful to consider why generally responsible individuals decide to drive after drinking. A study by Thurman, Jackson, and Zhao (1993) did just this. They investigated the decision process in 528 participants. They found the key components in deciding to drive were the extent of inebriation, alternative means of transport, weather conditions, and the distance to be travelled. Individuals were more likely not to drive in dry, sunny conditions. This weather effect on decision to drive after drink was also found in an earlier study by Turrisi and Jaccard (1991). Perhaps this is not really a surprising finding, but it is information that can be used in reducing drink–driving behaviour.

In essence the research on the effects of weather and climate has identified a range of variables as being implicated in the development of both physical and psychological disorders. However because of the complexity of the relationships involved the conclusions are still rather general. In fact there is room for a great deal of development of research in this area. In addition, the ever changing nature of our weather and climate as a process of both the natural evolution of the planet and the damage being done by pollution has hardly been recognised. It would appear that there may be support born out of necessity in the future for taking this issue more seriously. In the meantime it is a worthwhile area for research.

The impact of the environment upon our senses, whether in terms of noise, smell, colour, light, heat or weather, clearly has implications for predicting and explaining behaviour. They are factors that must be considered in environmental design and planning. In addition their impact on health and emotion have implications for other areas of applied psychology such as health, clinical, developmental, and criminological psychology. Much useful information has been gleaned from research in environmental psychology, but much is yet to be done.

CHAPTER FIVE

The human impact on the environment

Having explored the impact of the environment on people we now turn to the impact of people on the environment, which we will consider under two main headings, chemical pollution and technological or human-made disasters. These two areas are interrelated in that they are both consequences of human behaviour in one way or another, and they both have a major impact on behaviour at the time and major consequences for the future. Disasters come in two forms, natural disasters in terms of floods, earthquakes, hurricanes, etc. and human-made in terms of transportation accidents, nuclear explosions, and other major events which bring human death and suffering as a consequence of technological developments. Chemical pollution is a by-product of technological advance and often the outcome of technological disasters such as nuclear explosions and oil spills. At the time I write this people on a small island in the Shetlands are pursuing a public inquiry into the increased incidence of deaths from cancer which seems to have come in the aftermath of a nuclear accident at Chernobyl in Russia. It is being suggested that fallout from the accident has polluted vegetables grown on the island and that the link with cancer is through diet. In addition a fire at Chernobyl, which has spread through deserted villages in the exclusion zone, is threatening to spread radioactive particles carried in the smoke to originally safe areas all these years after the original disaster. About six weeks ago, one of the most beautiful stretches of seaside and beach in South Wales was almost destroyed by oil from a tanker which ran aground on the rocks. Large numbers of wildlife died as a result of the spillage. It is becoming increasingly difficult to remember a time when these type of events were not occurring on a regular basis. Hence the growing interest among environmental psychologists in exploring these issues.

THE HUMAN ATMOSPHERE—CHEMICAL POLLUTION

Chemical pollution is not new but it has become more widespread, more intense, and much more complex. The great industrial cities at the turn of the century suffered the effects of smog, when the billowing black smoke from factory chimneys mixed with the natural foggy weather and created a great cloud which could be observed to hang over the cities. The killer effects of smog only began to be recognised, however, in the middle of the current century. As one might expect, the variety of chemical elements which pervade the atmosphere has increased over the years, and these are dispersed mainly through air and water.

Box 23: Going on a gender-bender

It has been recognised that the sperm count in males has been falling over the past two decades or so. For example a recent study of 577 Scottish men showed a decline of 2% per year in sperm count in those born between 1950 and 1970 (Irvine et al., 1996). In addition there has been an increase in deformity of male reproductive organs and a decrease in size of organs at birth. A similar trend has been noticed among different animal species. A few years ago, biologists working on the Mississippi noticed abnormally small penis size among alligators. The resulting investigation led to a link with chemicals in the water, particularly DDT. DDT is a pesticide which has been banned in many countries but it is estimated it can continue to have a polluting effect for up to 100 years after it has been used. The breakdown of DDT and many other industrial and agricultural compounds in the environment produces environmental oestrogens. These have a demasculinising effect on the developing male foetus and in extreme cases young males may be born with genitalia which are almost female. Chemicals which produce this effect are commonly called gender-benders. Dr Luisa Dillner writing in the *Guardian* (7th May, 1996) provides some good news in that a recent study in the journal *Fertility and Sterility* shows that New York men have a much higher sperm count than males in other US cities, particularly LA. There is also some evidence of a slight increase in sperm count in US men over the past 20 years. While we shouldn't be complacent, perhaps we are seeing some evidence of a positive outcome of environmental awareness.

In the 1950s a plastics factory in Japan was blamed for a large number of deaths, disabilities, and birth deformities among inhabitants of the Minamata bay area. It was discovered that mercury released by the factory into the bay had been taken up by fish and eventually reached the local people, since fish from the bay were their main source of food. As a result 43 people died, 111 were severely disabled and 19 babies were born with congenital defects (Veitch & Arkkelin, 1995). Another famous example occurred in New York state, in a residential area now familiarly known as the Love Canal. It turned out that dwellings had been built on the site of a chemical dump and, although no deaths were directly attributed to it, the incidence of miscarriage, blood, and liver abnormalities and birth defects were noticeably greater in the area (Veitch & Arkkelin, 1995). In the area where I live there has been concern over a housing development and a leisure complex being built on areas that had been used as dumps. In fact both projects had to be delayed while the areas were cleaned up.

Veitch and Arkkelin suggest that at least seven lessons can be learned from incidents such as this. These are:

- Our society is producing chemicals at a rate which outstrips our ability to determine their health and environmental impact.
- We have not identified appropriate means for the disposal of many chemicals.
- The effect of chemicals is subject to individual differences.
- Pollutants may have thresholds which means that no effect is seen until the threshold is crossed, and then effects may be fast and furious.
- Some effects of pollutants are reversible, but some are not.
- The chemical form of the pollutant has a major effect on its toxicity, in that the form of the chemical being disposed of may be fairly harmless, but in reaction with other chemicals either naturally in the environment or from some other source, they may become lethal.
- The effect and level of a pollutant may change as it passes through the food chain. In Minamata bay the mercury didn't kill the fish, but it did kill humans.

(from Veitch & Arkkelin, 1995, p.183–184)

In fact the psychological consequences of chemical pollution may occur even if the chemical involved has no effect on health. David and Wessely (1995) report on the aftermath of an accidental dumping of 20 tons of aluminium sulphate into a water supply in 1988. Despite the fact that no evidence exists of any long-term health effect, many people reported somatic symptoms and increased levels of anxiety. The fear of chemical contamination may be on the increase. The incident reported by David and Wessely (1995) occurred at Camelford in Cornwall. As an addendum I have just read in the *Guardian* (17th May, 1996) that an unexpected and unusual cluster of cases of childhood leukemia has been diagnosed in one class in one school in the town. The effects of the pollution are to be reinvestigated.

Developmental effects of chemical pollution
Several studies have shown deficits in cognitive performance in children which can be linked to chemical pollution. A group of researchers at the Slovak Academy of Sciences (Halmiova & Potasova, 1994; Potasova & Arochova, 1994; Potasova, Kovac & Arochova, 1993; Potasova, 1992) compared a group of 83 children from an industrially polluted environment with 81 matched controls from a non-polluted environment, on a range of measures. The children were aged 8–10 years old. They found that children from the polluted environment had poorer short-term memory as indicated by the recency effect in serial recall, reduced attention span, and poorer sensorimotor skills. The Edinburgh lead study (Raab et al., 1990; Thomson et al., 1989) among others has clearly demonstrated the impairment of cognitive functioning in children as a result of exposure to high levels of lead in the environment. It is now generally accepted that lead from sources such as car exhaust fumes affects cognition and health. The widespread acceptance of this effect has led governments to take action to reduce the amount of lead emitted by car exhausts. Another area of concern is the effect of fluoride in water. Spittle (1994) reviewed the literature on the effects of fluoride pollution, and concluded that while the findings are not definitive, there is strong evidence of a link between exposure to high levels of fluoride and impaired CNS functioning, in terms of memory and cognitive deficits.

A process identified in an attempt to explain the developmental effects of chemical invasion on behaviour using the biological analogy is something called imprinting by Csaba (1980; quoted in Tchernitchin & Tchernitchin, 1992). It suggests that exposure to a range of agents, including chemical pollutants in the womb or shortly after birth, can permanently modify cells' ability to react to hormone stimulation in later development. Tchernitchin and Tchernitchin (1992) discuss this process and suggest a range of outcomes including changes in personality and temperament, modifications of mental abilities, and behavioural changes ranging from child's play to parenting behaviour in adult women. This sort of developmental effect alerts us to the particular vulnerability of children. Unfortunately damage to cells and chemical mechanisms, which instigate and control the different stages in the human developmental process, is irreversible.

More generalised effects

While the developing child is likely to be more vulnerable to chemical invasion, adults are also affected. Chattopadhyay, Som, and Biswas (1993) found evidence of both psychological and physical distress as a consequence of exposure to air pollution in an industrialised area of Calcutta, and Bullinger (1989) found evidence of pollution-induced impairment in reaction time and concentration in otherwise healthy adults.

Effects are not just limited to physical health and cognitive impairment. Palinkas et al. (1993) surveyed 594 participants in a number of Alaskan communities, one year after the Exxon Valdez oil spill. They found evidence of a breakdown in social and family relationships, increased drinking and family violence, and a decline in self-reported health. There was also evidence of affective disorder in some participants. It seems these effects may have been linked to the destruction of a traditional way of life.

Box 24: When ignorance may not be bliss

Bluhm (1992) argues that the stark images of polluted coastlines with dead and dying animals and birds, such as those portrayed in news coverage of the Exxon Valdez disaster, have an effect on our unconscious which colours our view of the world generally. There is a vast area of potential effects occurring below the level of conscious awareness that have not really been explored. Widely accepted evidence exists for subliminal processing of information, that is processing information of which we are unaware. Studies have involved participants watching images on a screen, among which experimenters have included images at an intensity which is below the threshold for visual perception. In other words these experimental images are not actually visible. However when participants are asked afterwards about what they thought as they watched, the invisible images are very often included in the report. The fact that images which we cannot see can invade our thoughts should make us even more sensitive to the effects of visible images. For example, Davey (1994) used video presentations as a way of manipulating mood in a study on worrying. Video recordings of negative news items produced depressed mood. If such a brief encounter with negative images can induce depressed mood in an experimental situation, one must wonder about the longer term consequences of the vast amount of increasingly vivid images of destruction and death which invade our lives these days. There is some evidence that watching news bulletins intensifies depressed moods (Potts & Sanchez, 1994).

The psychological effects of noxious substances are not often considered in diagnosing psychiatric illness. Individuals presenting with personality disorders and cognitive deficits like those posited by Tchernitchin and Tchernitchin (1992) may not be asked about their working conditions or the level of pollution in the area where they lived as a child, yet this may be an important factor in their illness. Dumont (1989) reviews the literature on psychotoxicology and concludes that there is a danger that psychiatrists may misdiagnose, if they are not aware of the possible effects of neurotoxins and don't include questions about exposure to toxic substances in their clinical interview. Additionally standard interventions may be useless and even damaging to such cases.

This summary indicates the paucity of research in the area while at the same time providing us with sufficient evidence of a range of potential effects of chemical pollution which need to be better understood. One problem in the area of course is that it is very difficult to produce research which allows definitive conclusions. We cannot realistically carry out controlled research on living participants (see Box 25).

Smoke gets in your eyes

While new and unknown chemical pollutants accumulate in our world, other more obvious pollutants have an effect as well. One of the major pollutants of indoor air is tobacco smoke. While the effects of smoking on smokers has been widely researched and is no longer in dispute, the effects of smoking on non-smokers who share the environment (passive smoking) is more controversial and less well understood. However it is clear that inhaling smoke from tobacco, whether actively or passively, is detrimental to health. The study by Hepper (1992), shows that passive smoking impairs the sense of smell. In fact one could expect that passive smoking might be more damaging since a major part of it is unfiltered, whereas the smoker actually sucks it through a filter. There is some evidence that partners and children of smokers have an elevated risk for lung cancer and respiratory problems (Veitch & Arkkelin, 1995). The evidence does seem incontrovertible with several studies showing that reducing the amount of cigarette smoke in the home reduces the risk of asthma and respiratory illness in children (Greenberg et al., 1994; McIntosh, Clark, & Howatt, 1994; Meltzer et al., 1993). Yet many people continue to smoke, and to rationalise or deny the health risk, something we will consider in a later chapter. At a societal level, there has been and continues to be strong resistance from governments to take radical action. The Australian experience is described by Winstanley and Woodward (1992). They describe the long and difficult campaign to have tobacco advertising banned in the media, and hail the ban introduced

---

Box 25: New directions, new ethical concerns

Ethics in research with humans and animals is of prime importance to all researchers. The hope is that we learn from the lessons of the past to ensure that no harm could ever befall the participants in the research process. When new areas of research evolve, we must always be alert to the possibility that some types of research in the area may be unethical. A timely warning can be taken from the paper by Molhave (1992) on methodological concerns in neurotoxicological research. Molhave considers experimental studies which have been conducted in which participants are subjected to controlled levels of polluted air, below the accepted threshold for any acute effects. However experience has shown that even at levels assumed to be safe, interaction with other environmental factors, or with individual differences in thresholds and reactions, can lead to harm. If we take this in conjunction with the David and Wessely (1995) study reported before, where psychological damage occurred as the result of an apparently physically harmless invasion of a water supply, we should be even more concerned. In other words even if safe levels are not breached, participants may suffer psychological damage as a result of fear of contamination. The evidence is that people generally overestimate the effects of pollution on health once they are made aware of it (Baghurst, Baghurst, & Record, 1992). Given the problems with use of fear appeals in changing attitudes, there would also seem to be an ethical issue involved in how people are made aware of pollution and its effects. Research shows that if the amount of fear generated is too high, people will avoid the issue (Janis & Feshback, 1953; Janis, 1967; McGuire, 1969).

---

in the 1980s as a victory for public health interests over the tobacco industry. The battle for the public health interests of those who suffer the general polluting effect is not yet being taken sufficiently seriously. The way in which smoke pervades clothing in crowded places such as public bars is some indication of its major polluting effect. Jarvis, Foulds, and Feyerabend (1992) explored the levels of nicotine in the saliva of 42 non-smoking bar staff and found a level equivalent to heavy smoking. On an optimistic note, the college where I work has just opened a non-smoking bar, one would hope the first of many.

It is clear that chemical pollution invades our physical and psychological world and has major consequences for at least some people, some of the time. The ways in which pollutants reach us are through the air we breathe, the water we drink, bath and swim in, and through the food chain and hence our diet. Currently in the UK we are in the middle of a major dietary scare concerning beef and beef products. It has been shown that a chemically induced disease of the nervous system (Mad Cow Disease, or BSE to give it its medical name), which was previously assumed only to affect cows, can actually be transmitted to humans through eating meat from infected sources. It appears that children are particularly vulnerable and exposure to infected meat as a child leads to CNS impairment and eventually death. There is clearly a case for being proactive rather than reactive in research and interventions since many problems, including mad cow disease, are irreversible. In many areas such as lead in the atmosphere, action is being taken. The promotion of lead-free fuels and so on reflect an acceptance of the need to protect our world and its people. However we seem often to be doing too little, too late. In a later chapter we will consider this issue of attitudes to the environment, why we often don't respond to problems in a preventive way, and what we can do about it. Before leaving the area for now, perhaps we could add an eighth lesson to the seven provided by Veitch and Arkkelin (1995). In chemical pollution, unlike the effects of weather, we are doing it to ourselves.

DISASTERS OR CATACLYSMIC EVENTS

Cataclysmic events are described as high severity events, affecting large numbers of people and generally of limited duration. These type of events are generally divided into the two categories, war and disasters. We will consider the latter. Disasters are defined as

> any event that stresses a society, a portion of that society, or even an individual family, beyond the limits of daily living (Gist & Lubin, 1989).

The history of the world we live in contains many reports of large-scale natural disasters perhaps the first of which was the (biblical) flood. Volcanic eruptions, earthquakes, floods, and wind storms have claimed thousands of lives and are evidenced on the physical canvas of our world. One such example is the Giant's Causeway in Northern Ireland which is the result of a volcanic eruption. Northwestern Europe has not experienced the natural disasters which have hit other parts of the world in the recent past. However it has not escaped the tragedy of more recent artificially created disasters.

Over the past 15 years there have been a series of disasters in and around Britain which have brought the issue firmly into public consciousness. We can all probably remember Zeebrugge, Piper Alpha, Hungerford, Lockerbie, the the M1 plane crash, King's Cross, and many more. The list goes on. Such cataclysmic events have consequences for a wide range of people from the survivors to the bereaved and those workers who are directly and indirectly involved in rescue services. These are all artificially created disasters in that they are the result of human error, deliberate human action, or technological breakdown, or all three. In places like the USA and Japan, natural disasters such as floods, earthquakes and volcanoes, have a similar effect. While the psychology of disasters has become more the domain of community psychology it is relevant here for two main reasons. First of all environmental psychology has provided the inspiration and much of the knowledge base for community psychology, and secondly environmental psychology has a lot to contribute both in determining how and why these disasters occur and in dealing with the consequences. It is one of those areas where the boundaries of fields become blurred in practice.

The effects of disasters

In the aftermath of a number of disasters in the mid 1980s several publications were produced which began to identify the consequences for individuals. It became clear that there were consequences that were not predicted. Immediate shock, grief, and psychological disturbance following a traumatic event is expected. However two main "surprising" findings were reported by workers like James Thompson at the Institute of Psychiatry in London. First of all psychological consequences were not always immediate, and often did not present until several months after the event. In many cases this could be 9–12 months after the disaster. Secondly the consequences were similar and as severe for workers involved at the scene as for the direct survivors who had actually been involved in the event. The latter finding led to the recognition that for workers involved in smaller accidents such as road traffic accidents such delayed, severe, and long-term effects were also both common and normal. This has major implications for both training and support systems for emergency personnel. In fact it is now recognised that even watching television news coverage of disasters or just being aware of traumatic events in one's neighbourhood can produce psychological distress. What is very clear is that (a) large numbers of individuals are affected by disasters; (b) these effects are not just limited to large scale events; and (c) we don't really know the extent of these effects.

In addition it became clear in the UK at least that rescue services and psychological support services were not adequately prepared to deal with such trauma on a large scale. The input from psychology comes from two foci, attempts to understand and deal with the psychological response to disasters, and attempts to understand the causes for technological disasters and accidents in terms of human error and person–machine interaction.

Understanding the consequences

In terms of understanding the psychological consequences observed the literature has focused on three groups, the survivors, the bereaved, and the workers involved at the scene. Much of what is understood came from response to crisis, where psychologists were involved in dealing with those who had been involved in major disasters. Such a response is evidenced at the Centre for Crisis Psychology in Yorkshire, directed by Peter Hodgkinson and Michael Stewart. These workers have provided a wealth of information from direct experience, but clearly much more needs to be done.

Surviving disaster

Those who survive disasters are often referred to as victims and there are two points that need emphasising about this term. First of all it highlights the fact that the consequences are often extreme and that in fact many who live through the event do not actually survive it. To survive is to return to a relatively normal existence comparable to that which existed prior to the event, and many do not make it. Secondly some writers object to the term victim because it implies helplessness and an inability to recover on the part of the person, and have instead recommended the use of "disaster affected person" as less connotive.

The first work on understanding the psychological consequences of disasters is attributed to Lifton (1967) who studied retrospectively some of the survivors of Hiroshima.

Lifton identified five categories of behaviours that typified this group. These were:

- The death imprint refers to a tendency to relive the event in vivid flashbacks either awake or asleep, as if the imprint of the event had been indelibly stamped on their memories.
- Guilt about surviving when others had died, and guilt about perhaps not having done enough to save others.
- Psychic numbing refers to the repression of feelings and emotions about the event, as if feeling had been turned off completely.
- Nurturance conflicts refers to the tendency to be angry and irritable with offers of help; to feel that others really could not understand and to isolate oneself, thus cutting off one of the most effective mediators of the process, i.e. social support.
- Quest for meaning refers to the fact that most sought desperately after meaning which could help them adjust to the event. Such a trauma contradicts totally our construction of reality which is to

some extent predictable, controllable, and with some degree of security. In the aftermath of such an event it is difficult to believe in anything. Hence the desperate and continuous search for meaning. This quest can be positive if it leads to a working through and acceptance of the event and a reintegration of the person into a new existence.

In addition there were long-term effects on relationships stemming from the tendency to withdraw and be mistrusting of friendliness. Many individuals became angry when help was offered and their nightmares and flashbacks led to the belief that they were developing some form of mental illness, a belief often shared by themselves and other family members.

These symptoms were incorporated into a recognised disorder in the the third edition of Diagnostic and Statistical Manual of the American Psychiatric Association, (DSM-III; 1980) called post-traumatic stress disorder (PTSD). This at once allows us to see the similarities that exist in consequences across a wide range of traumatic events, violence, rape, war, disaster, accidents, etc. It also legitimises the fact that individuals who develop these symptoms are indeed suffering extreme distress, and not just "whingers" or weak individuals. However the problems that exist as a result of any diagnostic or classification system are attached to PTSD. For example there is the question of whether such a wide range of symptoms, and the individual differences that exist in presentation of symptoms, really justify their clustering as one disorder. The argument is that perhaps we should focus on each pattern of symptoms as distinct. There is also the problem of misclassification in that there is a tendency to see symptoms which occur in individuals who have suffered a disaster as being part of the PTSD whereas they may in fact be something else entirely. For example many individuals will experience a range of other life stressors which would have occurred even if the disaster had not. Furthermore even "normal" behaviours may be seen as symptoms as a result of labelling as in Rosenhan's (1973) study "On being sane in insane places". In other words, once someone is labelled as traumatically stressed even normal levels of anger or depressed mood may be taken as confirmation of their illness.

There are three categories of symptoms associated with PTSD, re-experience phenomena, avoidance or numbing reactions, and increased arousal.

Re-experience phenomena incorporate Lifton's death imprint and include flashbacks whether sleeping or awake. Flashbacks involve a re-experiencing of the event in all its vivid reality and may be triggered by something seen on TV or by someone who resembles someone who died in the disaster. Disaster-affected persons often report seeing someone who died, just as the bereaved often believe that they have seen a missed loved one. You may have wondered why such a fuss is made about films on TV at particular times of year. For example there was an outcry about the portrayal of a plane crash in Emmerdale Farm (a British soap) which coincided with the anniversary of the Lockerbie disaster. One can see how these type of events on TV can cause a great deal of distress and even do a great deal of harm to those whose life experience has included such a traumatic incident.

Avoidance or numbing reactions incorporate both generalised avoidance of anything concerned with the disaster or anything that might be a reminder of it, and a general numbing or blunting of emotional responses and behavioural expressions.. These incorporate Lifton's psychic numbing. On the surface this set of symptoms reflect the classically conditioned response to traumatic stimuli which under-pin the two-process model of phobias (Mowrer, 1960). However they are more effectively treated at the cognitive level.

Increased arousal reflects a generalised anxiety which is exhibited in difficulty falling asleep, irritability and anger outbursts, and being continuously alert and vigilant, the latter involving exaggerated startle response.

It is important to recognise that PTSD is a psychiatric model, not a psychological one, though the distinction is often lost in discussion. The essential distinction is that that the psychiatric model implies that these are symptoms of a mental illness, while psychologists prefer to see it as a normal reaction to an abnormal experience. Diagnosis of PTSD is based on a specified number of symptoms from the three areas outlined, being present for at least one month before a diagnosis is made. One can see the arbitrariness of this decision process. It means that individuals whose combination of symptoms do not meet the criteria, despite the severity of their symptoms, will not be diagnosed. In addition the diagnosis ignores symptoms which are thought to be common to all survivors, such as survivor guilt and the nurturance conflicts discussed by Lifton. It seems more appropriate to focus on the coexistence of a pattern of symptoms within one individual rather than the existence of a limited range of symptoms between a group of individuals. In other words we need to consider each individual in a holistic sense and to understand how they have been affected, i.e. an idiographic stance. The search for generalisation of symptoms and for categories of disorder is understandable in the pursuit of simplification, however this nomothetic approach is less useful at the level of intervention.

Individual differences in response to disaster

Studies of the progress of survivors have demonstrated that not all persons will develop disorder, and that there are vast differences in how quickly or how well individuals respond to treatment. Attempts to identify what influences this differential coping have implicated variables at three levels, in the person, in the traumatic event itself, and in the recovery environment.

In the person, the focus has been on vulnerability and suggests that aspects of the cognitive appraisal and cognitive styles of the person mediate the process. This supports the stress model proposed previously. Hence responses to traumatic events are subject to differences within the person.

In the traumatic event the intensity of the event, the degree of loss and the level of threat involved are predictors of consequences. These are related to the degree of loss of control in the situation, and can essentially be explained in terms of the unconcontrollability of events. Where events are objectively more controllable the person will be less severely affected by them.

In the recovery environment the mediating variable identified is social support. Essentially where the person has a range of support from family, friends and health care workers, and where this support is accepted and used effectively, the person will suffer less severe consequences.

In essence what this means is that where the traumatic event is uncontrollable, where the person has a vulnerable cognitive style, and where there is poor social support following the event the consequences will be more severe and long term. Of course we cannot consider these aspects as independent of each other. For example one problem in social support in the recovery environment is that individuals may reject it. Nurturance conflicts are part of the symptomatology and are dependent upon the severity of the event and personal characteristics. It is important to acknowledge that this is an oversimplification of the experience. However identification of these variables has implications for treatment of survivors with a need to focus more on high risk individuals, and also for the possibility of prevention.

Bereavement and disaster

There will be two categories of bereaved persons following a disaster, those who are themselves survivors and who have lost loved ones in the tragedy, and those who have not been directly involved but who have lost loved ones in the event. A vast literature exists in counselling psychology on the grieving process and it is largely accepted that a range of typical behaviours and emotions are likely to occur. It is not useful to think of these as stages since the individual will experience them in no particular order and may move from one experience to another and back again. It is best to think of them as components of the grieving process which represent tasks that the individual must complete in order to work through the process. Individuals typically experience shock, disorganisation, confusion, denial, depression, guilt, anger, anxiety, helplessness, hopelessness, resolution, acceptance, and reintegration.

In bereavement resulting from disasters the experiences are intensified with the added distress of personal experience of the trauma for those directly involved. Again the consequences may not be immediate and may remain dormant for several months as with the post-traumatic stress experienced by survivors.

Rescue workers and disaster

As indicated above the effects on disaster workers were surprising to many, the surprise being the result of the "invulnerable" image attached to many rescue services. For example it is often seen as the norm for police, firepersons, and paramedics to be able to cope with anything and to distance themselves from it emotionally. This myth led to the covering up of many incidents where individuals had developed problems as a result of dealing with road traffic accidents, suicides, and other traumatic events. For example a police person may have to deal with a suicide on a railway line. The scene itself will be extremely traumatic. However, because of the normative pressure from her/his group the outward appearance of coping may be maintained. After several months the individual begins to experience flashbacks, nightmares, somatization, and anxiety which is dealt with by increased abuse of alcohol. At this stage colleagues are likely to have forgotten the event and the unfortunate person may themselves not make the connection between their symptoms and the incident. Thus there is an individual focus with a tendency to explain the symptoms in terms of personal weakness or psychopathology. The person may eventually retire due to illness. What I have just described is not a fiction, but reflects something that occurs with sufficient frequency to warrant concern within many helping organisations.

Hodgkinson and Stewart (1991) identify a wide range of potential disaster-affected persons as shown in Fig. 11.

In terms of service providers this ranges from the rescue personnel and investigation personnel who are present at the site of the disaster, to the support services for disaster affected persons and even those who provide support to the service providers. In addition many members of

	Direct exposure	Indirect exposure
Service receivers	Disaster survivors Bereaved disaster survivors	Bereaved relatives and friends Immediate community Wider community reached by media People who have experienced a previous disaster
Service providers	Rescue and emergency services workers Health service workers Investigators and people involved in identification	Psychological service workers/counsellors Support service workers Administrators and organisers in all services

FIG. 11. The range of disaster-affected persons (based on Hodgkinson & Stewart, 1991)

the local community and even those who watch the tragedy on news bulletins may be affected sufficiently to need some help.

Those workers most directly affected are the rescue services and they tend to be at risk in three main areas, from personal loss or injury, traumatic stimuli at the scene, and from mission failure.

Because they are first on the scene there may still exist danger of explosion or toxic material which may produce personal injury. There is the potential for injury or death of colleagues. As well as the physical aspects there is the potential for psychological loss. Hodgkinson and Stewart describe the loss of faith in life and the future as the result of witnessing such a terrible event, particularly where death of children is involved. Dead and mutilated bodies are undoubtedly traumatic stimuli and the rescuers are likely to experience a greater range of such stimuli than even the survivors themselves. Again seeing bodies of children are listed as the most traumatic. Because rescuers receive special training and develop a self-image of success in their job, failure may be even more stressful. For example where a great deal of effort has gone into trying to save a life only to see the person die is likely to be a major event for a rescuer. The media picture of the fireman emerging from the bomb site in Oklahoma City, USA, with an injured baby in his arms, which was flashed to TV screens around the world in 1995, illustrates much of the above. Yet it is often the case that such an event is expected to be treated as part of the job. There is also the potential for blame and guilt in that the rescuer or others may suggest that more could have been done. Often the debate about the disaster is carried on publicly in the media with politicians and others in administrative positions passing the buck by suggesting that rescue services were to some extent at fault. Typically the accusation of inadequate resourcing of services is met with the response that the problem is inadequate use of the resources. Coupled with public enquiries into disaster responses this can serve to exacerbate the guilt and self-blame already experienced by the individual rescue worker.

In the short term a wide range of physical, emotional, cognitive, and behavioural symptoms may be experienced such as nausea, dizziness, confusion, anger, and guilt. In the longer term many workers experience the whole range of symptoms associated with traumatic stress. It is suggested that only about 7–10% of workers will experience consequences sufficiently severe to warrant psychiatric diagnosis, however only about the same number will have no apparent negative consequences. In essence up to 90% will suffer some ill effect of disaster work.

The range and severity of effects which have only briefly been touched on for all disaster-affected persons stand testimony to the need for effective intervention and support services. It has clearly been acknowledged that such services are wholly inadequate, hence the support for centres such as the Centre for Crisis Psychology in Yorkshire from which the Hodgkinson and Stewart book has been produced. There is much to be done in the area but some useful conclusions can be drawn about the way forward.

First of all it is clear that one of the major problems for persons in the aftermath of disasters is the acceptance and normalisation of symptoms. The extreme symptoms experienced tend to be difficult for the person and their close friends or family to accept as normal. There needs to be acceptance that these symptoms are normal reactions to an abnormal event. Unless symptoms are normalised individuals are unable to return to a normal existence and are less likely to seek help because of the stigma attached to mental health problems.

Debriefing helps in this process. It involves education about what to expect and about the normality of the experiences. Sharing experiences with others who have been in the same situation makes individuals aware that they are not alone or different.

Attempts to treat individuals within their own groups or families and to remove the direct contact with experts helps to reduce the fear of stigma and greater acceptance of the normality of the experiences. This deprofessionalisation of treatment has been shown to be most effective.

It is also clear that individuals are not ready to accept help at all times. The nurturance conflicts identified by Lifton, where anger may lead to rejection of offers of help, is illustrative of this. Individuals must ultimately choose to be helped.

In order to deal with the symptoms typical of PTSD the person must go through what is known as "emotional processing". In other words there is a need to go through these experiences in order to reintegrate into a new existence. Grief cannot be effectively dealt with by suppression.

There are of course problems in the area such as the self-fulfilling prophecy, in that care must be taken not to create problems where none exist. There can be a tendency to force symptoms on those who are coping quite well.

Finally there is a need for training for disaster. It was only with the Piper Outreach team in 1988 that serious consideration was given to special training for those who might have to deal with this type of event. Recent evidence suggests that this training should also apply to those who deal with small-scale traumatic events such as road traffic accidents. What this training should consist of is not clear, but some suggestions can be made.

Individual differences in vulnerability have been identified in terms of cognitive styles, and factors that confer vulnerability such as inadequate support systems. Focus on these vulnerability factors is one part of the process.

Providing organisational support systems is another. The question is often asked by helping professionals, "who helps the helpers?". The question deserves an answer and an active response.

In addition to survivors, bereaved, and rescue service workers, disasters and traumatic events have effects on individuals living in the community, and is even spread further afield through media coverage. For example when the victims of a serial killer in Gloucester were uncovered a few years ago, sleep and emotional disturbances were noticed in children living quite a distance from the actual site. Greening and Dollinger (1992) show how adolescents living in the vicinity of a disaster felt themselves more vulnerable to future events for up to seven years after the disaster occurred.

It is clear that disasters have a wide range of effects on a wide range of people. In fact events which involve extremely traumatic stimuli have the same sorts of consequences, extending the area to include fatal or extensive accidents. We now turn to a consideration of the causes for human-made disasters and the potential to intervene at the preventive stage.

Transportation disasters and accidents

As already mentioned, weather conditions may play a role in transportation disasters, such as plane crashes (Helmreich, 1994); however such conditions are sometimes predictable and will also involve some element of human judgment. Baker et al. (1993) reviewed 118 accidents involving commuter planes in the period 1983–1988 in the USA. They found that 75% of cases involved pilot error, and 42% involved mechanical failure. The pilot errors were exacerbated by weather conditions, but it would be inaccurate to attribute them to the weather conditions. Another factor in many cases was over-complicated equipment and procedures, certainly allowing room for preventive improvement. The area of ergonomics which is defined as person–machine design, can usefully contribute here. Clearly the effective operation of any machine is an interactive process between person and machine. In a car, if we cannot reach the brake pedal we cannot effectively operate the machine. We have two options, either to alter the positions of brake pedals and seating, or to restrict the machine to people who are appropriately shaped. The former is of course often the more logical option given the great variety of shapes that human beings come in. A great deal of work has and continues to be engaged in in producing safer machines and useful lessons can be learned from accidents that have occurred in designing for the future. The process of machine design, however, is an ongoing negotiation between safety, comfort, and cost. The lesson would seem to be that safety should over- ride all other concerns.

Box 26: The sinister bias of hand dominance

While the majority of humans are right handed, a significant proportion prefer their left hand. In fact it is estimated that the split is about 90–10 in favour of right handedness. In terms of the English language it is unfortunate that right is also related to good. There is the right way to do things, and being in the right. On the other hand (pardon the pun), left often has negative connotations. There are leftovers, clumsy people have two left feet, and we can be left behind or left out. Left-handed people are often viewed negatively, and in fact it was the practice in schools and homes to try to force children who were left handed to use their right hand, even to the extent of tying their left hand behind their back. We are often unaware of the difficulties encountered by left-handed people in a society which is designed for right-handed people. There is evidence that left-handed people are more likely to suffer accidental injury and death (Coren & Halpern, 1991). MacNiven (1994) looked at handedness among head injury victims of accidents and found more left-handed individuals than would be predicted by chance. The suggestion is that design of machines, particularly cars, often reflects a bias towards right handedness.

Stress, fatigue, biological limitations and accidents
Of course while machines do tend to perform to a consistent level for the vast majority of the time, humans do not, which highlights the essential difference between a machine and a biological organism. Unfortunately the machine analogy is often applied inappropriately to humans. In the early part of this century the Industrial Fatigue Research Board (IFRB) was set up to investigate the biological limitations of workers. It provided a timely antidote to the machine analogy used in the scientific management movement and recognised that worker efficiency is reduced if workers are not allowed appropriate rest breaks. Over the years it has been widely established that a tired worker is not only an inefficient worker, but also a dangerous worker. This has led to strict legal controls being imposed on workers whose job involves risk. For example lorries and buses are fitted with tachographs which record the number of hours at the wheel. This is used to enforce laws concerning the periods of time spent driving and the length of rest periods taken between periods of driving. Even if driving is not one's job work-related fatigue may be a causal factor in increased accident risk. Disrupted sleep patterns and circadian rhythms caused by shift work have been implicated in driving accidents (Richardson, Miner, & Czeisler, 1990). However it is not only physical fatigue that is important. More recently the concept of psychological fatigue has been attracting research attention. Brown (1994) discusses the concept of psychological fatigue, defined as "disinclination to continue performing the task at hand", among drivers. It is not simply tiredness, but a combination of tiredness and motivational deficits, which accrue as the result of irregular and prolonged hours of work. The effect is not simply related to the number of hours at the wheel which is generally taken as the important factor. It indicates a need to consider the longer term picture in preventing accidents. For example the length of time one has been a pilot may be very important. It is clear that risk of accidents increases with increased psychological fatigue. Very much related to the concept of psychological fatigue is the emotional state of the person on a more immediate basis, or the day to day stress experience. Raymond and Moser (1995) review the literature on emotional stress in pilots and pinpoint it as a major factor in pilot error. Among drivers, stress has recently attracted attention under the guise of road rage. This describes a situation where drivers become so aggressive that they take risks with their own and others' lives. Typically it involves reactions to being cut up in traffic or to being impeded in some way by another driver. The actor Jack Nicolson appeared in court a few years ago on such a charge. He had smashed the windows and lights of another car whose driver had cut in front of him at traffic lights. Alcohol and drug abuse has also been related to

stress and to increased risk of accidents. Alcohol has been identified as a major factor in traffic accidents with a very high percentage of road accidents involving drivers who had been drinking before driving (Cherpitel, 1992, 1994; Romelsjo, Alberts, & Andersson, 1993). More recently police authorities have become concerned with the drugged driver, often a young person who steals a car and drives it recklessly on motorways. Unfortunately interventions often tend to focus on the alcohol or drug use which may actually only be the symptom and not the problem.

Industrial disasters

An other area of concern in person-made disasters is in the industrial setting. Accidents in nuclear power stations and in chemical industries, where noxious substances are allowed to escape, are a major source of threat. We have seen how chemical pollution of air, water and food chains can have major consequences for human populations. These disasters clearly involve human error. In many cases they are the result of poor planning and lack of knowledge as to containment and effects. Management decisions which have not been well thought out and general failure within the organisational system have been proposed as important aspects of industrial accidents (Wagenaar, Hudson, & Reason, 1990; Wagenaar & Reason, 1990), the lesson being that we shouldn't mess with what we don't understand, particularly if we are not personally involved at the hands-on level.

Ergonomics is not only useful in the area of transportation machinery. In industries such as nuclear power, complex machinery and control mechanisms need to be monitored in order to prevent accidents. Controls which are overly complex or confusing may overstretch human ability and lead to errors. It appears that the Three Mile Island nuclear accident was an example of this. The connections between various functions on the control panels had been so obscured by time that workers drew their own connections in pen in order to simplify the process. In addition buttons on the panel were so similar that workers attached different colour bottle tops to distinguish between them.

Fatigue, stress, and individual differences factors will also play an important role in the process.

Transportation of industrial materials

An area where transportation disasters and industrial disasters coincide is in the transportation of industrial materials such as oil and nuclear waste. The very recent oil spillage from a floundering tanker, the *Sea Empress*, off the Welsh coast is an example. We have already mentioned the effects of the *Exxon Valdez* spillage of oil on the Alaskan coastline (Palinkas et al., 1993). Such oil spills have become common place over the past few years. What is worrying is that lessons seem not to be learned from them. In a recent article in *Wildlife*, Tickell (1996) states that in the past five years there have been 33 near accidents and an average of 39 spills per year in loading and off-loading oil at Milford Haven in Wales, which is where the *Sea Empress* was bound before the recent disaster. The oil was being transported to fuel the Pembroke Power Station at Milford Haven. In the same article, Tickell suggests that National Power are considering converting the Pembroke Power station to a new and cheaper fuel, called Orimulsion. This is a cheap fuel refined from bitumen in the Orinoco basin in Venezuela. The problem with this fuel is that, while if spilled it would form into tar balls which would do less harm to seabirds, it contains a small percentage of a chemical which is a gender-bender (see Box 23). Each day large quantities of chemicals and chemical waste products are transported by road, rail, and sea. Given our incomplete understanding of their effects perhaps we should be more careful. If we must transport such materials we need to explore the potential consequences more fully, but we also need to reduce the potential for accidents to occur. It would appear that psychologists have a major role to play in both endeavours. Spielberger and Frank (1992) identify injury control, which is essentially accident prevention, as a promising area for psychological research and intervention.

CHEMICALS, TECHNOLOGY, AND PSYCHOLOGY

Very clearly chemical pollution and technological disasters are part of our modern world. Because of the immense physical consequences of such events it is inevitable that the first focus should be on alleviating these physical effects. However it is also very clear that these events have a major psychological impact and it is clear that the need for psychological input has not been yet met. Environmental psychologists have a major role to play in investigating the psychological consequences and in exploring potential interventions and preventions. As well as happening to people, chemical pollution and technological disaster are largely the result of human error. Environmental psychologists must also become more involved in research and practice in reducing such effects. In addition environmental psychologists have a responsibility to educate. It is very clear that we have a long way to go in terms of recognising what we are doing to ourselves and in taking positive action to change the future. We will return to this issue in a later chapter.

CHAPTER SIX

Urbanisation, movement, and space

In this chapter we turn to the social environment in terms of urbanisation, travel, and the use of space. Living in cities involves a range of experiences that differ from living in rural areas and we will consider these under sources of stress in the city and how cities influence behaviour generally in comparison to the effects of rural environments. We will then turn to the relationship between people and space, i.e. how people relate to the space in which they live, and to each other within that space. This subsumes the topics of personal space, crowding, territoriality, and privacy. Finally we will consider the experience of travel and the problems associated with commuting and travelling as part of the leisure domain of life.

URBANISATION

Statistics on human population of the earth make interesting and frightening reading. From a mere five million in 6000 BC, the earth's population has grown to a current approximate six billion. The rate of growth is also increasing. For example, it took 200 years (1600–1800) for the population to double in size. Currently it is estimated that the world population doubles about every 35 years. As Veitch and Arrkelin (1995) put it, the current rate of growth is the equivalent of a new city the size of Chicago every month. The vast majority of people live in a very small area of the world's surface. For example, it is estimated that 70% of Americans live in only 2% of the overall area of the USA. This concentration of populations is found in cities. The number of people living in cities means increased crowding, threats to territoriality, invasions of personal space, and reductions in privacy, and will be discussed in the sections to follow on people in spatial relations to each other. However there are some specific aspects of city versus country living which need to be explicated first. It is very clear from talking to people that previous experience is very important, in that most country people will find cities intolerable except for short periods whereas most city dwellers will long for the hustle and bustle of the city after short periods in the country.

One of the first researchers to focus on cities was Lynch (1960), who argued that urban planning must focus on the city as it is imaged in the minds of its inhabitants, and his work has had a major impact on urban planning which we will return to in a later chapter. McKechnie's (1974) model of environmental personality identifies urban versus rural preferences as one major dimension.

Stress in the city

The experience of city living involves increases in all of the major stressors already identified. For example noise and pollution are mainly urban phenomenon. Poverty tends also to be more obvious in cities than in rural areas and most cities will have slums and ghettos where unemployment, poverty, and crime (or at least the fear of crime) will coexist. Urban areas tend to be the focus of intergroup conflict and terrorism as is evidenced in the recent history of most countries in the western world. In fact it is in cities that the relationship between physical environment and social identity is of obvious importance. Recent work on prejudice, discrimination, and intergroup conflict has drawn on social identity theory as a useful explanatory mechanism (Brown, 1996; Tajfel & Turner, 1979). While research has recognised the physical location of intergroup conflict in urban areas (Reicher, 1984) the role of the physical environment in the construction and maintenance of social identity has not been really explored. This connection between urbanisation, social identity, and intergroup conflict may be an area for future research. Cities also create problems which encroach on the rural environment in terms of waste disposal, sewerage, and air and water pollution. The amount of stimulation provided in cities will impinge on the arousal and adaptation levels of individuals and may lead to the negative consequences associated with exceeding optimum levels as discussed in Chapter 2. As a result of overstaffing in terms of Barker's (1968) behaviour setting approach, cities present problems with providing meaningful roles for all inhabitants thus marginalising and alienating many people. In terms of the general model of stress, cities provide continuous, more intense and more complex sources of stress which challenge the coping resources of individuals. In addition cities are associated with increased isolation and smaller, less dense social support networks. As such it is not surprising that cities have often been credited with greater incidence and prevalence of mental disorders (Crowell et al., 1986). This is not however the complete picture since some studies do question the urban–rural difference in mental disorder (Freeman, 1986). Halpern (1995) suggests that studies may be confounded by the way in which people with disorders move from city to country and vice versa. For example highly anxious people may move to rural areas. Within cities higher rates of mental disorder tends to be concentrated in the poorer areas of the inner city (Dean & James, 1984; Levy & Rowitz, 1973). However this inner-city effect is probably better explained in terms of social drift (Cochrane, 1983). One interesting aspect of the urban–rural difference lies in the adaptation levels of individuals. There is some evidence that just as people in cities adapt to a faster pace of life by walking faster, eating faster and so on, they also increase their optimum arousal level. This process of adaptation must be considered in assessing the effects of stress. For example the effect of urban stress on an urban dweller will differ from its effect on someone who has just moved to the city from a rural area.

Social behaviour in the city

There is a general belief that city dwellers are less friendly, less helpful and engage in more antisocial behaviours than rural people. Anyone who has travelled on the London underground will not be surprised by the finding that city dwellers tend to avoid eye contact with strangers more often and are less likely to respond to a friendly gesture when compared to their country cousins (Veitch & Arrkelin, 1995). City dwellers are also less likely to help someone in distress, which may be more to do with the presence of others than city living per se (Korte & Kerr, 1975; Latane & Darley, 1968). Research also locates the major portion of crime in the city (Fischer, 1976; Halpern, 1995). In addition the size of the city correlates with the amount of crime, for example personal robbery is 50 times more likely in cities of over 250,000 people than in cities of less than 250,000 inhabitants. Interestingly the fact that violent attacks at night are associated with drinking behaviour allows some prediction of the most likely place for this type of crime to occur. According to Poyner (1983) most violent attacks at night occur on the principal routes from drinking places to public transport locations. However it is important to distinguish between the coexistence of events and causal relationships. The fact that one encounters less affiliative and prosocial behaviour in cities does not mean that city dwellers are less friendly or helpful people. There are many intervening factors. For example there is strong evidence that city dwellers learn to screen out information in order to cope with the hustle and bustle of city life. This leads to paying less attention to other people, hence often city dwellers may not be aware of a friendly gesture or a cry for help (Moser, 1988). In addition fear of crime is largely an urban phenomenon which leads to defensive reactions to strangers and strange situations. Furthermore, cities involve crowding, and as we shall see, there is a human tendency to be less helpful and more antisocial in crowds. Clearly urbanisation does have an effect on social behaviour, an effect which will be further explicated when we consider the interrelated areas of crowding, personal space, territoriality, and privacy.

The positive side of the city

While most people tend to idealise country living in terms of relaxation and more aesthetically beautiful surroundings, it is generally the case that employment opportunities, medical facilities, educational institutions, and cultural activities are located in cities. Veitch and Arkkelin (1995) quote a Gallup opinion poll from 1973 which reports that the majority of people prefer to live in or near a city. The result of any study is going to be confounded by the differential adaptation levels of city and country dwellers. On the other hand it is generally recognised that resistance to stress is the result of learned coping strategies rather than some innate trait, and cities do provide the opportunity for a wider range of learning. For example some studies on the effects of life events suggest that the experience of a wider range of events produces more positive problem-solving and coping styles (Cassidy, 1994a). This is not to say that stressful life events are a good thing, simply that the development of effective coping strategies depend to some extent on experiences of difficult situations. The positive and negative effects of city life have not been adequately identified since most research tends to adopt rather gross measures by necessity. City life involves a complex and dynamic series of effects and consequences and is very difficult to quantify. However many of the effects of urbanisation can be explicated by exploring the areas of personal space, territoriality, crowding, privacy, and travel.

PEOPLE IN SPACE

One major aspect of urban versus rural life is the difference in the amount of physical space available to each individual. While it is not always the case (consider a large rural family living in a one-room shanty compared to the city bachelor living in a large town house), it is generally true that space is at a premium in the city. Psychologists have explored this issue under four main headings: personal space, territoriality, crowding, and privacy. Traditionally these have been separate areas for research, however, as the literature has accumulated it has become very clear that they are very much interrelated and interdependent issues. We will follow tradition in exploring each separately to begin with, before exploring the possible integration of findings.

Personal space

The study of personal space is sometimes referred to as proxemics, and the field was founded by E.T. Hall (1966). Personal space refers to that invisible bubble we all carry around with us which defines how close we will approach other people and how close we will allow other people to approach us. To a very large extent it is a function of our relationship with the people involved and the society or culture to which we are accustomed. To some extent the terminology is misleading since in fact what we are considering is interpersonal space. It only becomes important when we interact with others. In addition we need to be aware that the bubble can expand or shrink. In essence we all have a construction of the amount of personal space that is appropriate between ourselves and other people in a range of situations. We only become aware of our personal space when it is invaded. In other words it is something which maintains an invisible control over our behaviour with others most of the time. Hall (1966) identified four categories of personal space, each of which can be subdivided into two, near and far.

Intimate distance

This tends to be somewhere between 0–45cm and is generally the domain of those who have an intimate relationship with each other, but also includes situations where the social rules allow contact, for example in a wrestling match. Hall distinguishes between near situations requiring body contact (lovemaking) and far distances which require being very close but not in contact (whispering). It is quite clear that the distinction is rather artificial since whether or not contact occurs will depend on a variety of things such as the social and physical setting.

Personal space
This ranges from 45–120cm and is the zone generally reserved for good friends or intimate partners in a social setting. Again Hall defines two aspects of this based on the level of friendship. The near aspect is reserved for couples or very close friends whereas the far phase is used by acquaintances or friends.

Social distance
This varies between 1.2–3.5m, and is the zone where those who are not acquainted interact or where business transactions occur. The near distance would be used by those being introduced or for informal business transactions whereas the far phase would be reserved for more formal business processes.

Public distance
This is described as 3.5m or greater; it is subdivided into near phase such as the distance between a speaker and an audience, and the far phase being the distance for example between the public and an important public figure.

These categories help to illustrate the different functions of personal space but on the face of it appear to be rather artificial. In fact it is likely that personal space spans a vast continuum which is determined by a number of factors including relationship with the person, cultural or societal norms, and the immediate environment. The important contribution of these categories lies in identifying the way in which they influence behaviour and experience. We do tend to maintain distances between ourselves and others and to reserve various distances for different people. If a stranger invades our intimate distance we feel angry or frightened. A serious aspect of this is the invasion of intimate space in the work place—see Box 27.

Different cultures tend to have different sizes of personal space bubbles. For example Middle Eastern peoples tend to tolerate closer distances than people from Britain. The caricature is the British and the Middle Eastern person who meet for the first time and end up going round and round the room as the British person keeps moving backwards to avoid what is seen as an invasion of personal space. Research also suggests that the personal space bubble is not circular, but elliptical, in that it is bigger in front and behind us than at the sides. This means that we will tolerate people coming closer to us at the side than in front or behind. It is perhaps not surprising that violent criminals tend to prefer very large areas of personal space behind them!

Box 27: Sexual harassment and the invasion of personal space

Over the weekend I read in the national press about a court case between a woman and her male boss. The woman (Jenny for the purposes of this chapter) worked in a restaurant. Jenny was British and her male boss was Italian. Over a period of time Jenny felt she had been the object of unacceptable sexual behaviour. This initially involved her boss touching and rubbing against her when they worked in the kitchen. Over a period of time the touching became more and more of a sexual nature, and during the touching her boss would revert to speaking in Italian. Jenny couldn't speak Italian, but she memorised some of what he said and later looked it up in a dictionary. She was very distressed to discover that he had been making lewd and inappropriate remarks. She complained and was sacked. She took her boss to court for wrongful dismissal and sexual harassment. In court her boss argued that Jenny had misinterpreted his touching which was only meant as a friendly gesture and would have been perfectly appropriate in Italy. Jenny won her case, but only because of the lewd language that had been used. This highlights the problem of cultural differences in personal space when people from different cultural backgrounds interact.

Personal space (or interpersonal distance) is a mechanism of communication and as such it cannot be understood independently from other aspects of nonverbal communication such as orientation, touch, and eye contact. For example, on a crowded train we may be forced to allow others to invade our personal space for periods of time. However, consider the difference between having to stand very close to someone in front of you who turns slightly to one side, tries to avoid touching you, and avoids eye contact, as opposed to someone who faces you head on, makes no attempt to avoid squashing against you, and looks you straight in the eye. In addition being inappropriately far apart is also uncomfortable. We know a loved one is angry with us when they sit apart, and we feel uncomfortable if someone tries to hold a conversation with us across a room. Considering these differential effects leads one to become aware of how good we generally are at reading and using nonverbal cues, including personal space, and how unaware we are of our skill. The title of Hall's first book on personal space, *The Silent Language* (1959), was very appropriate. Personal space even invades our spoken and written language in that we talk about being close to someone when we are good friends with them. We talk about keeping in touch or being distant. In essence, we use personal space to communicate our relationship with others, to protect our territory, and to generally regulate our social interaction.

Factors that influence personal space

Personal space is an infinitely flexible mechanism, which is influenced by a wide range of cues in the situation, our personal characteristics, the nature of the relationships, and our social and cultural experience. In a world where we interact with similar people, whom we know on a regular basis, invasions of personal space are generally unlikely. However in a world where we meet new people everyday, who come from a variety of different social and cultural backgrounds, and where space is often at a premium, an understanding of personal space is important. We encounter situations every day where some discomfort is experienced from perceived invasions of personal space. For example, when we book a seat in a cinema, which is relatively uncrowded, and we find that we are all sitting in one block with lots of empty seats around. Or we go to a restaurant, which has only one already occupied table, and the waiter seats us right next to it. As you will see when we discuss territoriality, it is often difficult to distinguish between territoriality and personal space. In fact we shall argue that it is neither necessary or useful to treat them as independent phenomena. Research has identified some of the factors which lead to differences in personal space requirements, and hence the differences in response. Gender differences have been identified, which suggests that males interacting with other males require the largest interpersonal distance, followed by females interacting with other females, and finally males interacting with females (Gifford, 1987). However such generalisations need to be qualified. Most of you will have already thought, well it depends on the situation, or the relationship, or the age group and so on. Indeed this is what the evidence also suggests. While traditionally differential socialisation has tended to encourage physical closeness, and touch more in females than in males, such effects are being influenced by changes in role models. It is more common these days to see men hugging each other or even kissing in films and on television. In fact Severy, Forsyth and Wagner (1979) concluded that gender on its own is not a very good predictor of personal space, and is only really clearly observable in conjunction with other factors such as race, age, and relationship. Some evidence suggests that personal space gets bigger as we grow older (Hayduk, 1983). Children tend to be quite happy to be physically close to each other, something which changes as awareness of adult sexuality develops. In addition the gender difference does tend also to appear at this time. However as with gender, age differences are best understood in interaction with other factors. Perhaps the most important factor to come out of this type of research is the evidence of cultural differences. Hall (1959) identified the importance of cultural variation. He suggested that while all cultures use personal space to communicate, and tend to conform to the different categories, the size of the space within the categories varies across cultures. Hall also identified the essential issue in intercultural difference as the tendency to interpret invasions of personal space as an indication of aggression. Consider the effect of this on international relations, where many different cultures meet. Smith and Bond (1993) provide an overview of the evidence and conclude that Hall's proposed cultural differences are well supported for those that are acquainted, though there is some lack of clarity regarding personal space between strangers. The coexistence of different aspects of nonverbal communication is also important here, since it seems to be generally found that closer proximity tends to also involve increased eye contact and more touching. As you might imagine it is difficult to assess which aspect, the proximity, the eye contact or the touch, is most uncomfortable. The important effect of differences in personal space is illustrated in a study by Collett (1971) where English men were trained to stand closer and engage in more eye contact with Arab men. The outcome was that the English men were better liked by Arab men. In these days of multinational organisations, international conferences, and the general fall of barriers to travel, cultural differences in the use of personal space must be an important consideration. There is some evidence of personality differences, though as with all aspects of personality, effects here need to be treated with caution given the situational dependence of traits. Extraverted and gregarious persons tend to require smaller personal space, while cold and quarrelsome people require a larger interpersonal distance (Gifford, 1982). The relationship between interpersonal space and problem behaviours is perhaps a more interesting area. It is generally found that violent criminals require larger interpersonal distances. The evidence for psychiatric patients is that interpersonal distance depends on the specific symptoms and severity of the disorder. For example Sommer (1959) found that schizophrenic patients tend to vary from one extreme to the other, i.e. from very small to very large interpersonal distance. Since many psychiatric disorders involve withdrawal from social interaction, one would expect such disorders to include greater interpersonal distance. In addition many disorders involve attention seeking, which would appear to predict interpersonal closeness. These differences in specific symptoms do not appear to have been thoroughly investigated.

Situational effects on personal space have tended to focus on the social rather than the physical setting. It is generally found that where attraction between individuals is strong, where friendships exist and where the general tone of the interaction is friendly, we are more willing to decrease our personal space requirement (King, 1966; Little, 1965).

Alternatively where people dislike each other, and where the tone of the interaction is unfriendly, people move further apart (Guardo & Meisels, 1971; O'Neal et al., 1980). While this is not unexpected its relevance lies in the way our personal space interacts with the valence of our attitudes, i.e. whether they are negative or positive. Thus interpersonal space betrays our prejudices. Levels of prejudice have often been assessed using the Social Distance Scale (for example Cover, 1995). This is done by asking people about how closely they would associate with particular groups of people. For example whether they would be happy to have them live next door, in the same street, in the same town and so on. The rationale behind the measure is that we are more prejudiced against those that we would restrict to a further distance. The use of this scale reflects a generally accepted belief among social scientists that interpersonal distance and prejudice are interrelated. The harsher evidence however comes from studies which have looked at how we treat those who differ from us in a variety of ways including race, ability, and appearance. It doesn't take a scientific study to show that people with disability, the mentally ill and those who appear and behave in different ways, tend to be shunned in the social arena. Interpersonal distance between ourselves and these groups tends to be much larger than for individuals who appear similar to ourselves. A particular instance of this is the way we react to facial disfigurement. A series of studies by a group of British psychologists led by Ray Bull at the University of Portsmouth has provided a great deal of evidence here. They found that people moved away from a confederate who was made up to appear as if their face had been disfigured (Bull & Stevens, 1981; Rumsey, Bull, & Gahagan, 1982). They also found that the effect can be ameliorated by whether the disfigured person appears to be married to a facially attractive partner (Bull & Brooking, 1985) and by social skills training with facially disfigured individuals in order to alter their expectations of how the general public will react (Rumsay & Bull, 1986; Rumsay, Bull, & Gahagan, 1986). The strength of the message communicated by increased interpersonal distance as a response to disfigured individuals is evidenced by the very negative expectations and feelings of rejection engendered in the disfigured individual. Although choosing to sit or stand apart, or to move away, suggests dislike in the absence of other cues, choosing to sit or stand close together is not generally interpreted positively. As illustrated in Box 27 inappropriately small interpersonal distances between males and females is likely to be seen as harassment. In fact if we want someone to like us we are better advised to use appropriate interpersonal distances when interacting with them. Herein lies the problem, because what is appropriate to one may not be appropriate to another. Because of the subjectivity of personal space, it is important to stress the need to consider individual differences in any analysis. As Fisher and Byrne (1975) demonstrated, our liking for someone as a function of their use of interpersonal distance in interacting with us depends on gender among other things. In addition, as demonstrated by Sommer (1969), the best way to get someone to leave or move is to invade their personal space. However as invasions of personal space arouse emotions one may be prepared for a less than welcoming response.

Other important aspects of the situation are the status of the interacting individuals and whether they are involved in cooperation or competition. The cooperation versus competion effects on personal space interact with orientation. In other words, as well as differences in interpersonal distance in cooperative interactions as opposed to competitive ones, we will tend to differ in whether we are face-to-face, side-by-side, or somewhere in between. Generally people in cooperation will select a smaller interpersonal distance unless the competition requires interpersonal contact (Cook, 1970). Perhaps the most interesting effect was that demonstrated by Tedesco and Fromme (1974). They had participants interact either in competition or cooperation with each other. They then observed the same participants' interpersonal space in another room after the study. Those who had been in the cooperative encounter chose a smaller interpersonal distance than those in the competitive condition. This generalised effect on interpersonal distance as a result of competition or cooperation is important given the information conveyed about attitudes and potential aggression in our choice of interpersonal distance. The general finding for status focuses on differences in status and it appears that the greater the difference in status between individuals, the larger the interpersonal distance used. There doesn't seem to be any evidence regarding personal space between same status individuals at different levels. In other words it is not clear if high status individuals require a greater distance when interacting with other high status individuals, than low status individuals in interaction. We also use interpersonal distance to assess the differential status of individuals in interaction. Burns (1964) showed that in a filmed interaction in an office setting, someone standing further away when conveying a message was judged to be a subordinate, whereas when the same individual stood closer they were judged of equal status.

Our anticipation of the type of person we are going to meet in a situation also influences our choice of interpersonal distance. When we anticipate meeting a warm and friendly person we tend to choose smaller distances (Kleck, 1969). We are also less likely to offer help to someone if our personal space has been invaded (Konecni et al., 1975), however if we perceive the person's need to be great the negative effect of the invasion may be offset (Baron, 1978).

It seems very clear that use of interpersonal distance is an important part of the regulation of interaction and has important effects on the relationships and hence effectiveness of the interaction. In a world where interaction is an important part of everyday life, at work, rest or play, we need to be aware of the potential positive and negative aspects of the use of interpersonal distance. The use of interpersonal distance will be a function of the design of the physical environment. For example library seating which is cramped, the number of people sharing a small office, and the size of the aisles in a shop layout will all determine the level of interpersonal space invasion that occurs. We will discuss this aspect of personal space when we look at environmental design in a later chapter.

We have seen that the use of interpersonal space is important in interpersonal communication, that it regulates the interaction and allows us to defend our personal territory. In essence personal space provides us with comfort in interaction, and protects us from physical invasion. In other words we need enough space to be able to move our bodies, flex our muscles and so on, without restriction. Just as we dislike uncomfortable clothing, we dislike too little personal space. However it is much more than that. Being too close to someone obscures our ability to read their nonverbal cues. As we come to know someone, and trust them, there is much less need to read the nonverbal cues and hence we allow them to come closer. An interesting view on the function of personal space is provided by Argyle and Dean (1965) in their affiliative-conflict theory. This suggests that we have both a desire to be close to others, and a desire to move away, much like the approach–avoidance conflict in regard to novel stimuli observed in behavioural studies with animals. The goal of interaction is to reach a compromise in the conflict which means an equilibrium point. An alternative view with a similar outcome would be to apply the social constructionist perspective. This would suggest that a particular personal space involves reaching some shared representation of what is appropriate through negotiated interaction. Invasions of personal space tend to produce physiological arousal, and within the arousal-level or adaptation-level perspectives we can see personal space as some form of achieved homeostasis. In addition we can draw on the lability model of emotion here, in that an invasion of personal space produces generalised physiological arousal which leads to an appropriate emotion as a result of the cognitive appraisal of the situational cues. Hence if the invader is a loved one the physiological arousal may turn to passion, whereas if it is a stranger we may become angry. Essentially, invasions of personal space are potentially stressful depending on their context and personal appraisal, and as such are important aspects of maintaining health. However, personal space invasions which are associated with effects on mental health occur within the context of crowding and will be discussed in more detail in that section. In addition the use of personal space involves aspects of control over territory, to which we now turn.

Territoriality

Related to personal space is the concept of territoriality, which originated in work on animals. The acquisition, marking, and defence of territory is essential to the survival of animals in the wild in terms of both provision of food and drink and in enabling the continuity of the species through mating. Very often animal territoriality involves group territory rather than individual territory and watching any of the wide range of nature programmes on television will give you an idea of the processes involved. Territoriality can be observed in domesticated animals as well. A cat will mark out the boundaries of its territory by urinating around the borders and will defend that territory against invasion by other cats. In human societies territorial behaviour can be observed at its most horrific in wars. However it occurs on many less obvious levels as well. We build houses, erect fences or other markers and defend this claimed territory against invasion. In many places a great deal of anger is generated over parking places in a street. People tend to regard the space outside their house as theirs and will resent another driver parking there. The strength of resentment will vary from person to person. People leave towels on sun beds at the beach to mark their territory and in libraries students place books and other belongings on desks to mark the spot which they intend to occupy. Territoriality on this level is closely related to personal space in that markers serve to indicate territory and to reduce the likelihood of an invasion of personal space. We have probably all experienced irritation when someone takes our seat and observed others being irritated when we have encroached on their territory.

Again psychologists have tried to measure and define territoriality and the most commonly used categorisation is that produced by Altman and Chemers (1980) which identifies three types, primary, secondary, and public territory.

Primary territory refers to space that is felt to be owned by an individual or an interdependent group on a relatively permanent basis and is central to their daily lives. One's home is a primary territory and so also could be one's nation. It is not the size that matters, but the psychological importance which will be indicated by the strength of feeling aroused when the territory is encroached upon and the strength of the defence response.

Secondary territories are generally less important to the person and are likely to be only owned on a temporary basis, for example a locker in a changing room. The distinction between a primary and a secondary territory is not an objective one, but rather depends on the individual's perception of its importance to them. Hence to distinguish between what was primary and secondary territory for one person we would need to know how the person felt about it.

Public territories are more distinct in that they don't belong to any person and are generally accessible to anyone, for example a beach.

Objects and ideas also come into the arena of territoriality. We mark objects and go to great lengths to ensure that they remain with us. Similarly we defend our ideas through copyrighting of the written word, patenting and rules about plagiarism. The latter raises the issue of the legal system and indeed many aspects of territoriality are subject to laws in many societies. Invasion of another's home is trespass.

There is some debate about why we behave in territorial ways and part of the debate hinges on the nature–nurture controversy. Some theorists from the sociobiological perspective argue that territorial behaviour is inherited and is a carry-over from our evolutionary past. Others argue that it serves an organising function and is learned. The latter explanation is based on the basic notion from cognitive psychology that our cognitive processes operate to simplify the world and do this through categorising information. These cognitive processes are based on the biological processes in the brain and central nervous system which provide the "hardware" for psychological functioning. In this explanation what is inherited is a brain which is physically designed to categorise. The types of categories, hence the types of territorial behaviour, are a function of our experience in the world, that is the content is not programmed in at birth. Territorial behaviour is very much dependent on social and cultural factors.

Factors that influence territoriality
As with personal space, territorial behaviour is modified by personal and situational factors. It appears that males prefer larger territories than females. The finding has been consistently demonstrated in studies of behaviour on the beach, and in dormitories (Gifford, 1987). In traditional families different rooms in the home were often seen as male or female or shared territory. The study was often the domain of the father while the kitchen was seen as under the control of the females. Given this one can see how it is quite likely that male–female expectations of territory are part of the socialisation process. In support

of this learning influence are studies which show that individuals who were brought up in larger homes tend to mark out larger territories for themselves as adults (Mercer & Benjamin, 1980). The same study suggests that gender interacts with personality in the process. However less attention has been paid to these aspects of territoriality, but one would expect that size of territory expected or required would be very closely related to size of personal space. Hence one can argue that the data on personal space can usefully be generalised to territoriality. One aspect of territoriality that has gained some public acclaim is the way in which people from different nations compete for beach space on holiday. Smith (1981) compared Germans, French, and Americans, and concluded that there were both similarities and differences. In general males claimed more territory than females regardless of nationality, and groups tended to claim less space per person than couples or people on their own. However the study did suggest that the Germans engaged in much more marking of territory in erecting boundaries, and also tended to claim larger territories than either of the other groups. Shapes of territories were similar however, with individuals marking elliptical territories and groups marking territories that were circular. Another behaviour which would appear to differ across cultures is queuing. While queuing behaviour does not seem to have been studied, experience in everyday life does suggest variations between people. Queuing can be seen as controlled access to territory and appears to cause a great deal of distress when not adhered to. Perhaps it can be seen as an area for future investigation. Essentially territorial behaviour does show some variation between cultures, genders and personality; however the similarities set it out as another important control over behaviour and experience.

Situational aspects of territoriality

Territoriality by definition is concerned with the division and defence of situations. However it is an interaction rather than a one-way effect. In other words, while territoriality works to structure the use of space, the physical location of that space will determine the types of territoriality behaviour. For example when homes are owned rather than rented, people are generally more territorial about the entire area. Home owners are more likely to be concerned about litter in the street in their area, outsiders using the parking space, and people repairing cars on the street. People in rented accommodation tend to be concerned only with the actual piece of property rented. The situational effects on territoriality are very well captured in the work of Newman (1972) on defensible space.

Using territoriality to fight crime

A concept that has attracted a lot of attention in regard to crime prevention is the notion of defensible space. The idea is that space which was originally public space is organised so that residents feel some sense of ownership of it. It is based on the observation that much crime in the community is centred around public space. While offenders are unlikely to congregate in someone's front garden they are likely to occupy public spaces such as street corners or pathways. Newman (1972) studied crime rates in two housing projects in New York. While both projects housed the same number of people, one (Brownsville) was organised in smaller blocks catering for five to six families while the other (Van Dyke) was high rise. In Brownsville the buildings were built around courtyards while the large Van Dyke blocks were separated by large parks. In essence the area around the Brownsville blocks was defensible while the Van Dyke parks were public and became a base for juvenile gangs. In Brownsville people knew their neighbours and a sense of community developed whereas families in Van Dyke kept to themselves. The difference in crime rate was such that the rate in Van Dyke was 50% greater than that in Brownsville. While it is difficult to be exact about the causes for such a difference in the natural environment because of the number of possible variables, it has been suggested that four factors are important (Newman, 1972).

1. Zone of territorial influence refers to markers which indicate to outsiders that an area is private rather than public.
2. Opportunities for surveillance involve two aspects. First of all a physical arrangement of the environment so that intruders can be easily spotted, and secondly knowing who is and who isn't an intruder. The latter is enhanced by smaller groupings and a sense of community.
3. Image refers to the identity portrayed by the design of the building. High rise blocks tend to be similar wherever they appear and don't portray a sense of individuality. In fact there is often little difference externally between them and multistorey car parks! Individuality also suggests privacy and is linked to the zone of territorial influence.
4. Milieu refers to the surroundings of the buildings, or the setting. Buildings that are set in the middle of open public space are more likely to attract vandalism than those organised around more personalised space such as the courtyards in Brownsville.

The issue of defensible space is important in designing environments and will be returned to later. However this is a useful time to stress once more the relationship between social and physical aspects of the environment in terms of how physical environments enhance or destroy communities.

Territoriality and community

Central to the effect of the environment on crime is the facilitative effect of the environment in generating a sense of community in inhabitants. People must be able to feel some sense of ownership of the environment and hence a sense of responsibility for it. Terence Lee (1984) described a new development where a new motorway was built through a town, effectively dividing it in two. A subway was built to allow access between the two parts of town. Crime rates in the town escalated with much of it being based around the subway which became a haven for street gangs and a source of many violent crimes. A survey revealed that people felt they had lost a sense of community. People who had once visited each other regularly and were now separated by the motorway ceased to visit and rarely saw each other. It was as if there were now two separate towns with a sort of no man's land between them. This serves to illustrate the consequences of change in the physical environment and the need to consider the effect on human behaviour in planning environments.

Marking, personalisation, emotion, and behaviour

Territoriality is expressed through marking whether physically or verbally and often involves personalising. Fences, boundaries, and other indications that the territory belongs to someone, without identifying who that person or group is, are markers. Markers which indicate the identity of the person (name labels) or which distinguish the territory in some unique way (house names) reflect attempts to personalise territory. Marking territory in the public domain such as your seat in the library, or your space on a beach, is where invasions and distress are most likely to occur. It is less likely that your home or garden will be invaded, but the same is not true when the space is in the public domain. Often when a territory in the public domain is invaded we just move somewhere else. However the invasion will engender physiological arousal and anger, and may lead to conflict. It is this aspect of conflict over territory in both animals and humans which attracts most attention. The extreme and tragic example is war. However, one must acknowledge the way that for the vast majority of time territoriality serves to produce a positive outcome. In other words violent conflict over territory is the exception rather than the rule. Ethologists would argue that human war and the atrocities that go with it are the result of technological developments which allow us to kill or injure others at a great distance. This, they claim, overrides the natural control mechanisms for aggression built into our nonverbal communication. For example when animals are in conflict, they have ritualistic displays of aggression and submission which they use before any physical conflict occurs. The effective use of these displays often means that no physical conflict does occur. It is interesting to speculate, but very difficult to test, if in fact human war would be less frequent if long distance weapons were not available. Certainly in face-to-face disputes over territory, violence is generally the last resort. Marking of territory occurs in many ways that are not entirely obvious to us. Street gangs use graffiti and slogans sprayed on walls to define the boundaries of their territories and such markers do tend to engender fear in those who stray into the area. Studies have shown that we touch our plates in restaurants more when they are served by someone else in what is seen as territorial ritual (Truscott, Parmelee, & Werner, 1977), and that people who display signs such as "Private Property" on their houses respond much quicker to a knock at the door than do those who are less obviously territorial (Edney, 1972). While we might be surprised at such territorial behaviour which occurs below the level of our awareness, we have probably all felt some emotional reaction on discovering that our favourite seat on the bus or in the refectory is occupied, or a parking space which we often use is taken, even when we have no claim to these territories.

The positive side of territoriality in regulating our interaction and helping to establish some sense of control in an increasingly complex environment should not be underestimated. Clearly infringements of territorial rules increase physiological arousal, and have the potential to result in aggression. In addition they lead to perceptions of lack of control which is a central factor in the stress process. As with personal space the rules of territoriality are subjective and involve negotiation through social interaction. Evidence for the reduced stress effect of effective territoriality comes from studies which have looked at territorial behaviour in psychiatric hospitals. Holahan (1976) showed that the mood of both staff and patients was improved when patients were allowed to personalise their territory. Personalisation of office space at work, using family photographs, amusing quotes and so on, are a very common aspect of work life, though no evidence appears to exist concerning the relationship between personalisation and job satisfaction or levels of stress. Personalisation is by definition related to identity. For example young adults tend to personalise their bedrooms with pictures of pop and film idols and current affiliations. Often colours and decorative schemes are chosen which appear the antithesis of parental preferences. The reflection of social identity in territorial behaviour is recognised but not very well researched.

As with personal space, it is the aspect of understanding and obeying the informal rules of territoriality, which is of most importance in understanding human behaviour and experience. These rules are subjective, and are constructed through interaction in the social arena. However they are about the physical environment and subject to its influence. Again we will explore this in the chapter on environmental design. As with personal space, territoriality is of prime importance in the context of crowding, because crowding is essentially the outcome of perceived invasion of personal space and/or territory.

CROWDING

Crowding is closely related to previous topics since it is suggested that the effect of crowding on behaviour and experience is largely through its effect on personal space and territoriality. In other words people feel crowded because their territory or personal space is being invaded by others. Crowding is at once a fairly simplistic concept, in that we all have some experience and personal view of crowding, and a complex concept when we come to consider its impact on us. Imagine several different situations, for example, an airport lounge when several flights have been delayed, a London underground train or Greek bus in the rush hour, an office party, a discotheque, and a live concert. We could envisage all of these situations having a very great deal of similarity from the outside observer's point of view, yet differing greatly in terms of the experience of an individual in the middle of it all. We can imagine a lot of anger and distress being experienced in the airport, the bus and on the underground, but a great deal of enjoyment and pleasant experiences occurring at the party, the discotheque, or the concert.

The difference just outlined leads to a major distinction which has been drawn by environmental psychologists between crowding and density as a result of their research findings (Stokols, 1972). Density refers to the number of people in a prescribed space, for example the number of people per square kilometre in a city, and is an objective measure. Crowding refers to our experience of the number of people in a given setting, and is a subjective, psychological concept. The importance of the distinction lies in how useful each concept is in predicting behaviour and experience. From the example outlined, a measure of density would predict a similar experience in all six situations and would therefore be of very limited use. To measure crowding we would need to ask people about their experience. There are a great many variables that will influence our experience of crowding.

These will include our relationship with the people involved, the duration of the experience, the physical context of the experience, and the meaning of the experience. We are likely to feel less crowded in a group of friends than in a group of strangers if we have chosen to be there. However there may also be situations where the opposite is true. For example it may feel more uncomfortable to be crowded by a work colleague we know but with whom we are not intimate than by a total stranger on a train. Again we tend to be more tolerant of crowding if we know it is short term and will soon end. Research suggests that the correlation between density and crowding is often quite small. For example Edwards et al. (1994) compared density and crowding in 2017

Box 28: The behavioural sink

While there are many problems with animal studies in terms of both the ethics involved and the generalisation of findings to humans, a series of studies by Calhoun (1962, 1973) is pertinent to the effects of crowding on behaviour and experience. Calhoun built an environment for rats where they were provided with abundant food, water, and nesting material and allowed to live and breed freely. As the population of rats grew in size Calhoun was able to observe the effects of increased crowding. In fact the behaviour of the rats under crowded conditions deteriorated so much that Calhoun coined the phrase behavioural sink to describe the effect. Despite a quarter of an acre of space with no predators the population levelled off at 150 while such a space might have been predicted to accommodate several thousand. The reason for this was the very high level of infant mortality caused by the aggressive attacks from adult males on pregnant females and often cannibalism in eating the newborn. The females lost their maternal instinct and often abandoned their young. In general there appeared to be a vast increase in psychopathology. Aggression was rampant, and aberrant sexual behaviour was common. Some animals became hyperactive while others became withdrawn and appeared depressed.

In the study reported in 1973 Calhoun replicated his earlier study with mice. Again despite adequate facilities for 4000, the population never went above 2200. Disruption of reproductive processes eventually led to the extinction of the complete colony. There have been many criticisms of Calhoun's research not least because of the distress caused to the animals. Critics have suggested that the environment was not natural even for rats or mice and ultimately that findings from animal studies cannot be generalised to humans. However these studies inspired much of the work on crowding in humans that followed and there is nothing to contradict the suggested relationship between extreme crowding and psychopathology. One would expect that a human replication of such extreme conditions would not be allowed to occur.

households in Bangkok, Thailand. They found a very modest relationship, which was non-linear and produced a ceiling effect. In other words there was a level above which density had no further impact on crowding. Furthermore an important moderating variable was how much control individuals perceived they had over the use of household space.

Research on the effect of crowding on behaviour and experience has produced quite substantial evidence of a negative effect of crowding in a range of areas.

Developmental effects of crowding

Some research suggests that adults are likely to experience crowding at lower density levels than children (Sinha, Nayyar, & Mukherjee, 1995). This study used the Crowding Perception Test (Desor, 1972), which uses a wooden box divided into two sections with a connecting door and containing miniature furniture. Participants use dolls as people and are asked to populate the space. In this study children and adolescents were asked to imagine they were inviting people to a party. Children consistently introduced more people than the adolescents did. There are of course problems of ecological validity with this type of study, but it would appear that we require more personal space as we get older. However, perceptions aside, crowded home environments tend to have negative effects on children. Goduka, Poole, and Aotaki-Phenice (1992) found that parents' education, occupation, and crowding were the three important predictors of cognitive development and self-concept in 300 black South African children. Mascie-Taylor (1991) found crowding to be a predictor of physical underdevelopment in British children. Powell (1990) explains the poor performance of African-American children in science and mathematics in terms of learned helplessness induced by high density living and uncontrollable noise in their environment. In a study of Haitian-American infants, Widmayer et al. (1990) found that low birth weight and household crowding were the best predictors of psychomotor development at 12 months old.

Levels of crowding in the home have also been shown to influence the level of mother–child interaction with more crowded homes reducing the levels of involvement, verbal stimulation, and more frequent disciplining of children (Fuller, Edwards, Vorakitphokatorn, & Sermsri, 1993a), and responsiveness of mothers towards their child. Crowding is just one of a cluster of variables that will coexist in a child's home background, and it would be impossible to disentangle the effects. However, the design of living accommodation should take into account density and, even more importantly, crowding.

Crowding in corrective institutions

Over the recent past, overcrowding in prisons has become a major problem in the UK. Riots among inmates and stress among prison officers have both been attributed to overcrowded conditions, before the effects on the prisoners themselves are even considered. The problem has been experienced more widely in the USA (Kinkade, Leone, & Semond, 1995; McKenzie & Piquero, 1994; Pontell & Welsh, 1994). The possibility of alternative strategies for criminals and young offenders who do not require totally controlled incarceration has been explored. Residential treatment centres and day-reporting centre programmes have some potential (Koehler & Lindner, 1992). As with all aspects of psychological functioning, responses to crowding are subject to individual differences. Anson and Hancock (1992) suggest that aggressive potential and prior evidence of violence need to be considered in prison space allocation. As previously pointed out violent criminals tend to require larger amounts of personal space than non-violent individuals. The research on corrective institutions tends to focus on density rather than crowding and it is very clear that such a focus limits application. It is the interface between crowding and individual differences in regard to aggression that are most useful in informing application.

Crowding and psychiatric institutions

Anyone who works in institutions which deal with individuals with psychiatric problems, or with individuals with mental disability, will be aware of their sensitivity to large numbers of people. In my own experience with clients with challenging behaviour, incidence of aggressive behaviour tended to be related to the number of other clients and staff around at the time. This is supported by a study by Palmstierna, Huitfeldt, and Wistedt (1991) who monitored the behaviour of 163 acute care psychiatric patients over a period of 25 weeks and found that a major predisposing factor in cases of aggressive behaviour by patients was an increase in the number of patients on the ward. Brooks et al. (1994) looked at the relationship between the use of seclusion and restraint as a result of violence and the population density of six psychiatric units and found a strong significant positive correlation. Lanza et al. (1994) investigated environmental factors which coincided with patient assaults on other patients or staff in two acute and four long-term psychiatric units, and concluded that crowding as measured on the Ward Atmosphere Scale, rather than density, was a major factor. In a comparison of psychiatric patients and controls, Kamal and Gupta, (1988) found that the psychiatric patients exhibited a higher sensitivity to crowding. This effect was common to patients suffering from schizophrenia, affective disorder, and neurosis. It would appear that crowding is a variable that needs to be better understood and managed in psychiatric settings.

Crowding and the home

We have already seen that crowding in the home is one factor in both impaired cognitive development and in slowed physical development in children. Early studies of crowded home environments and psychological distress produced conflicting findings (Galle, Gove, & McPherson, 1972; Mitchell, 1971). Gabe and Williams (1987) suggest that one reason for this conflict is the confounding effect of living alone. In other words single person occupancy would appear as low on an index of density, yet living alone brings its own problems. It would appear that the relationship is curvilinear when density is the measure. Other reasons why some studies don't find a strong relationship between crowding and health may be because they don't account for individual and cultural differences and moderating variables such as perceived control and social support, all factors which have been found to be important.

More recent research does allow us to conclude that crowding in the home tends to be a source of stress generally and to coincide with more unstable and conflictual relationships (Fuller et al., 1993a) but to have no real effect on sexual or reproductive behaviour between couples (Edwards et al., 1992). Crowding is also associated with a general decrease in satisfaction with the area one lives in (Bonnes, Bonaiuto, & Ercolani, 1991). Because crowding is a source of stress, it has an effect on physical health as well, with poorer physical health coexisting with the experience of crowding (Fuller et al., 1993b). The Fuller and Edwards, Edwards et al., and Fuller et al., results are produced from an intensive study of 2017 households in Bangkok, where population density is a recognised problem. In an interesting study among autorickshaw travellers in India, Ruback and Pandey (1992) investigated the effects of temperature and crowding. They interviewed passengers under three levels of temperature and three levels of crowding and found both main effects and an interaction effect on affect. Higher temperatures and more crowding produced more negative affect. They then manipulated the effects by telling some passengers about the effects of temperature, some about the effects of crowding, and some were not told anything. They found that knowing about the effects of temperature produced a greater sense of control and mediated the negative affect. However this did not work for crowding, indicating that being made aware of the effects of crowding does not enhance our ability to cope with it. This is supportive of the role of appraisal of cause effects in the stress process proposed by Halpern (1995). Lepore, Evans, and Palsane (1991) compared social hassles and crowding in the home, in American and Indian samples, and found that although there was a relationship between the two, crowding was a better predictor of psychological distress. Homma (1990) reviews the literature on crowding and coping in Japan, and concludes that crowding is generally recognised as a negative experience, and that recent cultural and social changes (mainly Westernisation), has reduced the effectiveness of coping strategies.

So far we have focused on the effects of internal crowding, that is crowding inside buildings such as homes, prisons, and hospitals. It does appear that psychological distress, physical health effects, and generalised stress effects are more closely related to internal crowding. However crowding also occurs outside the home, in the neighbourhood, the local community, and in nations. Perhaps the most noticeable ways in which external crowding effects impinge on us are to be found in travel (which is discussed later in this chapter), leisure activities, and crime.

Crowding and leisure
I was recently asked by a national radio station for my views as a psychologist on problems associated with Bank Holidays. The main thrust of the questions concerned the problems of crowding at leisure venues, such as seasides and leisure parks. We are all aware these days of bank holiday traffic congestion, queuing for rides in amusement parks, and densely populated beaches. In addition we find sports facilities and fitness suites where we have to queue for facilities and where changing rooms are often more intimate than is comfortable. Andereck and Becker (1993) studied the crowding experience of 1687 visitors to a national monument where they had to travel on boats at various levels of density. They found that participants' expectations of crowding at the monument and on later visits was influenced by their first experience. This sort of finding in conjunction with the level of annoyance experienced by crowded leisure facilities would lead one to predict that people might stop using crowded facilities. However, neither practical experience or research supports this. Kuentzel and Heberlein (1992) tested this in people using a leisure facility in the USA. They found that crowding experience in 1975 had no predictive effect on use of the facility over the following 10 years. In other words feeling crowded did not prevent people returning to the spot. In many ways this seems to be a central problem in the area in that it is not self-regulating. This leads to ridiculously long queues of traffic on motorways on Bank Holidays. Part of the problem seems to be that most people have their

---

Box 29: Crowding the consumer

The effects of crowding on consumer behaviour is something we often experience these days, but appears not to have attracted researchers. It is recognised by some in the business world, for example one large supermarket chain recently introduced a promise to customers that there would never be more than three in a queue for a checkout. They intended to do this by opening a new checkout every time queuing reached the specified limit. One study by Hui and

Bateson (1991) investigated participants' responses to hypothetical scenarios about a consumer's experience in a bank. Density and consumer choice were varied in the scenario and participants were then assessed by questionnaire as to their ratings of pleasantness–unpleasantness of the encounter and their attitudes to using the bank. Participants' ratings were mediated by control, in that they were only put off where the choice was limited.

---

leisure time at the same time. The effect of crowding in leisure facilities seems to be mediated by perceptions of control (Propst & Kurtzz, 1989).

In a study of the size of exercise classes Carron, Brawley, and Widmeyer (1990) found a curvilinear relationship between size, perceived crowding, and satisfaction with social interaction. It appears that small and large classes were perceived more positively than medium-size classes. The size of classes varied between 5–46 participants. Perceived crowding was also identified as a factor in reduced satisfaction in larger teams in a study of participants in a college basketball league (Carron, Brawley, & Widmeyer, 1990).

Crowding and crime

There is a widespread belief that crime and economic deprivation go hand in hand, hence by proxy, crowding and crime might be linked. However, just as with the link with poverty, crime is not necessarily a result of crowding. The clearest indicator of this is the comparison by Gifford and Peacock (1979) between Toronto and Hong Kong. The latter has about four times the population density of Toronto, yet has only about one quarter the crime rate. Crowding is associated with increased levels of aggression and violent behaviour and may be a contributory factor in assaults on spouse or children in family settings although the evidence is not conclusive (Fuller et al., 1993b). Crowding appears not to have been investigated in relation to specific crimes, but some link would seem to be indicated. First of all crimes such as pickpocketing tend to occur in crowded situations. We are all familiar with the increase in this sort of crime at holiday resorts during peak periods, on busy rush hour trains, and at large outdoor events. A more insidious effect of crowding is the effect on helping behaviour. The widely known bystander apathy effect (Latane & Darley, 1968; Latane & Nida, 1981) is related to the number of people around (see Box 30).

Although there is not a lot of evidence in the area, one other important effect needs to be mentioned—that is that fear of crime does appear to increase with population density (Gifford, 1987).

Crowding, emotion, and behaviour

Crowding, both in laboratory studies and in real world situations, leads to increased physiological arousal and stress (Epstein, 1982). Because of this it is not surprising to find increased incidence of high blood pressure and faster heart rate in crowded situations (Epstein, Woolfolk, & Lehrer, 1981), and increased levels of physical illness (Fuller et al, 1993b). Because of its effect on arousal, crowding instigates the process of emotional responding and could produce aggression or elation depending on the social cues. However positive social cues rarely occur

---

Box 30: Safe in the madding crowd

Most people would tend to associate crimes against the person (rape, assault, mugging) with dark deserted alley ways. While it is still good advice to avoid such situations, in reality violent crime often occurs in the middle of the day when there are lots of people around. The infamous case of the horrific murder of Kitty Genovese, which occurred while 38 other inhabitants of the apartment block listened to her screams throughout her 30-minute ordeal, led Latane and Darley (1968) to carry out a series of studies on what they came to call bystander apathy. In their studies they had a confederate fake a heart attack on the New York underground under various levels of crowding and found that when there were lots of people around help was less frequently offered. Recent reports of crimes include a young woman dragged by two assailants along a busy railway platform and raped in a doorway just out of sight, and another woman taken from a telephone box in a busy London street into a local park and raped. Both crimes occurred in the middle of the day and no one intervened or even called the police. Why might this occur? Various explanations have been proffered ranging from fear of embarrassment, to diffusion of responsibility (i.e. leave it to someone else to help). The work of Latane & Darley shows that when people are alone they are most likely to help, supporting the diffusion of responsibility explanation. The evidence would indicate two foci for intervention. First of all observers need to be clear that help is required, and secondly observers must be made aware that no one else is going to help, therefore they should take responsibility.

with crowding (although they may occur with high density as at the rock concert) and anger and aggression seem to be the most likely emotional responses. The alternative is apathy, social withdrawal, and learned helplessness (Powell, 1990). Both effects occur. Studies in correctional and psychiatric institutions implicate crowding as a factor in aggressive behaviour. The Powell (1990) study and the effects of crowding on social support indicate the social withdrawal option. In essence the effects of crowding on emotion can be explained in the same way as other external stressors such as noise and temperature. As well as increasing aggressive behaviour, crowding also reduces helping behaviour. The Evans and Lepore (1993) study discussed below linked lower helping to crowding in the home. More generally crowding reduces liking and the desire to help others (Gifford, 1987).

The effects of crowding on performance appear to fit with the general arousal–performance relationship discussed for other variables. Sinha and Sinha (1991) found that density impaired performance on complex tasks, but not on simple tasks, supporting the Yerkes–Dodson law. This replicates the earlier work of Evans (1979), Knowles (1983), and Heller, Groff, and Solomon (1977). The effect of crowding on performance can be at least partially explained in terms of audience effects (Zajonc, 1965, see Box 21).

All of the effects of crowding on human behaviour and experience will coexist with many other factors in the environment. For example the effects of crowding in the home will coexist with effects of lower socioeconomic status, unemployment and general social and economic deprivation. In addition social (or people) stressors such as invasion of personal space and territoriality and lack of privacy are all aspects of the crowding experience (Gutheil, 1992). It is difficult to disentangle these effects, but they combine to influence all sorts of behaviours and experiences, as we have seen. In fact their major effect may be in terms of their influence on cognitive and motivational responses which may reproduce the same sort of economic deprivation across generations (Cassidy & Lynn, 1991). In addition not everyone is affected by crowding in the same way. The ways in which some people cope effectively with crowding can perhaps provide us with more useful information. We will first of all explore individual and cultural differences and then focus on two moderating variables that have been identified, control and support.

Individual and cultural differences in response to crowding
The studies that we have reported have been drawn from an international sample. Studies from areas such as India or Thailand, where population density is very high can inform us about the effects of extreme crowding, whereas studies from Canada are less informative

about this effect since population density is low there. Thus the first cultural difference lies in the differential experience of crowding across cultures. This is important because studies have shown that prior experience and expectations influence both our sensitivity to crowding and our coping response (Lepore, Evans, and Schneider, 1991; Webb & Worchel, 1993). Cultural effects in terms of sensitivity will reflect cultural differences in personal space preferences generally. Some evidence exists of more sensitivity to crowding among Blacks compared to Hispanics in Chicago (Gove & Hughes, 1983) and among foreign students compared to Indian students in India (Odera & Hasan, 1993). However studies are too diverse to allow any real conclusions. What such studies should alert us to is the importance of situation. With increased movement of peoples worldwide many countries contain a mix of people from different cultures. People who have experienced high levels of crowding in their previous environment are likely to respond positively to reduced density in a new environment and vice versa. Perhaps previous experience of crowding is what we need to consider, rather than culture. Similar conclusions can be drawn for gender differences, but some additional aspects do need to be considered. For example a study of the effects of crowding in dormitories on student behaviour and experience by Karlin, Epstein, and Aiello (1978) found that three people living in rooms designed for two felt more stressed and produced poorer performance than uncrowded students. An important outcome of this study was the observation of gender differences in behaviour. Males tended to leave the dormitory more frequently and spend much more time in other settings, while females generally tried to base themselves mainly in the dormitory. Thus males felt less impeded by the crowded conditions than females. In addition many of the males still operated in their triad even after the semester, while most of the females disbanded. On the other hand the study discussed in Box 31 suggests that females cope better with crowding in the home than males. An explanation might be expectations in each situation. The home is a long-term commitment, and requires different behaviours, than the short-term experience of a shared dormitory.

While cultural and gender differences are important, they are perhaps less informative and useful than other individual differences in terms of previous experience, expectations, and current commitments.

Crowding, control, and social support
One way of coping with crowding is to withdraw from social interaction, almost a seeking of internal privacy when opportunities do not exist in the external world. Such withdrawal can be interpreted in terms of an attempt to restore some sense of personal control over the situation.

Box 31: Too many men for well-being

The evidence strongly suggests that men are less likely than women to talk about emotional problems, and tend to be less supportive in terms of emotional crises. A study by Ruback and Riad (1994) provides more evidence of this. They accessed the social density of males and females in households and the level of social support reported. Results show that occupants of homes with higher social density of men liked their home less and reported more psychological distress. While reported social support levels were not related to the social density of males, it was positively correlated with social density of females. This supports the buffer theory of social support with higher levels of support, in more densely populated female homes, being related to more positive well-being. In some of my own research, there appears to be a relationship between warmth of family relationships, conflict in the family home, and the sex distribution of siblings. In homes with more female siblings participants report warmer relationships and less conflict. Aiello, Nicosla, and Thompson (1979) found that as early as nine years of age females are better able to share the distress caused by crowding than males, which ultimately leads to better psychological health for females.

Evans and Lepore (1993) compared participants from crowded living conditions with participants from uncrowded homes, under stressful conditions in a laboratory situation. They found that those from crowded homes were less likely to ask for support from, or to offer support to, colleagues. Evans et al. (1989) concluded from a study of 175 heads of households that the effects of crowding are mediated through its effect on social support with negative consequences occurring where social support systems within the family have broken down.

In a longitudinal study Lepore, Evans, and Schneider (1991) found that students exposed to crowded living conditions went through an initial phase at two months where perceived social support was related to individual levels of psychological distress, to a stage at eight months where the buffering effect of social support was eroded. At the latter stage in fact, social support itself seemed to be eroded. Lepore, Evans, and Schneider (1992) studied the effects of crowding, social support, and perceived control on psychological distress in students. They found that while there were no obvious effects of crowding on social support, perceived control did significantly moderate the relationship between crowding and psychological distress. As in the Ruback and Pandey (1992) study, participants who had higher levels of perceived control, were less affected by crowding. In another study Ruback and Patnaik (1989) found that crowding leads to increased vandalism and destruction of property when perceived control was low. Generally studies have considered one or other variable but not explored control and support together. One study which did this (Jain, 1993) found both social support and control to be moderators of the effect of crowding in a study of 960 participants. As we saw in Chapter 4 social support and control are important factors in mediating the stress process. Crowding appears to impair social support and constrains the amount of control individuals have over their world. Individuals who create more support systems for themselves as the females in the Ruback and Riad (1994) study did, will cope better. Alternatively asserting control, as the males in the Karlin, Epstein, and Aiello (1978) study did by choosing to spend more time outside the dormitory, also improves one's chances of coping. It seems fairly clear from the research that social support and control are the major mechanisms involved in determining whether crowding has negative consequences for individuals. Crowding effects seem to be the accumulation of infringements of personal space and territory. A more recent concept which can be usefully applied to explicate the interdependence of these processes is privacy.

PRIVACY

Privacy is something we are very much aware of these days as we observe the ongoing debate about invasion of privacy by the media. The concept of privacy is something that impinges on each of us daily. People talk about being given "space" in which to grow and develop. In research on relationships it is recognised that even intimate partners need time away from each other. In essence privacy is about seeking respite from the direct influence of others. Altman (1975) defines privacy as "selective control of access to the self or to one's group" (p.18).

The definition suggests that privacy is much more than personal space or territoriality. It involves social access as well in terms of information about one's self or one's group. Research on the development of relationships identifies the process of disclosure as central. When we meet someone for the first time we tend only to disclose superficial facts about ourselves. If this is reciprocated we may begin to disclose a bit more. If the relationship is to develop we will both get to a stage of disclosing more intimate information about feelings. This negotiated route from fact to feeling is often engaged in without our awareness of it. Disclosure involves selective control over the type and amount of information about ourselves that we are willing to allow another to access. We use the process of disclosure to exclude by refusing to move beyond the level of fact, the intention being to give a clear message to others not to proceed. We try to manage the expression of our emotions and we engage in impression management (Goffman, 1959) in other ways as well. In fact we use the whole range of verbal and nonverbal communication, including personal space, in an attempt to ensure that others see us as we want them to see us. Hence privacy involves the control of access to both our external and internal worlds, to the objective and subjective territories and spaces that we reserve for our personal use. As with most areas of psychology the concept of control is important, and identifies the psychological aspect of privacy. It is not necessarily the case that the person desires to isolate themselves; simply having the option to do so as and when required may be sufficient. It is when this option is removed that psychological distress ensues. In other words as long as we perceive ourselves to have control over access to ourselves we do not feel distressed. In fact we generally do not even think about it. As with personal space, and territoriality, it is only when someone encroaches on our privacy and we feel unable to prevent them, that we become aware of the process. Also in common with personal space, territoriality, and crowding we need to be aware that measurement is not an objective procedure but involves the phenomic world of the person. This includes the level of privacy preferred by the person, and will be a function of their experience, personal characteristics, cultural heritage, and the current social and physical contexts.

Some issues of privacy

Personal desire for privacy will range on a dimension from total withdrawal to very public interaction. Some individuals by virtue of their position in society (members of royal families, film stars) are often considered public property and denied the right to seek privacy. It is interesting that denial of privacy applies to both ends of the social status spectrum, with the down and out and homeless also having little privacy accorded to them. For example Rizzini and Lusk (1995) identify an important aspect of the life of children on the streets in South America as the fact that they live in "an environment without privacy". In fact the privacy of the patient in psychiatric institutions is a matter for concern to many with information ranging from how much they have eaten to the size and timing of their last bowel movement sometimes being discussed in front of other patients and staff. Counselling practice involves confidentiality as a central mechanism, thus protecting the privacy of the client, and many professional relationships involve rules that protect access to information. For example, client–lawyer, patient–doctor, penitent–priest, customer–banker and so on. So to some extent privacy is protected either by law or professional obligation.

Box 32: Privacy in research

Protecting the confidentiality of research participants is one important aspect of ethical concern in research and is addressed in the ethical guidelines of all professional bodies. It is general practice to record data anonymously or to ensure that access to names is only available to a professional whose code of practice ensures confidentiality and after consent from participants and/or those responsible for them. This means that no individual can be identified. However what about the privacy of a group? Scarr (1994) considers the issue of adoles- cents' versus parents' rights in research. The information generated from studies often generates general statements about groups, such as a particular percentage of adolescents engage in sexual activity. Disclosing this sort of information, assuming that it is accurate, may influence parents' and others' attitudes towards individual adolescents. The sort of information produced about groups from research needs to be considered in terms of how it might infringe the right to privacy of an individual member of the group.

The importance of remaining private

Research identifies the importance of privacy in a range of areas. For example there is evidence that privacy conflicts in the family are related to psychiatric symptomatology in undergraduate students (Johnson, 1993). Families where individual privacy is respected and accorded without conflict tend to occur more frequently among students with no noticeable symptoms. In the area of AIDS and HIV infection, privacy is also an important issue. Research suggests that loss of privacy is a factor in the distress caused by having AIDS (Powell-Cope, 1995). In addition concerns about privacy and perceptions of the possible release of information affect decisions about having an AIDS test (Greene, Parrott, and Serovich, 1993; Phillips et al., 1995).

In a world where terrorism and other forms of violence exist and where drug trafficking is a major issue, laws which allow officials to over-ride the right to privacy are a cause for concern to many. For example in Northern Ireland over the past 20 years it has been common place for police and army personnel to carry out searches of houses, cars, and even intimate body searches. The degradation of being searched in such a way if one is innocent is quite distressing. Recently in the UK police have been given the power to stop and search pedestrians on suspicion of criminal activity. Many of you may be unaware that officials of water, electricity, and gas authorities have the right to break into your home in emergencies or if they suspect any illegal use of services. Clearly the relationship between the legal system and individual privacy is an issue of concern (Kagehiro, Taylor, & Harland, 1991).

Factors influencing privacy

As with other factors that have a subjective element, not everyone will react in the same way in regard to privacy. Anyone who has moved through bedsit (or flat) land, will be well aware of this fact. Some people like to keep both their physical belongings and their thoughts or feelings very much to themselves, while others are less concerned about such things. Not recognising these differences can be a major problem in sharing with others. One such factor is the gender difference. As we saw in the study by Karlin, Epstein, and Aiello (1978) males and females reacted differently when sharing three-person rooms. Females tended to try to use the room as a base and felt more distressed, while males tended to spend most of their time out of the room, only returning to sleep. This is supported by Walden, Nelson, and Smith (1981) who compared males and females in two- and three-person rooms. Males in two-person rooms became more conscious of issues of privacy because they spent time in the room, but when in threes males tended only to use the room as a place to sleep. Females however tended to use the rooms in both cases, and coped better than males. It is difficult to argue a case for any one explanation here. The study suggests that females felt less threatened in regard to privacy. However it could be because they are less concerned with privacy, have more ways of protecting privacy, are more comfortable with the intimacy which would involve more invasions of personal space, or as the study by Ruback and Riad (1994) suggests perhaps females are better at providing social support for each other which might buffer the effects of reduced privacy. In fact it is quite likely that all of these play a role. Whatever the difference when same sex participants interact, clearly privacy is an important aspect of cross-gender interaction. Although it hasn't attracted research, sharing accommodation between males and females who are not involved in an intimate relationship tends to lead to problems. Cross-gender patient–doctor or client–counsellor relationships often become problematic and are generally protected by professional guidelines. While not researched in this context it seems reasonable to suggest that issues most often involve the distinction between public and private in the relationship. In other words the negotiated boundary is perceived differently by both. There is evidence that males tend to be less accurate in reading nonverbal cues than females which is likely to be a major part of the problem. One area where some evidence is available is in cross-gender supervision in prison (Alpert & Crouch, 1991). This study identified invasion of privacy as an important source of problems. What does seem very clear from research is that females in the young adult and middle years tend to engage in more intimate disclosure with other females, than males of the same age do with other males (Rubin & Shenker, 1977). In essence the stereotype of males as being less willing to talk about their emotions seems to be supported by the evidence. As discussed above this has an effect on social support and ultimately on psychological health. It is interesting that there is some evidence that the gender difference in disclosure is reversed in older adulthood, with older females disclosing less and older males disclosing more (Gifford, 1987). The age difference in privacy requirements raises the issue of privacy as a developmental process. It seems generally clear that infants' need for privacy is quite small, however the process whereby privacy becomes important has not been widely researched despite the fact that the parent of any teenager will know it is often a source of strain between parents and children as they grow older. Wolfe (1975) explored the meaning of privacy in different age groups of children. She found that as children get older the need to be alone; control of access to information and autonomy become important in how they define privacy. In addition control over place tends to take on prime importance in the 8–12-year-old group. It appears that all of the 10–17-year-old participants in one study closed the bathroom door (Parke & Sawinn, 1979). Though underresearched, it does seem that privacy needs and the development of adult sexuality are intertwined. Some workers have explored personality effects in regard to privacy with need for privacy being seen as an individual difference factor. There is a suggestion that higher need for privacy goes with lower self-esteem

---

Box 33: The sound of closing doors

For many people living in the UK the control of access to the self is enhanced by being surrounded by walls and having doors which we can close. However it has not always been like this, and for many people, even in the UK, it is not the same. We saw above how being homeless leads to environments without privacy. In the past families often lived in cramped accommodation with several children sharing the same room and even the same bed as adolescents. It appears that when doors are not available we develop alternative mechanisms. In other words we still desire privacy but we have to achieve it by different means. This adaptation was observed in the studies of students sharing rooms, where males tended to satisfy their privacy requirements in other places. Gifford (1987) describes an unwritten rule among Gypsy groups where one can maintain privacy by not washing one's face. It is only after a person has washed their face in the morning that others will disturb their privacy. Hence by choosing not to wash her/his face a Gypsy says "stay away!". Other groups devise ways of dressing and undressing which protect their modesty and develop norms about turning one's back or looking away so as to respect the privacy of others.

(McKechnie, 1974). However the approach–avoidance conflict or the affiliative-conflict model of Argyle and Dean (1965) is evident in the work of Pedersen (1982) who found that individuals with a high need for privacy also appear to have a strong need for intimacy with their family. In situations where individuals perceive their neighbourhood negatively this tension is also observed in that two common features of the experience reported are lack of privacy and a sense of isolation. In the relationship between social support and health, privacy is also a factor. As Halpern (1995) suggests, positive effects of social networks depend on finding a comfortable balance between good neighbouring and privacy.

Situational aspects of privacy

Clearly situational effects are also very important. On a night out with a lover we often seek intimacy in the form of a table for two in a secluded restaurant. On a boys or girls night out we probably seek less private situations. Satisfaction with privacy, which according to Altman (1975), occurs when achieved privacy is equal to desired privacy is related to psychological health and its effect can be explained in terms of optimum arousal levels and stress (Halpern, 1995). It therefore follows that environments that restrict privacy or provide too much seclusion will be perceived as stressful and psychologically damaging. For example the higher levels of distress among flat dwellers as opposed to house dwellers is likely to be due more to lack of privacy than reduced social support as is commonly thought (Halpern, 1995). Privacy in the work place and how it relates to mental health has attracted some research, particularly since factors that increase stress and reduce mental health also reduce performance and efficiency. We spend up to a third of our life at work and the work environment is perhaps the one which individuals have least control over in terms of its design or layout. For those who are involved in designing work buildings all the factors relating to use of space and many more are important. One question that is often addressed is whether it is better to provide one large open office for staff in a department or if the best design is to provide everyone with their own office. These questions are generally driven by considerations of the effects of different types of office design on performance and productivity. However these days it is widely recognised that performance is only one part of a dynamic system of human behaviours and experiences. In other words performance is related to levels of motivation, job satisfaction, absenteeism, job turnover, stress levels, and even physical healthiness. Hence factors that influence one will influence others as well. In terms of the debate about open plan or individual offices research seems to point to privacy as a major factor (Sundstrom, Burt, & Kamp, 1980; Sundstrom, Herbert, & Brown, 1982) This research found that perceived privacy significantly decreased for employees moved from secluded to open plan offices and concluded that satisfaction with privacy is related to how open or closed the physical environment is in the work place. These researchers found that regardless of job type, workers generally preferred individual offices and identified privacy as a major concern. In fact satisfaction with privacy correlated positively with job satisfaction, satisfaction with the work place, and job performance. While correlational studies do not allow any definitive conclusions about causality they do indicate factors that planners need to consider in their work. The evidence is that open plan offices have more disadvantages than advantages mainly because they impinge on workers' need for privacy.

Box 34: Sick buildings without walls

An interesting question which has caused some recent debate is whether buildings can make one physically ill. This is demonstrated by the experience of one British company in the design of their new headquarters. They opted for the open plan office design based on economic factors and a popular trend at the time. Basically it is cheaper to build one large office, space can be more effectively utilised without obstructing walls, less supervision is required since people can be easily observed, and there was some belief that communication between individuals and groups could be facilitated. However occupation of the new office was followed by an increase in levels of symptoms of illness, absenteeism, and in turn a general reduction in motivation and performance. The conclusion drawn from the experience was that the building itself was the source of the problems—something that has been labelled sick building syndrome. This is a relatively recently identified phenomenon which recognises that particular buildings because of their design can cause physical illness in workers. Currently a debate is in progress as to what factors are most important (Ryan & Morrow, 1992). Some theorists focus on psychological factors (Bauer et al., 1992), others explore the physical aspects such as air quality (Skov et al., 1990; Norback, Michel, & Widstrom, 1990), while other studies indicate interactions between job-related factors and personality (Skov, Valbjorn, & Pedersen, 1989). It is unlikely that any one factor will emerge triumphant and that a number of interdependent factors are involved. However the identification of sick building syndrome is strong support for the need to plan work environments with a range of possible influences on people in mind. Sick building syndrome is not necessarily associated with open plan offices and the example above just serves to show how a change of office design can have a major effect on people at work and the fact that the effects of work environments on behaviour are not likely to be in terms of any single dimension or aspect of the design. Within the process the evidence suggests that privacy considerations will be an important factor.

Generalising from the evidence on students sharing rooms suggests that sharing an office may lead to dissatisfaction with privacy and therefore distress. One factor that influences our reaction to privacy is our expectation, which is a function of our previous experience (Walden, Nelson, & Smith, 1981). In addition we do adapt to less privacy as was demonstrated by Firestone, Lichtman, and Evans (1980) in their study of patients in private versus open wards. Those on open wards actually reported desiring less privacy. However as Gifford (1987) suggests this might be fatalism rather than a real adaptation. Fatalism could alternatively be defined as learned helplessness, a response to lack of control. With privacy control is all important. Altman (1975) whose work is the most prolific in the area suggests that privacy has three important dimensions. He describes them as a boundary control process, an optimisation process, and a multimechanism process. In other words privacy is about control over the boundary between ourselves and others; its aim is to optimise the balance between solitude and intimacy; and we use a wide range of physical factors and behaviours in establishing the control. These latter range from verbal communication through the complete range of nonverbal cues to the use of walls and doors to physically exclude. The physical environment's role in the process will be considered in the chapter on design, but in essence the physical environment will enhance or restrict our control over access to ourselves and hence privacy. There is clearly a need to explore privacy more fully in terms of the development of the need for privacy, the role of privacy in stress and health, and the structure of privacy. The latter seems to be somewhat unclear. Research shows that privacy is about a balance between solitude and intimacy and therefore involves an approach–avoidance conflict. In addition it involves the need for control. When people define privacy they talk of being alone, controlling information, autonomy, a need for intimacy, and so on. The question remains as to whether privacy is a multidimensional concept or whether control and intimacy are independent but related factors. What research has been done identifies privacy as an important aspect of human behaviour and experience which is related to the general issue of interaction with others. We now turn to a consideration of how the issue of spatial relations might be integrated.

An integration of space

From the discussion above it should be clear that it is often difficult to distinguish between effects of crowding, personal space, territoriality, and privacy. In fact it seems a rather futile exercise to even try since each will also involve elements of the others. In other words crowding involves invasions of personal space, privacy, and territoriality and arguably it is only when such invasions occur that density becomes crowding. Similarly one cannot research personal space and territoriality without considering crowding and privacy issues. This raises the question if in fact they are different mechanisms. It would appear that they are all concerned with control of access to one's space and are all concerned with obtaining a balance between too much and too little space. In addition they are a subjective response to other people and involve communication. The space being controlled can be a large area which one feels one has some claim to, the immediate space around one's body, or the internal space which controls information about the self. In themselves these aspects of our space are interdependent, so the mechanisms that control them are unlikely to be explicated in isolation. Some theorists have tried to integrate personal space, territoriality, crowding, and privacy within one model. The flow model shown in Fig. 12 from Altman (1975) is one such attempt. In line with Altman's particular interest it focuses on privacy and provides a model of the relationship between personal space, territoriality, crowding and privacy. According to this model the process of obtaining a balance between desired privacy and achieved privacy will be mediated by the different processes which control access to the self. Included in this will be personal space and territoriality as well as other aspects of the communication process. If these operate to produce an achieved privacy which is less than our desired privacy we will experience crowding. Alternatively if our achieved privacy is more than we desire we will experience social isolation, loneliness, and a lack of social support. If the control processes operate effectively then achieved privacy should be more or less equal to desired privacy and hence homeostasis or optimum levels. Attaining this optimum level means less stress, and better health, satisfaction, and general well-being. It is a useful framework which links the different aspects of interpersonal space which have traditionally been studied separately. As such it guides research towards more integrative practices. However it is important to recognise that it is just a beginning. We still have to operationalise and measure the factors identified. In addition it doesn't incorporate the physical environment which, as we have seen, plays an important part in the process. The mechanisms of interpersonal control must be seen in terms of an interaction between the person and their environment. As we have already suggested it also relies on a clear definition of privacy which, it is suggested, is a multidimensional concept. We have reviewed a varied range of evidence which supports the contention that failure to control access to one's desired space instigates the stress process. Hence personal space, territoriality, crowding, and privacy all have implications for both mental and physical health. In addition much can

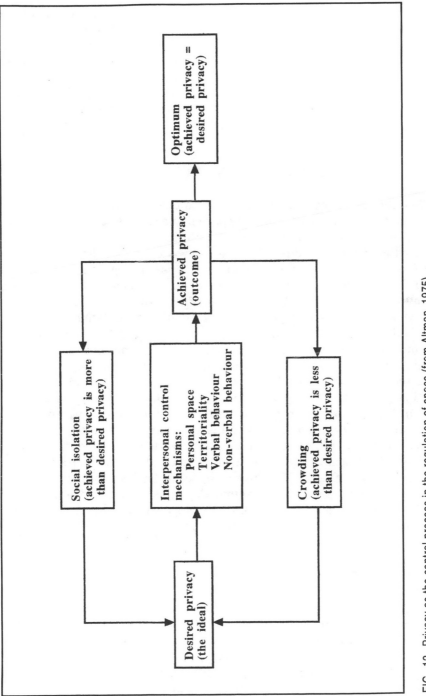

FIG. 12. Privacy as the central process in the regulation of space (from Altman, 1975).

be learned about our skills in communication from the ways in which
we do control our personal space very effectively most of the time. Space
has physical boundaries which may either enhance or restrict our
control, and these boundaries need to be fully understood and applied
in designing physical environments. One area where space is of the
essence is in travel, whether on a crowded commuter train or bumper
to bumper on a crowded Bank Holiday motorway. Let us look at what is
known of the effects of travel on human behaviour and experience.

THE PLEASURE AND PAIN OF TRAVEL

When the M25 circular motorway around London had been in operation
for just a short while it became apparent that it was totally inadequate
to meet the demand in terms of traffic volume. The horrendous
congestion that ensued led Chris Rea to write a song called *The road to
hell* in its honour. Comedians referred to it as the largest car park in the
world. More recently government agencies have released plans to add
another lane. This is just one example of problems that occur in sharing
the world with others. Reports from road traffic organisations these days
in the UK make depressing reading. It seems that if the number of cars
on our roads keep on increasing at current rates, motorways in the UK
will grind to a standstill sometime early in the next century. We saw in
the section on crowding that people are not put off by traffic jams at
holiday periods. In other words it is not a self-regulating process. One
might expect that the dreadful experience of Bank Holiday traffic might
lead many to try to avoid using roads at such times. Yet the evidence is
that we do it time and time again with no apparent learning from the
process. On the more optimistic side, a national cycle network has been
set up in the UK. SUSTRANS, which stands for sustainable transport,
has been funded by the Millennium Commission with national lottery
money. The aim is to develop a national network of cycle routes through
major towns and cities, thus enabling many to use cycles rather than
cars.

The stress of commuting
The problem identified by the M25 example has been researched under
two main interrelated areas—driver stress and the experience of
commuting. The latter has included considerations of the experience of
using public transport. To some extent this is an area where it is easier
to identify the need for psychological input than to produce evidence of
its effectiveness. In the UK it would appear that psychologists have not
played an active role in the design of transport systems on the broad

scale, though the evidence would suggest that they have a lot to contribute. Travel to and from work is certainly a source of psychological distress and would appear to present a threat to both work and family life (Cassidy, 1992). In a review of research Costa et al. (1988) state that numbers of commuters have increased rapidly across the European community, that distances travelled have increased, while time taken has generally decreased. British Department of Transport (DOT) figures for 1989 for London indicate 161,000 car commuters, 96,000 bus commuters, and 473,000 rail commuters entering London each day. This massive movement of people has many clearly visible effects, one important one being death and injury through accidents. The figures for car accidents for London again from DOT figures for 1989 were 460 deaths and 8840 injuries. The less visible aspect are the psychological casualties. It is generally accepted that commuting in large conurbations is a source of stress, yet while some research has been carried out in the area it would appear to be disproportionately small compared to the large literature that has accumulated on work stress. In fact we seem to have accepted large-scale and long-distance commuting as a fact of technological advance. Yet for many, apart from the extra inconvenience, it has added time to their working day. For some this can be up to an extra four hours per day. Can you imagine the reaction if we were asked to stay at work for an extra 2–4 hours each day? As with many aspects of change it has occurred gradually over a period of time, and hence has not attracted quite so much attention. Costa et al. (1988) stress that the consequences of commuting stress in terms of long-term effects on health have not been adequately researched and the few studies which are available have focused more on describing effects rather than defining casual links and hence opening avenues of intervention. What data is available suggests that not only is commuting a source of stress in itself, but that it has consequences in the way it interferes with family and leisure activities, and increased absenteeism from work. In their study of commuter stress, Costa et al. (1988) show that commuters generally experienced a more stressful life style, with increased psychological and physical health problems. They also show an effect of commuting in increasing absenteeism from work and reducing engagement in leisure activities. The majority of commuters in their study used public transport. Another study which identified the generally stressful effect of commuting was that by Koslowsky and Krausz (1993), who looked at stress symptoms as a function of commuting in 682 nurses. They found that time taken to commute was correlated positively with stress in both car drivers and users of public transport. In addition this had a negative effect on employee attitudes for the car drivers. Commuting was shown to increase stress levels and reduce decision-making effectiveness in the home in dual career commuter families, an effect possibly mediated by the traditional division of labour in the home (Anderson & Spruill, 1993). Novaco, Kliewer, and Broquet (1991) show commuting to be a source of stress and to affect satisfaction and mood at home for both male and female commuters.

There is a need to identify the specific sources of stress and to incorporate this knowledge into design. In the USA psychologists have been involved in the design of transport systems, the most famous being the San Francisco Bay Area Rapid Transit system commonly known as BART. This system has been in operation since 1972 and has had a psychological input both in its design and in more recent evaluation of its effectiveness. On the whole BART has not been a resounding success and has been attacked on a number of fronts including its failure to reduce road traffic congestion, its lack of financial viability, and the fact that it exposes the backs of houses which some felt invaded their privacy. It is probably best considered as the source of learning about how not to design a transport system. An example of an innovative approach to the problems of traffic congestion and commuter stress is the neighbourhood work centre (NWC) approach in Sweden (Becker, 1984). The aim is to bring the worksite to the people rather than have people commute long distances. This does not work for every employer but many can benefit from having small work centres in the community thereby reducing the need to travel and enhancing family and community life by giving back the time normally taken to commute. This looks like a growth area for environmental psychologists.

Driver stress

Gulian et al. (1989, 1990) looked at driver stress which they describe as:

> an aggregate of negative feelings, cognitions and behaviours, heightened aggression, increased alertness close to anxiety, a dislike of driving and, not least, frustration and irritation provoked by the interaction with other road-users, mainly in relation to overtaking.

They identify a dimension of alertness which differentiates stressed drivers, and ranges from a positive alertness to a potentially dangerous anxiety. They conclude that the experience of stress for drivers is dependent on age, driving experience, health conditions, sleep quality, time of day, time of week, attitude towards driving, and appraisal of driving. The latter reflects the general conclusion from stress research

---

Box 35: Road rage: Aggression on the move

This morning's main news story concerns a man who was killed in a knife attack by another motorist after an altercation on the M25. Another victim of what has been termed road rage. While it generally doesn't result in such a tragic and violent end, the incidence of road rage seems to be on the increase. Road rage describes displays of aggressive behaviour by drivers towards other road users, often involving very dangerous driving or threats of physical violence. It seems to be related to driver stress and is most frequent on busy motorways, particularly when traffic flow is obstructed.

---

first highlighted by Lazarus and Folkman (1984) that what makes an experience stressful is its appraisal by the person.

The role of individual differences in driver stress while commuting was investigated in a series of studies by Matthews, Dorn, and Glendon (1991) and Dorn and Matthews (1992). Using the Driver Behaviour Inventory (Glendon et al., 1993; Gulian et al., 1989) they show that driving aggression and dislike of driving were the most significantly correlated dimensions with experienced stress. They also show that driving stress is significantly correlated with neuroticism, frequency of daily hassles, and poorer self-rated attention. They identify cognitive appraisal of coping capacity as a likely cause for adverse emotions experienced as a result of driver commuting (Matthews, Dorn, & Glendon, 1991). Schaeffer et al. (1988), also focusing on commuting by car, found that systolic and diastolic blood pressure was increased and behavioural performance decreased on high impedance routes. However this effect was mediated by the level of control individuals had over the commute. The interesting aspect of their study was that they focus, not on drivers, but on car passengers using a car pool. The proposition was that drivers have higher perceptions of control than passengers.

Control and impedance

The concept of impedance has emerged as a possible explanatory mechanism in the area. For example Schaeffer et al. (1988) define impedance as "anything that would hinder a commuter's movement towards the destination, as a function of total distance travelled and total time in transit" (p.946).

The study by Schaeffer et al. (1988), shows that when the commute was more impeded stress levels increased and behavioural performance decreased. Further support for the mediating role of impedance in the negative physical and psychological consequences of commuting are presented by Stokols et al. (1978). They found that among car users impedance was an important contributor to the experience of stress. The concept of impedance was further developed by Novaco, Stokols, and Milanesi (1990) and Novaco, Kliewer, and Broquet (1991) in terms of objective and subjective elements. They describe physical impedance and subjective impedance. They found that physical impedance and subjective impedance have some differential effects, but are essentially overlapping in their relationship with outcome measures. Physical impedance was defined as objective levels of impedance agreed generally by the population being studied. Subjective impedance was defined as self-ratings on an impedance scale. Novaco, Stokols, and Milanesi, (1990) found physical impedance related to task performance, absenteeism, job turnover, mood at work, and physical health. Subjective impedance also related to a number of physical and psychological variables, most notably evening home mood, and reported chest pains. The study again focused on driving as the mode of transport. Novaco, Kliewer, and Broquet (1991) found that subjective impedance was the strongest predictor of negative mood and relationships in the home and levels of stress. There was a close relationship between physical and subjective impedance, but one interesting difference was that on the high physical impedance routes females were more negatively affected than males.

The Stokols et al. (1978) study also showed that commuting distance, commuting time, and number of months travelling this route correlated significantly with measures of blood pressure. In other words commuting appears to have some long-term effects. Their prediction that Type As who experienced high levels of impedance would show elevated blood pressure and lower frustration tolerance was not supported. In fact it was Type Bs in the high impedance category who were most affected. In my own work (Cassidy, 1992) it was found that longer term and longer distance commuters tended to be more effective in coping with stress, and higher in achievement motivation. It is difficult to know if the experience of commuting longer term and longer distances makes one more stress resistant, or if the preponderance of stress resistant individuals in this group is because more vulnerable individuals drop out of the commuting process earlier or at shorter distances. It is quite likely that both occur. The achievement motivation effect suggests that it is important to consider the value of the job to the person. Perhaps when a job is an important part of our life we will learn to cope with the stress of travel in order to maintain it. One other interesting effect to come out of this area is the finding in some studies that car drivers seem to report less stress than users of public transport, and higher levels of perceived control (Cassidy, 1992; Schaeffer et al., 1988). It appears that because they feel they have more control, even if the objective aspects of the journey appear quite stressful, drivers can alleviate the stress effect. Alternatively train users appear to feel less in control, something that one might expect, and therefore experience more distress. The way in which this perception of control may lead more people to use their cars, even when public transport is regularly available, needs to be considered in interventions in the area.

Commuting and travelling

The studies summarised above focus mainly on commuting by car but do provide strong evidence that commuting has a major effect on health and support the need for research in the area. Commuting is a complex phenomenon which is part of many people's daily experience. Studies tend to focus on a narrow definition of commuting as travel to and from work. However people travel daily under congested conditions for other reasons as well. Parents taking children to school, school children travelling to and from school, students travelling to and from university, and travel for leisure purposes all fall within the same rubric. In addition the effects of commuting cannot be fully understood by focusing on individuals. Just as work and organisational psychologists have accepted that work behaviour can best be understood through multiple levels of analysis and within an open systems model of organisations, so commuting needs to be looked at from a similar perspective. The experience of commuting needs to be understood as a person-in-context process in terms of Lewin's (1951) $B=f(P,E)$ equation. Furthermore it is only one part of a person's experience and will be involved in reciprocal relations of causality with other aspects of the person's life (e.g. work, home, family, leisure).

What the foregoing studies present are pieces of a large and complex jigsaw, which is a useful and necessary part of the preliminary investigation of a relatively new research area. What is needed is a guiding framework so that all the bits can be fitted together. Such a model is proposed by Novaco et al. (1990) and a modified version is presented in Fig. 8. Novaco et al. (1990) tend to focus more on the environment. This modified model adds the leisure domain, and includes individual difference aspects in terms of the cognitive appraisal and coping abilities of the individual.

The research suggests that travel under conditions of impedance is a source of stress and leads to negative effects on health, emotions, performance, and relationships. Its negative effects are mediated by perceptions of control. In addition the damage to relationships may have effects on social support networks and needs to be further investigated. As a new area of research, and one which is driven by necessity in terms of the growing problem of travel, a reasonable foundation has been laid.

However lots more needs to be done. In the context of the present chapter, though travel is a fairly obvious candidate, it hasn't really been explored in terms of spatial relations. Although some work on crowding has shown that crowding during travel is stressful, the effects in terms of personal space, territoriality, and privacy have not been explored. Territoriality is obvious in travel. People place markers on their seats and often on the seat next to them in an attempt to discourage others from sitting there. Have you ever encountered a situation where on a crowded train you have been forced to ask someone to remove their baggage from a seat so you can sit down? Did they comply gracefully and with a smile? People on the London underground avoid eye contact and display other cues to maintain privacy and generally manage to survive travelling in quite close proximity, often when bodies are in physical contact, without breaking the unwritten rules of personal space. Many people reduce the stress of commuting by trying to do something useful on the journey. Using a laptop computer or learning a new language from an audio cassette are just two examples. It would appear that there is a great need to explore the sorts of spatial relationship issues that are important to people in travelling and to try to incorporate them in design. Population increases and changes in work and leisure facilities have brought with them situations which make it more difficult for us to use our boundary control mechanisms effectively. As a result we become more distressed with negative outcomes such as aggression, violence, and reductions in mental and physical health. We have a great deal of skill in using these mechanisms, but we need to have a care that our environments don't make that skill obsolete.

CHAPTER SEVEN

Environmental design

We have seen how a wide range of aspects of our world produce a range of feelings, attitudes, and behaviours in individuals. Many of these aspects are largely beyond our control, such as weather and climate, although even these are to some extent being dominated. For example we now have large indoor holiday parks where everything is under cover and temperature controlled. In this chapter we will focus specifically on the physical environment and how research can inform us in regard to future design. It is impossible not to be influenced by the design of our environment, whether in terms of homes, work spaces, parking lots, schools, hospitals, or the larger scale urban or rural environment. Over the past few weeks the local council have been redesigning a road junction close to my home. Most people were unaware of the impending change until workmen arrived and erected temporary traffic lights. The work itself caused a great deal of distress with long lines of traffic in the rush hours. When it was complete it turned out that turning right on the way out of town had been prohibited, meaning that for several hundred people, including myself, returning from town meant finding another route. This is a minor junction in a small area, but one can see that the design process could have been made less stressful for local residents. The landscape of many cities bears evidence of the failure to consider human behaviour and experience in the design process. For example the oft quoted example of Pruitt-Igoe, a building project in St Louis, USA, which was acclaimed in 1954 and demolished in 1972. This vast development of high rise accommodation became a centre for crime, fear, high levels of mental illness, and eventually underused to the extent that it was considered better to remove it permanently. It is just one example of the many such failures in cities across the world which attest to the need to consider people in the planning process. This concern for people is referred to as social design to distinguish it from the more formal design process (Gifford, 1987). However social design needs to be incorporated within formal design. The need for social design could be argued to be a product of industrial development, just as the loss of traditional communities has led to the need to create social support networks. Within many communities in the past, buildings were on a smaller scale, often built by the local community in collaborative effort, therefore involving the people who would use the building in all stages of the process. This democratic process seems to have been lost in our industrialised and technologically advanced world.

The contribution from psychology

The role of the applied psychologists in the 1990s can best be described as a person with a method. In other words applied psychologists do not have prepackaged cure-all remedies which can be taken three times a day therefore solving the problem. Nowhere is this more evident than in environmental psychology. In fact the role of the psychologist as expert is often damaging because the popular image of the psychologist is of someone who deals with the mentally ill. Therefore to need a psychologist's help is to admit to having a psychological problem. Indeed one might suggest that two of the groups in our society of whom the least accurate stereotypes exist are the mentally ill and psychologists. Though the image is changing people still react negatively to the idea of psychological intervention. In the advent of a more realistic attitude towards psychologists and psychology, psychologists can often do their best work by giving psychology away. The idea of giving psychology away was formalised by Miller (1969) in his presidential speech to the American Psychological Association. Giving psychology away is based on the premise that psychology happens naturally in the social world. In other words all of the theories that have been proposed by psychologists over the years are put into practice by people in living their everyday lives. People form groups, provide social support for each other, reward and punish each other, and so on. Psychology can be more effectively applied and reach more people through being shared than it can if it is held by psychologists. A nurse who has a knowledge of the role of her relationship with patients in their recovery can be more effective. Similarly an environmental planner who has a knowledge of how buildings affect behaviour and experience can more effectively design environments which provide satisfaction. It brings to the fore the consultative role of the psychologist. However giving psychology away does not mean providing people with ready-mixed solutions which can be applied in all settings, rather it involves providing them with a knowledge of the sorts of things they need to look for in assessing a problem, and the tools (or methods) to find them. Essentially psychology can provide the methods to find solutions rather than the solutions themselves. In terms of the psychological input to design in the context of the person with a method model, we need to view design as a process which begins with assessment of the problem, leading to choice of design, implementation of the design and evaluation of the effectiveness of what has been achieved. There are different ways in which this process could be described, all of which will incorporate similar aspects. One such process is outlined in terms of five stages, programming, design, construction, use, and evaluation by Zeisel (1981).

Programming stage

This is the stage where a need has been identified and the specifics of that need must be elaborated. It is the stage of analysis of the specific details of the users of the finished product and will incorporate some attempt to predict future needs. The building(s) must fully meet the needs of users when complete and be able to sustain those needs in the future. A common problem in design is where the needs have changed or expanded beyond the capacity of the building by the time it is ready for occupancy. If problems are not to occur the building must not only be physically large enough to house its occupants, but must provide a healthy and satisfying environment which enhances their behaviour and experience. Essentially information must be obtained on the full range of future occupants in terms of all relevant dimensions. There will be a need to know the number of people using the space, the range of things they will need to do in that space, their different needs and wants, how much time they will spend in the space, and the overall purpose of the space. This will differ depending on whether we are building a prison, a hospital, a factory, a car park, or a new housing area. As well as assessing the potential users, there will be a need to incorporate information on previous buildings of similar purpose and what research has shown about the effects of different aspects of the physical environment on behaviour. While it would be naïve to design a building without an understanding of the needs, desires, and characteristics of those who will use it, it would be equally naïve to assume that they will be able to supply all the necessary information. People often want things they don't need, and also need things that they are unaware they want. Most people are unaware of the specific effects of air quality, noise, colour, light, and so on on their health. On the other hand people may want factors incorporated in the design which are not beneficial to them. For example if given a choice most people would probably choose a comfortable easy chair rather than a typist's chair, yet using an easy chair if one was a typist would have detrimental effects on health. Planners and designers must be open to information and advice from all possible sources at this stage.

Design stage

This is the stage where the information gained at the programming stage is integrated in producing a design that maximises the different needs. Practical experience and research has shown that this is a complex process. Design is often restricted by current economic concerns and it is tempting to treat the process as the provision of the minimum necessary to facilitate the task requirements. However we know this to be a false economy. The evidence from years of research and practice in organisational change and developments shows that one must maximise task and socio-emotional aspects (King & Anderson, 1995). Design must not only meet economic and practical needs but must also enhance the psychological and physical health of all who use the building(s). The evidence that we have reviewed in previous chapters indicates the wide range of factors that need to be incorporated into an effective design. As well as physical shape and size, we will need to consider noise levels, lighting, colour, air quality, temperature, and control of access to the self in terms of enhancing privacy and personal space needs.

Construction stage

If the programming and design stages have been thorough and effective, the psychological input at the construction stage becomes minimal. However it is important to recognise that the design process is not totally predictable and things may not go as planned. There is always the possibility that something has been overlooked in programming and design. In addition the translation of an idea into a physical reality is not a simple straightforward process. It is likely that any new building(s) will differ from any that have previously existed in that they have been designed to meet new needs or have been designed to overcome problems experienced in previous designs. In order to get some idea of how the overall product will look when completed, designers have in the past used scale models. Currently computer simulation tends to take over this function. These simulations are often used to help potential users to provide a more informed response. While simulation can be useful, it cannot replicate the total experience of the environment (Stamps, 1994). Change agents in organisations have learned that one must continue to monitor the change throughout its implementation and be flexible enough to respond to any issues that arise. So too with the construction phase in the design process. It is much better to modify the design in response to a problem at the construction phase, than to have to live with the problem when the building is occupied.

Use stage

When the project is completed people move in and occupy the space. There will be a period of adaptation beginning with a sense of excitement for many in response to the novelty of the environment. You may have experienced the initial excitement on moving into a new office or house, which may be replaced later by disappointment once you had adapted to the place. It is important to recognise this phase in the process because as a transition it is unlikely to be an accurate reflection of the effectiveness of the building. The building may seem too hot or too cold, people will need to negotiate territories, and they will need to orient to the building generally in terms of finding their way around. For example most new buildings smell differently from old ones. This will be a combination of fresh paint, new furnishings, and differential air circulation. In an experimental study where 66 healthy males were exposed to odours typical of new buildings a high level of general discomfort was reported (Otto et al., 1990). Research has generally not targeted this phase, but it is important to identify whether adaptation has occurred before evaluation of the effectiveness of the building is carried out.

Evaluation stage

This is a phase that has produced a growing research literature over the past 20 years and is referred to as post-occupancy evaluation. The growing interest reflects the importance attached currently to the continued monitoring of the design process. In any area of applied psychology the job is not complete until the effectiveness of the intervention has been assessed. Evaluation of the intervention will indicate the success of the intervention and allows the designer to modify the process if it is not successful. Ultimately the information gained will feed into the process of designing future interventions. In post-occupancy evaluation the psychologist is interested in answering three main questions: does the building effectively serve the purpose for which it was designed?; how does the building affect the behaviour and experience of the people who occupy it?; and what lessons can be learned for future designs.

In one such evaluation, Becker and Poe (1980) looked at the outcome of their recommended changes to a hospital building and targeted three categories of variables:

1. organisational climate (attitudes and feelings of staff and patients);
2. ratings of the changes in terms of a range of dimensions;
3. changes in behaviour.

Items 1 and 2 were assessed using questionnaires, while item 3 was assessed by observation. They found that organisational climate had improved for all, but most noticeably for staff. Ratings of changes were favourable, again most noticeably for staff. In terms of behaviours they found that facilities, such as the solarium, were used more frequently and that there was a general increase in verbal interaction among the users. The only negative feedback was the initial reaction of visitors. Becker and Poe had been involved in the design process from the beginning and the post-occupancy evaluation allowed useful feedback on the success of their work.

Environmental planning and design is a multidisciplinary process and each discipline will have its own perspective and its own needs and goals. Architects will be concerned with the aesthetics of the building, industrialists will be concerned with economic viability and psychologists will be concerned with human behaviour and experience. If the end product is to be successful all the differing concerns must be recognised and maximised. In practice economic considerations often take precedent and human concerns are often low on the list of priorities. Increasing evidence is providing a convincing argument that the two are very closely related and that human needs should be a priority for economic reasons as well as more humanitarian concerns. From a social scientist's perspective the major focus is on the relationship between environmental design and mental health. Given the general consensus that mental health effects are mediated through the stress process, this also leads to a concern with physical health effects. The premise is that physical and mental health are rather more closely related than was thought in the past. As a relatively young field environmental psychology needs increased and continuous effort in research. However in the spirit of Lewin let us not forget to treat theory building and practical application as two interdependent parts of one whole. Hence we must attempt to draw forth from each area of research, the elements of knowledge that can be usefully applied in designing and planning better environments. Through this application we may learn more about how to do our job well.

INDIVIDUAL DIFFERENCES AND DESIGN

There are two good reasons for starting with a look at how research on individual differences might be usefully applied in planning and design. First of all an extensive literature exists which supports Kluckhohn and Murray's (1953) contention that while at some levels we all differ, at other levels there are similarities between groups of individuals. While these similarities might be very heavily situation dependent as argued by people like Barker and Wright (1955), they may be usefully combined to allow some predictability in the design process. In addition taking account of differences makes for a more satisfactory design process. The second good reason to highlight individual differences at the outset lies in the fact that all of the different factors of the environment that influence human behaviour are subject to individual differences. People react differently to the same levels of noise, pollution, light, personal space, privacy, and so on. The design process is doomed to failure if we assume otherwise. It is important to bear this in mind as we try to glean some general guidelines for design from the various pieces of research reviewed.

In environmental psychology individual differences have traditionally been investigated in terms of personality (McKechnie, 1974). As discussed in a previous chapter McKechnie developed an eight factor Environmental Personality Inventory (ERI) and this has been used to identify differences in preference for particular types of environment. It provides very broad measures of different factors such as one's preference for urban versus rural settings, or one's need for privacy. While much more specificity is needed, these measures provide a good starting point. It would be just as naïve to expect someone who scores low on the urbanism factor to be satisfied with an urban environment as it would be to send an introvert to get some life into a dull party. The problem lies not so much in using such measures, though issues of reliability, validity, and situation dependence need to be considered, but rather in the underlying assumptions. If one makes traditional assumptions that these dimensions are temporally and situationally stable then our conclusions from scores on the measures are likely to be problematic. However if used within the context of cognitive styles which are learned and modifiable then such measures can be very useful (Pervin, 1995). In other words if we consider that stability in behaviour is a function of the person, the environment, and the interaction between the two, our predictions about behaviour and experience in the design process are likely to be more accurate. Craik (1976) suggests that measures of individual difference can be useful for three different functions; description, comparison, and prediction. They

---

Box 36: The pessimist, the partial pessimist, and the optimist

The design process to a large extent depends on the designer's beliefs about human nature. Many people believe that psychological characteristics and hence happiness or satisfaction are stable traits. In other words there are happy, satisfied people who will be happy and satisfied regardless of circumstances, and in contrast there are unhappy, neurotic and depressed people who will be so regardless of environmental circumstances. This view is very pessimistic and suggests that there is no point in designing environments to try to improve mental health. Another view suggests that satisfaction is relative. In other words we are satisfied and happy as long as we are doing better than others. It is when we find that we are deprived relative to our neighbours that we become dissatisfied, unhappy, and depressed. This perspective isn't quite so pessimistic because it suggests that improving environmental conditions will improve mental health. However it suggests that there is little point in such intervention since if we improve the environment for one person, others will then become dissatisfied, and if we improve the environment globally then we don't really influence mental health at all. Thus it is ultimately pessimistic. The third view is that the environment directly affects the mental health of each individual and that improving the environment will improve mental health as long as we can identify and improve the aspects that have the effect. This is the more optimistic view. It seems that design often appears to be based on the pessimistic view, either in the extreme form or with elements of the relative perspective. The evidence from psychology would suggest that design needs to be guided mainly by the optimistic view with an awareness that relative effects also occur. One contribution which environmental psychologists can make is in trying to move designers from the former to the latter.

---

help us to describe people in relation to different environments, they allow us to make comparisons between people across and within environments, and they allow some prediction of future behaviour in particular environments. For example the ERI has shown validity in predicting which medical students will emigrate (Gifford, 1987). While generalisations to the total population are not possible from research on individual differences, generalisations to specific subgroups may be useful in the context of a multiple-level analysis approach. For example the ERI measure of need for privacy may be incorporated into the design of office space. What is needed in the area is the development and use of measures designed to assess the more specific individual difference factors that are supported in research, for example the perception of control over various aspects of the environment. We now turn to research on more specific features of the environment.

Noise, light, temperature, odour, and colour

As we have seen noise, light, temperature, odour and colour all influence behaviour and experience. If they do not match individual needs they have detrimental effects on human emotion, performance, and health. Our sense modalities operate to threshold levels. Environmental stimuli need to be sufficiently intense to be detected by the senses, but equally they need not to go above a level with which our senses can cope. Overload leads to physical damage. However well before the level of physical damage has been reached there will be a level where discomfort begins. Stimuli will have a comfort threshold. For example the physical effects of heat are often discussed in terms of thermal comfort. Thellier, Cordier, and Monchoux (1994) describe a thermoregulation model which can be used in building simulation programmes to assess the comfort level of different temperatures within a building. This sort of model can be used as part of the process of design outlined above. Westerberg (1994) argues the need for architects' assessment to include the subjective element of thermal comfort among other factors in urban design. While too much heat, light, noise, colour, and smell cause discomfort, are sources of stress, and impair our performance, too little have a similar effect. The question is what is too little or too much, which highlights the subjective element. Traditionally designers have focused on preventing negative consequences, which is a laudable aim. However what has been ignored is that all of these factors have the potential to enhance human experience and behaviour. We have discussed evidence that particular types of lighting enhanced performance at school (Hathaway, 1995), and that the colour pink enhanced physical development and mood in children (Hamid & Newport, 1989). Design needs to consider both the negative and positive effects of the range of environmental stimuli that impinge on the senses.

Air quality, pollution and weather

The quality of the air we breathe and the chemicals that pervade our water and food are becoming a growing concern. One of the often worrying aspects of this is the great deal of confusing and contradictory information available. As we saw in the Camelford incident (David & Wessely, 1995) even when assurances were offered people still suffered psychological distress. Air quality in buildings has been linked with Legionnaires' Disease and with sick building syndrome. The effect of pollution from chemical waste is illustrated by the experience at the Love Canal (Veitch & Arkkelin, 1995). Cigarette smoke as an air pollutant has been shown to have major health effects on smokers and non-smokers (Hepper, 1992). A question that designers may face is whether the building(s) are to be smoke-free zones and if not the consequences of smoking must be considered in planning in terms of factors from fire risk to passive smoking effects in enclosed spaces. Weather is a factor that is often only considered in the context of weather proofing in environmental design. In addition we generally feel the weather is beyond our control, and in many ways it is. However the effects of weather on behaviour and experience need also to be included in design. For example in new housing projects it is accepted that leisure facilities for children are important. Yet in many parts of the UK where wet and windy weather is the norm, planners continue to provide unsheltered facilities which can only be used for a very small percentage of the year. In addition certain configurations of buildings can produce exaggerated wind effects which in turn affect the behaviour of people in the area (Cohen, Moss, & Zube, 1979; Poulton et al., 1975). The quality of the air and pollution whether within buildings or in the external environment, as well as the effects of weather, need to be more fully incorporated in the planning process.

Control of access to the self

Personal space, territoriality, crowding, and privacy are interrelated and interdependent aspects of control of access to the self. The evidence is that we have conflicting needs to withdraw and approach other people. We need social interaction and to feel that we have social support. Our perceptions of reality are socially constructed through interaction and social comparison processes (Festinger, 1954). On the other hand we need to be able to be alone, to defend our personal space and territory, not to feel crowded, and to have our private space and time. What is important is to feel we have control over this process, so that we can choose to be alone or to be with others. It is when this control is removed that psychological distress occurs. This is of course an over-simplification, since the ways in which the physical environment enhances or restricts control are many and varied. However designers need to identify the ways in which their designs may affect control of access to the self and to incorporate those that optimise control into the design process.

Urbanisation and travel

Those watching news broadcasts during late May and early June 1996 in the UK will be well aware of the problems of travel in cities. Road rage was highlighted by the death of one person and at least two other serious physical assaults, leading people to ask why it was becoming such a commonplace event. Explanations favour the stress hypothesis and the extreme nature of the aggression attests to the high levels of stress experienced these days in travel. As we saw in Chapter 7 it seems to be the increased lack of control due to the high levels of impedance experienced on overcrowded city roads and trains which is the major source of stress. It would follow that planners of transport systems need to reduce impedance where possible and reduce its effect on perceived uncontrollability where not possible. Cities generally bring with them problems of population density and crowding, whether in transit or not, and through reduced control of access to the self produce negative emotional effects. Planners must therefore consider how control of access to the self can be enhanced in city living. In addition cities increase anonymity, and isolation of individuals, replacing the small dense social networks of rural areas with larger less intimate networks where people are more often familiar strangers than close friends. This issue of social support in the city must also be on the planner's agenda. Finally cities tend to have areas where economic deprivation, homelessness, mental illness, and crime appear to concentrate, whether through social causation, social drift, or both. There is obvious need to address these problems as well as their associated aspects in terms of fear of crime. The factors mentioned above need to be considered in planning city environments in order to reduce the dissatisfaction of residents, before factors such as aesthetic appeal which increase resident satisfaction can be usefully applied. In essence a focus on factors that provide satisfaction, without removing the factors that cause dissatisfaction, will not be effective. A beautiful building will not resolve the problems of deprivation and fear of crime.

Design in hospitals
Hospitals in this context refer to the wide range of institutions which cater for those who have been categorised as physically or mentally ill. This includes the entire age range from the newborn infant to those who, having grown old, are no longer able to live independently and are passing their winter years in a nursing home or hospice. As you can see the needs of such a range of people will differ greatly, yet one is often struck more by the similarity than the difference between the buildings within which they reside. A common perception for example is that such places have a distinct and recognisable odour, a combination of the chemicals used to heal and those used to clean the building. Some attempts are being made to provide for different needs in different types of physical environments, but changes are slow, hampered by finances and the inflexibility of many of the old style buildings, which were built to last. However it is sometimes the case that this inflexibility of physical structures is exacerbated by lack of creativity among designers and administrators. The early work of Osmond (1957) on sociofugal and sociopetal arrangements of space are an example of how creativity can

make an inflexible building more effective. A sociofugal arrangement of seating tends to restrict social interaction whereas sociopetal arrangements are more intimate and enhance interaction. Sommer and Ross (1958) demonstrated how a change from sociofugal to sociopetal arrangement (see Fig. 1) in a nursing home day room improved the quality of life for both staff and patients. The danger with this however is that many seem to have assumed that sociofugal is bad and sociopetal good in all situations. Clearly this is not the case and the need for privacy of patients must be considered as well. This was demonstrated in a more recent study by Cherulnik (1993) in which it was shown that interaction among patients in a psychiatric hospital increased as a function of the combination of sociopetal seating arrangements and the partitioning of sleeping rooms. In this study patients' control over access to the self was enhanced by allowing privacy in sleeping quarters, whereas the need for intimacy was enhanced by the seating arrangement. Research on privacy which we discussed earlier has clearly identified these two aspects of privacy. We need to be able to control the process so that we can be alone if we wish to, but we can also have access to interaction with others. It is this balance between the need for intimacy and the need for isolation which is important to us, and environments which allow us to exercise autonomy in the process will optimise our experience and behaviour. Changes such as those described above can be relatively inexpensive and very quickly carried out and can have a major effect on human experience within a hospital. In a review of the area, Winkel and Holahan (1986) argue that there are a range of identifiable factors which contribute to the prevention of psychological and social problems for patients in both acute care and psychiatric hospitals. These include the spatial layout of the environment, privacy considerations, personal control and independence, sharing information, social relationships within the hospital, and environmental stimulation. Some studies have demonstrated the positive effects on patient interaction and behaviour of redesigns in psychiatric hospitals which adopt an environmental psychology perspective (Holahan & Saegert, 1973; Whitehead et al., 1984). In the main these studies tend to involve changes in spatial layout, increased privacy and general redecoration of wards, which makes it difficult to isolate specific causal relationships.

Noise, windows, and special needs
Despite the clear evidence for the effect of the physical environment and the need to research this effect in hospital settings, relatively few studies seem to have been carried out (Sundstrom et al., 1996). The effect of noise for example has not been widely investigated despite the fact that many hospital situations will be filled with a variety of sounds

both human and technological which from the evidence reviewed would be predicted to influence the distress levels and performance of both patients and staff. One study by Lawton, Fulcomer, and Kleban (1984) showed that the positive effects of a new and innovatively designed nursing home were offset somewhat by the noise from the intercom system. This is a good example of how failure to integrate all aspects in the design process leads to less than satisfactory outcomes. There is some evidence that higher levels of noise in the post-operative period coexist with more experienced pain among patients (Minckley, 1968). Nurses' performance can also be negatively affected by noise (Topf, 1989). Increased post-operative problems have also been shown to occur in windowless intensive care units as opposed to those with windows (Wilson, 1972). The special needs of patients must also be considered, which is a strong argument for different designs for different patient groups. One area of concern is the difficulties encountered by dementia patients in finding their way around hospitals and nursing homes. One way of dealing with this is to use building codes (Van-der-Voordt, 1993). Many of the occupants of nursing homes will be suffering some form of disability, so it is important that they are not further handicapped by the physical design of the space they occupy.

Conflicts of interest
One of the problems in designing hospital environments is that there may be a conflict of interest between staff and patient needs. For example an operating theatre requires hot, humid conditions for the patient, which reduces the thermal comfort for staff (Veitch & Arkkelin, 1995). In addition the location of nursing offices on the ward is important for patient observation and speed of response, but actually reduces privacy for both staff and patients. There may also be conflicts of interest between staff and visitors in hospital. Bunker-Hellmich (1987) found a conflict over use of space between nursing staff and visitors on a neonatal intensive care unit. It is difficult to design an environment where the balance between interaction and privacy is achieved when only a single group is involved. When there are several groups with different interaction/privacy needs, the task becomes even more difficult.

New challenges in design
While research has identified some ways in which the physical environment can improve the hospital experience, what is most noticeable is the lack of research in the area. It would seem to be a fertile area for future research. When the impact on people has been considered in the design process in hospitals, the outcome has generally been

positive. As well as improving the quality of life for patients and staff, design changes have been shown to increase the amount of visiting and to improve the quality of the visiting experience, something that is of particular importance for the elderly and those in long-term care. In the area of mental health new challenges are arising for designers within the context of more community-based approaches. For example, in Italy, where the move from institutionalisation to community treatment for mental illness has been more successful than anywhere else, one of the factors that hampers progress is that many of the community mental health centres are still physically housed in the old mental hospitals (Jones & Poletti, 1986). The need for smaller rehabilitation centres with space for meetings and recreational activities is highlighted by Scala (1990). An evaluative study of the move from an old hospital building to a new community mental health centre showed a significant increase in morale and effectiveness in those staff who moved compared to those who didn't (Folkins et al., 1977). It would appear that in some areas it is not sufficient to be creative in the use of traditional buildings; rather, new designs are required.

Designing prisons

Sommer (1976) identifies eight different perspectives on the function of prisons, each reflecting a different philosophy. They are deterrence, incapacitation, reform, rehabilitation, retribution, restitution, re-education, and integration. Clearly the design of prisons will depend very much on the philosophy of those directing the design, ranging from a very simple cage design in the case of incapacitation to a much more complex multifaceted design in the case of integration. In fact it is also likely that different types of criminal will attract different philosophies. For example most people seem to agree that re-education is appropriate for nonviolent juvenile offenders, while incapacitation is often the favoured approach for dealing with the persistent violent criminal. In addition differences in needs will exist between groups of prisoners. For example age segregation of prisoners has been shown to benefit older prisoners (Moore, 1989). Yet as with hospitals all different types of criminals are often incarcerated together. The tragedy is that this often leads to the naïve, first offender learning how to be an expert criminal while in prison. Prison buildings tend to be fortress-like with walls, fences, and window bars much stronger than those used to hold even the strongest animal in a zoo. Arguably such exaggerated use of oppressive and punitive environments leads to more destructive behaviours in the criminal (Holley & Arboleda-Florez, 1988). As Skinner (1953) demonstrated, punishment used in excess or inappropriately leads to suppression of all behaviours including positive ones.

The issue of privacy

One of the major problems facing those who control prisons is overcrowding. Over the past few years in the UK a spate of riots has occurred in prisons which have arguably been a result of simply too many prisoners in the space available. The small amount of research that has been produced has tended to focus on this issue. There seems to be fairly clear evidence that higher levels of psychological distress and more aggressive behaviour occurs in more densely populated prisons particularly where prisoners are housed in open dormitories (Paulus, 1988; Paulus et al., 1975; Schaeffer et al., 1988). It appears that having one's own cell, or at least having an area clearly partitioned in a dormitory, is the most desirable accommodation. Again the explanation that best fits is in terms of control of access to the self, or privacy. The evidence is that designs which enhance privacy or control of access to the self are associated with more positive outcomes in general (Cherulnik, 1993). There seems to be some general consensus from what research exists that control is a major factor with designs that allow more control having more positive impact (Veitch & Arkkelin, 1995). The effects of the wide range of factors including noise, light, colour, smell, temperature and so on, which clearly have an effect on behaviour, have not really been investigated in prisons. For example the effect of colour on aggression, as indicated in the review of the literature on Baker–Miller pink, would seem to be an area usefully applied to prisons. Again one can only reiterate the need for much more research and application of psychological theory in prison design.

Designing places of work

Most of us spend a great deal of our waking life in work places of one design or another. In fact many people spend as much time at work as they do at home. In the industrial or business world the effect of the physical environment on behaviour has been recognised for quite some time. One has only to look at the architectural detail on some of the very early factory buildings to recognise that more than their instrumentality was considered in their design. While the principles that guided design were not based on psychological knowledge, they did consider the comfort of workers as important. In fact one might be tempted to suggest that this is something that is lost in more recent designs. Spreckelmeyer (1995) reviews the design of office buildings in America and argues that the current dominant design model focuses too narrowly on instrumental aspects of work places and often ignores cultural and social factors. Some of the very earliest work reported in work and organisational psychology was on the effects of lighting on behaviour (Roethlisberger & Dickson, 1939), a study that fits clearly within the remit of environmental psychology.

DEMOCRACY IN DESIGN

A major lesson learned by those involved in planned organisational change can be usefully drawn on in the context of designing work environments. The lesson is that if the process is to have any chance of success it must be democratic. In other words people at all levels within the organisation must be consulted and allowed to participate in decision making from the beginning (King & Anderson, 1995). Evidence suggests a similar conclusion in regard to design changes to the physical environment, in that participation in the process is an important factor in determining the level of satisfaction with the outcome (Spreckelmeyer, 1993). An area that has attracted some attention is the issue of open plan versus enclosed office space. As discussed in Chapter 7, it seems clear that open plan offices reduce control of access to the self and lead to lower satisfaction, higher levels of psychological distress, and reduced performance. In regard to the control of access to the self, the most effective design will allow the person autonomy in the process. It will maximise opportunities for isolation and interaction. In office accommodation this might be achieved through providing individual enclosed offices and larger communal areas where people can meet for breaks or to discuss business as and when necessary. Drawing on research on group processes it seems clear that people need to have a sense of group identity and the opportunity to negotiate the process of group formation (Brown, 1988). For example, one cannot expect an academic department to operate as a team if they have not developed a sense of group identity, involving a shared vision and shared goals. The physical environment must enhance the type of interaction necessary for group formation. In addition members of the group will need individual space for individual work. It is often the case that one or other need is satisfied by the physical space, but not both. Where it is not possible to provide individual offices the need for privacy can to some extent be satisfied by the creative use of furniture and partitions to mark out individual workers territories as was shown by Cangelosi and Lemoine (1988).

Status and automation

Environmental factors will also differ in importance across different levels within a work organisation. For example one series of studies found that the physical environment and social environment interacted with job status in predicting work involvement and job satisfaction. For managers the physical environment was positively correlated with involvement and satisfaction, while for workers at other levels it was the social environment that was positively correlated with these measures (Zalesny & Farace, 1988; Zalesny, Farace, & Kurcher-Hawkins, 1985).

One major change for many in the work place over the past 20 years has been the increased use of automation, particularly the now commonplace use of personal computers. Stellman et al. (1987) provide evidence that increased use of automation does not improve the quality of life for clerical workers. They compared video display terminal (VDT) users with typists and clerks in a total sample of 1032 female clerical workers and found that the VDT users reported greater levels of stress.

As with hospitals new challenges have begun to arise for work place designers. For example there has been an increase in home-based work enhanced by developments in communication (Ahrentzen, 1989). Designers need to turn their attention to how space in the home may be effectively used to enhance work satisfaction and performance (Christensen, 1989, 1993). The increased problem of commuting needs also to be considered in design, with a particular problem in parking in the already overcrowded cities where many work places are sited. We have only touched on a few aspects of work place design, but again the relative lack of research and the important effects of design aspects on health, emotion, and performance evidences a need for increased psychological input.

Box 37: In a world without windows

One aspect of the work environment that has attracted some attention is the effect of working in environments without windows. It seems that the absence of windows generates some distress (Nagy, Yasunaga, & Kose, 1995) and leads to attempts to compensate (Biner et al., 1993). One study compared workers in windowed offices with a group working in windowless offices and found that those without windows used significantly more visual material to decorate the walls of their offices and were much more likely to use landscapes than cityscapes.

In an experimental study with 40 students mood and performance was actually better in a windowless office, though this might have been because participants experienced more privacy without the windows (Stone & Irvine, 1993). The general conclusion is that windows are important, but they should not impinge on privacy.

Designing schools and educational institutions

As adults we spend a large part of our lives at work; as children we spend spend a large part of our waking hours in school. For increasing numbers these days this is extended into young adulthood with significant amounts of time spent in college or university. In fact for some it may be that as adults we return to such environments for periods of time. We have seen that noise, colour, light, temperature, air quality, and control of access to the self affect our behaviour and experience in the educational setting. The evidence suggests that the physical environment in schools affects the performance of teachers (Cooper, 1985). In a review of studies published between 1970 and 1983, Borger et al. (1985) identified eight variables that determined effective schools as defined in terms of academic achievement. Among the eight was the physical environment. Different studies have tended to focus on different aspects of the physical environment, hence no simple generalisations can be made. For example in one study a comparison was made over a five-week period of college students allocated to either an experimental or a control classroom (Wollin & Montagne, 1981). The experimental room was brightly painted, had softer lighting, had plants and wall decorations in the form of posters, kites and rugs. The control room had none of these. Students' performance was measured on a range of academic tests. In addition their attitude towards their environment, their evaluation of their teachers, and the amount of teacher–student interaction was measured. Students in the experimental room did significantly better on the tests and rated their teachers more positively. They also felt more positive about their room. There was no effect on student–teacher interaction. While this study may actually demonstrate a reduction of performance in the control room, rather than an increase in the experimental room, what is clear is that an effect occurred. It appears that a range of factors including seating position, classroom design, density, privacy, noise, and the presence or absence of windows are implicated in the process.

Open plan school rooms

As with work space, the idea of open plan environments has also filtered into the design of schools. It would appear that similar problems have ensued with teachers generally responding negatively to the reduced privacy. Studies have shown that both students and teachers report more disruptive noise in open classrooms (Brunetti, 1972; Rivlin & Rothenberg, 1976). In contrast a study comparing open plan versus traditional classrooms in New Zealand found no differences in behaviour or performance (Gill, 1977). This study did not however measure either teacher or student satisfaction. Arguments for open plan classrooms tend to hinge on economic issues in that they are cheaper to build and more flexible to furnish. There seems to be no real evidence for their educational benefit. Given that open plan classrooms exist, some researchers have looked at how they can be made more satisfying and effective. Weinstein (1977) demonstrated how behavioural goals may be achieved through structured manipulation of the physical layout. Evans and Lovell (1979) suggest that the physical layout can be manipulated to demarcate territories and provide areas of privacy for teachers. As with open plan offices, the design must allow control over access to the self, and maintain a balance between interaction and privacy.

Seating position

There is some evidence in higher education that seating position in lecture theatres and seminar rooms is related to amount of interaction with tutors and to academic attainment. Becker et al. (1973) found that students sitting in the front and centre of lecture theatres attained better grades than those sitting at the back. A similar effect was found in a study where students were not allowed to choose their own seats, therefore suggesting that it is not simply because uninterested and unmotivated students choose to sit at the back (Stires, 1980). However the effect on academic attainment is questioned in a review of the literature by Montello (1988).

Again the evidence from the research already produced suggests that design has an important effect on motivation, mood, and intellectual development within educational institutions. Studies have shown that design interventions can be effective but much more needs to be done. More recently new problems have begun to develop. In the UK over the past 5–10 years student populations have grown dramatically and innovative design is required to ensure effective delivery of education. In addition advanced communication technology, coupled with the recognised need in industrial societies for ongoing education and training, either in short bursts or as a continuous part time activity, has led to distance learning. A great deal has yet to be learned about the effects of such changes and how psychology can be used in enhancing the process.

Designing a consumer environment

One has only to visit any large town or city during the day to discover the large numbers of people who are engaged in the business of shopping at any one time. In fact the way in which so many people can negotiate the space available to them bears witness to our expertise in the use of nonverbal communication. While some frustration will be experienced, particularly at very busy times such as the period leading up to

Christmas in the UK, in the main people do it very successfully. This is not to say that crowding in shops has no negative effects, in fact it affects us in the same ways as crowding in other situations (Harrell, Hutt, & Anderson, 1980). Research in the area tends to focus on attracting consumers and selling products (Schuler, 1981; Winter, 1974). For example the use of bright colours, and stacking products on shelves by colour code, enables consumers to locate products more easily and therefore benefits the trader. In a review Bellizzi, Crowley, and Hasty (1983) argue that colour is a major factor in attracting consumers and influencing their attitude towards the store. In addition stores are often designed so that one has to pass by many less necessary products in order to get to the necessities, a strategy designed to encourage increased spending. One problem with design driven by retailers is that it tends to draw on the same pool of ideas about how to attract and influence consumers, and leads to a high degree of similarity between shops in a shopping mall. While it is easy to distinguish between a clothing shop and a supermarket, it is not always so easy to discriminate between two supermarkets or two clothing shops. With this high degree of similarity there is often a distinct lack of landmarks which are so important in finding our way around our physical environment. Cognitive maps, which guide us through complex environments, begin with landmarks.

Clearly there is a need to reduce the frustration experienced by the consumer, and recently this has begun to be taken more seriously by sellers as its effects on buying behaviour become recognised. One such frustration is the ever popular queuing phenomenon. Wherever we go these days we seem to have to queue. Many places, such as post offices, attempt to control the process by providing barriers which identify the queuing space. Other places, such as special product counters in supermarkets, provide tickets which are numbered and one has to wait until that number is called to be served. Veitch and Arkkelin (1995) discuss queuing theory which is concerned with attempts to calculate the most efficient method of queuing. One way which this can be done is to estimate the rate at which people join queues and the time it takes before they are served. From a large number of observations one can then estimate the average length of time anyone will need to wait and hence the number of people who can be served in any period of time. The trouble with averages as we all know is that they rarely translate into real life experience. One supermarket chain in the UK has given a promise that there will never be more than three people in a queue at their stores. They aim to do this by opening a new checkout as soon as there are three in a queue. Two things seem to be indicated by the above. First of all there is a clear need to research more fully the needs of

---

Box 38: Children in shops

Parents who take their children shopping will be well aware of the nightmare that this can be, and indeed many large stores and shopping malls recognise the problem and provide creche facilities to help deal with it. The practice of placing sweets and other goodies by the checkout has been identified as a factor in the problems for parents with children in stores, and some major chains have accepted responsibility and removed them. One major consideration both for parents and shop owners is the safety of the child. The death of a child when an overloaded trolley capsized in a DIY store a few years ago led to a major information campaign by stores regarding risks to children. The provision of safety belts on trolleys is becoming standard procedure, but as one might expect, many people do not use them. One study showed that prompting, particularly if this was done through personal contact, both increased the use of safety belts and was appreciated by parents (Ferrari & Baldwin, 1989). Another aspect of child behaviour in shops was raised in a study by Barnard, Christophersen, and Wolf (1977) where they helped parents to train three children in appropriate shopping behaviours. Given the complexity of the shopping process these days and its major role in the lives of many people, it seems to have become another aspect of the socialisation of children.

---

consumers. Secondly that need is being recognised by those in the business of selling and offers some opportunity for future developments. In large towns and cities shopping tends to be concentrated in large shopping malls, which have become much more than just clusters of shops. For many people, particularly older children and young adults, and older citizens, shopping malls play an important part in their social life. The use of shopping malls as meeting places for young people often leads to problems when their presence conflicts with the image desired by those who run the mall. For older people the mall may be their main source of contact with other people (Brown, Sijpkes, & MacLean, 1986).

Designing leisure environments
In many areas of the industrialised world, leisure has created an industry of its own. Leisure tends to be defined in relation to work, with leisure time being the time when we are not at work. However this subservient role for leisure has not always been the case. For example in ancient Greece leisure was seen as superior to work. Work tended to be done by slaves leaving the rest of the population free to pursue athletics, music, and philosophy. An essential ingredient of leisure seems to have been activities done for their own sake which involved personal development. For the ancient Romans, leisure was often less

intellectual and involved lions and Christians. With the industrial revolution, work became the superior pursuit and for many leisure time became a respite or recuperation from work. Throughout the industrialisation process, many leisure pursuits became commercialised, and in today's society we have a music industry, a sports industry, and ultimately a leisure industry. This often means that for the less economically advantaged, only the cheaper leisure pursuits are available, such as watching television. In fact for many, their leisure time is a period of inactivity, and hence unhealthy. The evidence suggests that structured use of leisure time is also associated with more effective coping with stress (Cassidy, 1996). For environmental psychologists leisure activities raise issues of design on several fronts. First of all the growth of the leisure industry has led to competition for resources. Bank Holiday traffic jams, massive queues for rides in leisure parks, and the growing problems of crowding at leisure centres attest to the need to pay heed to design. Secondly there is the need to provide useful and effective leisure facilities for those who have time on their hands. This ranges from providing safe and developmentally appropriate play facilities for children, particularly in already crowded neighbourhoods, to the growing problem of young adults who have no employment. In addition there are also growing numbers of older adults who have retired from work and whose leisure needs are often overlooked. It seems generally accepted that, as William Cowper said (in Milford, 1934, p.122),

> absence of occupation is not rest
> a mind quite vacant is a mind distressed.

The design of leisure facilities must also consider the preservation of the environment which is a third area of concern in environmental psychology. With increased numbers problems have developed such as damage to the countryside, pollution and littering, and the damage to the natural beauty of the environment from unsightly leisure complexes. Despite the need, again psychologists have been under-utilised in the process.

Facilities for children

It is widely recognised that children learn and develop cognitive and social skills through play, and the physical environment will play a major role in determining the effectiveness of the process. This applies to the micro-level environment in terms of things like the use of partitions as opposed to free play within a play room (Gehlbach & Partridge, 1984) and to the macro-level in terms of differential provision of play facilities in different neighbourhoods (Berg & Medrich, 1980). A study by Hayward, Rothenberg, and Beasley (1974) compared a traditional, a contemporary, and an adventure playground and found that they attract different user groups. The adventure playground attracted more 6–13 year olds, whereas the other types were mainly used by adults and preschool children. It is not clear if this reflects what actually attracts children, or the protectiveness of parents towards preschoolers. There are of course issues of safety in regard to adventure playgrounds. The type of play also differed. In the adventure playground it involved more social interaction, whereas the others involved more of a focus on individual use of the equipment. All of these studies raise the issue of the need to involve users in the design and to use more structured design drawing on psychological evidence where available. The paucity of evidence highlights the need for more research. Where collaboration occurs between parents and designers positive effects can be produced even in the most basic conditions (Weinstein & Pinciotti, 1988). In general the lack of involvement of local communities in the design of facilities has been one factor blamed for the underuse of facilities (Gold, 1977). Another likely factor is the lack of a sense of community. This is indicated in a study where more outdoor socialising was observed in an old well-established neighbourhood than in either a traditional high rise neighbourhood or a new more innovative project (Holahan, 1976). The evidence is that involvement in the design of communal facilities enhances individual's involvement in their communities (Kaplan, 1980). Again the inseparable relationship between the physical and social environment is highlighted.

Designing dwellings

The most recent review of environmental psychology (Sundstrom et al., 1996) suggests that the type of housing choice in North America is a single-family home which is located away from a central city. In addition they identify the common themes which are associated with satisfaction as:

> the importance of adequate space, convenient location for services, sense of security associated with distance from inner cities, attachment to neighbourhood and people, and environmental support for changing work and family roles.

In addition the involvement of those who will live in the dwellings in the design process is essential if the design is to work (Conan, 1987; Kaye, 1975; Lawrence, 1984; Sime, 1986). It is very clear that size, shape, use of space, control of access to the self as well as thermal comfort, colour, light, levels of noise and smell all combine to create a subjective impression of one's home. This is often referred to as the atmosphere of the home and involves the feelings engendered by the home (Pennartz, 1986). A more technical way in which this may be expressed is in the level of place attachment and place identity (Proshansky, Fabian, & Kaminoff, 1985). It is essentially what turns a house into a home. Quite a bit of research has explored the meaning of place and hence home for individuals (Groat, 1985). Research on meaning, place attachment, and place identity provides useful information for architects and designers of more global housing environments in terms of communities, neighbourhoods and cities, but is less informative in terms of designing individual dwellings and the interior design process. Research on interior aspects of homes has tended to focus on the way in which space in the home is used, and on the effects of various stressors on the behaviour and experience of family members. As we have seen, crowding has been the major research topic and has shown that ultimately negative effects are mediated by the balance between desired and achieved privacy. In essence where individuals are satisfied with the level of social support provided and feel they have control over access to the self they are better able to cope with density, noise, and other sources of stress in the home. For example Altman, Nelson, and Lett (1972) suggest that we need to distinguish between open and closed families as defined by the family need for privacy as opposed to individual members' privacy needs. Descriptive research on the amount of time spent in different rooms by different people can be usefully applied in determining the size, and amount of time, effort, and attention to detail that needs to be spent in designing different areas of the home (Kira, 1976; Mehrabian, 1976; Parsons, 1972; Steidl, 1972). However psychologists have been slow to extend the research to more detailed aspects of the design of homes. It would seem that there is a great deal that psychology can contribute to an understanding of the effects of colour, light, physical layout on the behaviour of families and how such design features can best be used to ensure effective functioning within the family. With the changing structure of families, more single-parent families, same-sex couples, and people from a range of cultural backgrounds living in the same neighbourhoods, or even the same building, the input from psychology would seem even more necessary. Dwellings exist in neighbourhoods, communities, and cities and hence cannot be researched or designed as totally independent units. This interdependence is illustrated in the finding that satisfaction with specific aspects of one's dwelling is a strong predictor of satisfaction with one's neighbourhood (Windley & Scheidt, 1982), and that in turn satisfaction with one's home is dependent on being satisfied with one's neighbourhood.

Designing communities and neighbourhoods

While individual families will be influenced by the design of their home, they and many other families will be influenced by the larger neighbourhood or local community. As illustrated above the relationship between satisfaction with one's home and satisfaction with one's community suggests that it is more important to live in what one perceives as a "good" community or neighbourhood than in a good home. Halpern's (1995) analysis supports this conclusion. Essentially this argument hinges on the way in which the physical design of a neighbourhood influences the social interaction and hence the amount and quality of social support accorded. It is widely accepted that social support is important for mental health, whether through buffering the person against the trials and tribulations of life or in that absence of social support is itself a source of stress.

New town blues

The early work of Young and Willmott (1957), on the break up of communities and the move from extended families to nuclear families was a landmark in this area. They showed how working class families were dependent on extended families for social support and predicted the effects later found in new towns throughout the UK. Essentially these new towns are very strong evidence that communities cannot be created, but rather evolve over time. The early experience in many of these new towns was of increased social isolation, poorer mental health, escalation in crime rates and fear of crime, and general dissatisfaction with the neighbourhood (Hare & Shaw, 1965; Higgins, 1984; Martin, Brotherston, & Chave, 1957; Taylor & Chave, 1964). This effect has been variously referred to as suburban neurosis (Taylor, 1938) and new town blues (Halpern, 1995). There are problems with the interpretation of these results mainly because of inadequate control comparisons. For example comparing those who moved with those who stayed behind is fraught with many possible confounding variables. Generally those who moved were younger and often newly married or with young children. In addition it is likely that those who were already ill stayed behind. Comparisons with other populations may involve differences in social class or may be comparing a group who are experiencing stability with those who have experienced the stressful effects of the move itself. However the finding among these studies that symptoms in new towns were significantly higher than national figures provides worrying evidence that something was not quite right. Moving people from slums to new towns was based on the assumption that slums engender poorer physical and mental health. While the physical ill health effects might be more objectively quantifiable, it is very clear that mental health effects can only be ascertained by adopting Kelly's (1955) maxim and asking people how they feel. As Gans (1963, quoted in Halpern, 1995) concludes, "A physical slum does not imply a social slum" (p.159).

A moving experience

The finding that mental and physical health was in fact worse in new towns suggests that either the assumption about slums was wrong, or that the new towns have a detrimental effect. In fact it is likely that the real explanation draws on both. The evidence from the life events literature (Brown & Harris, 1989) is that moving house is one of the top three sources of stress, hence one would expect that the move to a new town would in itself be experienced as stressful. Studies which explore the health and well-being of people who have just arrived in a new town may therefore be assessing the stress of moving rather than the effects of the new environment. On the other hand new towns with improved housing will provide people with more space, more thermal comfort, and generally better physical living conditions—hence any ill effects are unlikely to be due to physical environmental stressors.

New communities

It appears that the most likely source of any continued distress, once the immediate effects of the move have been mastered, will be to do with the disruption of social networks. Indeed in interviews with individuals who are distressed in new town settings it is this loneliness as a result of loss of contact with family, friends, and neighbours which is most often expressed (Halpern, 1995). The fact that evidence also suggests that the initial ill effects for some new towns gradually disappeared over time and that this reduction coincided with the emergence of traditional more closely knit communities identifies the need to consider how new towns may influence the social behaviour of dwellers (Halpern, 1995). Halpern provides an excellent discussion of the interaction between the design of neighbourhoods and social behaviour, identifying a number of important considerations.

The homogeneity dilemma

One major question planners need to consider is whether neighbourhoods should be socially homogeneous. In other words should new developments only house people from the same social class, cultural background, or whatever social categories are considered important in the particular society? Or alternatively would it be better if each neighbourhood contained a representative mix of all the different social categories? The evidence is conflicting. There appears to be fairly strong evidence that groups with lower population density in a neighbourhood experience higher prevalence of mental illness (Halpern 1993). This effect has been demonstrated in terms of ethnicity (Halpern, 1993), occupation (Wechsler & Pugh, 1967) and religious category (Cairns, 1988b). As Halpern argues, this effect seems to be the result of increased vulnerability to stress through prejudice, and decreased levels of social support. In addition where neighbourhoods are heterogeneous there is a danger that a sense of community will be inhibited, or that open conflict may develop as was the case in some new towns in Northern Ireland. The evidence would suggest that homogeneous neighbourhoods are more likely to develop into closely knit communities, to provide more effective social support, and to result in reduced levels of mental illness. On the other hand where physical divisions enhance social divisions other problems develop, something that was clearly evidenced by the riots in several UK cities in the past 15 years. It is quite clear from the vast literature that has developed on social identity theory over the past 30 years that intergroup conflict will be exacerbated by anything that reinforces the social categories that exist and form the basis of the many intergroup prejudices within any society (Abrams & Hogg, 1990; Brown, 1996; Tajfel & Turner, 1986). It appears clear that to reduce this intergroup conflict some form of intergroup contact must occur. Brown (1996) sets out the conditions which must be met if this contact is to be successful:

> there should be social and institutional support for the measures designed to promote the contact; the contact should be of sufficient frequency, duration and closeness to permit the development of meaningful relationships between members of the groups concerned; as far as possible the participants in the contact situation should be of equal status; the contact should involve co-operative activity (p.269).

It is very clear that homogeneous neighbourhoods do not meet the necessary conditions. Attempts to reduce intergroup conflict through desegregation of education in places like Northern Ireland and North America provide some hard-earned lessons. One reason why attempts have failed is because of the lack of social and institutional support. In simple terms while children from different social groups interact in school, the rest of their lives are lived in homes, neighbourhoods, and societies which actually reinforce segregation. In addition the most successful desegregated schools tend to be in communities or neighbourhoods where housing is also desegregated (Cairns, 1988a). There is no easy solution to the social homogeneity dilemma. Halpern

(1995) suggests that some sort of balance between homogeneity and heterogeneity is the best solution.

The question of numbers

The evidence from several studies suggests that the physical layout of a neighbourhood can either enable or constrict the development of social networks (Blake et al., 1956; Festinger, Schachter, & Back, 1950). The general conclusion is that designs that provide opportunities to meet are more likely to lead to the development of relationships. In addition a size effect has been shown, with neighbourhoods containing larger numbers of dwellings having less dense social networks (Lefebvre, 1984). Halpern's (1995) very thorough review of the evidence combined with his analysis of data from the Social and Community Planning Research (SCPR) (1978) which involved 7500 participants, provides some very practical conclusions. First of all the sheer presence of people does not predict supportive relations. In fact it is generally the case that the larger the number of dwellings in a development the smaller and less dense the social networks of individuals (Willmott, 1963). Individuals must have the space and opportunity to interact, but also the opportunity to control the level of interaction by choosing to be alone. Physical environments must enhance this. Individuals who live in environments that don't allow them control over access to the self tend to become adept at stimulus screening (Mehrabian, 1976) in order to cope. Stimulus screening involves deliberate screening out of information and is thought to be a major explanation for the apparent lack of friendliness and unwillingness to help those in distress among city dwellers. As a coping strategy it is likely to have negative consequences since it fosters a tendency to develop less dense social networks and hence to reduce the quality of social support available.

Traffic, noise, and social cohesion

One factor that disrupts the social cohesion of a neighbourhood is the amount of traffic in the street. This is confirmed from the SCPR data (Halpern, 1995) and the study by Willmott (1963) which found that cul-de-sacs and shorter, narrower streets tended to have a stronger sense of community. On larger streets, particularly where these were main thoroughfares people interacted less with their neighbours. More traffic means more noise, and noise has been shown to increase stress levels and reduce helping behaviour. However, traffic in a street also impedes social intercourse in other ways. Traffic makes it difficult for people to sit outdoors, or to converse in the street. In addition more traffic means more strangers in the area. What is clear is that there is a complex relationship between density, noise, reduced social support, and mental health and it is very unlikely that any single factor will emerge victorious in an attempt to disentangle the interaction. One reason why there might be more traffic and more strangers in a residential area is if that area is located near areas of commercial land use, something we will return to in the next section.

Neighbourhoods and social support

The brief look at the literature on neighbourhoods above provides fairly clear evidence that a major factor in determining whether neighbourhoods will be positively experienced by the inhabitants is the degree to which the neighbourhood meets their needs for social support. To do this effectively the physical environment must create opportunities for social interaction, while maximising opportunities for privacy. In other words the physical environment must enhance an individual's autonomy in regulating the level of social interaction in which they engage.

Autonomy and empowerment

This issue of autonomy or control is also evidenced in other areas of neighbourhood research in regard to two main findings. First of all research suggests that an important factor in differentiating between positive and negative experiences of new towns is whether the move to the new town was voluntary or not (Kasl, 1974). An analysis of an imposed move from a slum area in Boston in the early 1960s shows how much distress can be caused when planners make decisions without consulting those involved (Fried, 1963; Hartman, 1963). This lack of consultation exposes the conflicts that can and do occur between the perceptions and interests of planners and the people involved. On the planning side will be governments or city councils whose remit is to manage the finances, health and welfare officials who are often concerned with getting people out of what has been designated an unhealthy environment and may be less concerned with the psychological effects of new environments, and architects whose concern is to design physical structures and are likely to be more concerned with aesthetic qualities than psychological effects. The evidence is that architects' tastes differ significantly from the general population (Devlin & Nasar, 1989; Halpern, 1987). One major aspect of this difference is that architects generally intend their designs not to be tampered with. In other words they do not allow personalising, which as we saw from the work on territoriality, is such an important aspect of human social behaviour in exerting control over their physical environment. In fact many housing developments seem to be based on principles of homogeneity. In addition to the issue of volition in the process, there is clear evidence that participation in the design process is essential if it is to be effective. As we have seen in all the areas of design, from prisons to leisure facilities, participation of users is an essential ingredient in the design process. A lack of consultation is likely to lead to misinterpretations of the needs of residents, particularly given the different motives and tastes of those involved in the design process. It is very clear that having such an immense change as moving to a new area imposed on one leads to feelings of lack of control and helplessness even if the new area is a vast physical improvement on the old. When this lack of power is combined with severe disruption of one's social network it is not surprising that mental health effects will occur. As Rohe (1985) suggests participation in the design process has effects on the two main mediators of mental health, control and social support. Being involved provides a sense of control and empowerment and if done effectively allows some real control over the process. Involvement also increases the amount of interaction between residents, provides a sense of shared goals and purpose and ultimately increases the sense of community and social support. The central role of control and social support in the mental health of communities is well established in the more general literature (Orford, 1992). The evidence discussed above suggests that in designing neighbourhoods, designers need to explore ways in which both can be enhanced.

Designing urban environments

Everything that has been discussed under designing neighbourhoods and communities applies to and is generally only applicable to urban environments. However there are other issues in urban design which need to be considered, many of which impinge on neighbourhoods and communities. Cities are not only made up of dwellings. They are also places where people work, shop, travel, and play, and combining all these activities successfully in one large physical environment brings special problems. One such problem has been investigated under the area of mixed land use which refers to where buildings designed for different use (dwellings, shops, industry) are placed beside each other. For example Baum, Aiello, and Davies (1979) found that the presence of a shopping area at the end of a residential street reduced social interaction and community spirit and reduced residents' sense of control over privacy. Halpern's (1995) analysis of the SCPR data replicated this finding with only 58% of respondents who lived next to a commercial area rating their neighbours as helpful, compared to 82% in a purely residential area. As discussed in the previous section it is likely that commercial land use next to a residential area has its effect through increased traffic and number of strangers in the area. The effect of traffic and its related increase in noise and pollution, and the increased presence of strangers reduces the social cohesion and sense of community. As a consequence individuals experience less social support and control which has major implications for both physical and mental health. Another effect of an increase in the number of strangers in an area is an increase in fear of crime (Fowler, 1987), something we will discuss more fully. On the other hand the separation of places of work, and shopping, from residential areas is also problematic. It increases traffic flow on routes between the different areas thus increasing noise, pollution, and other related problems for those living along such routes. It increases the need to commute longer distances thus introducing another major source of stress. More recently a great deal of concern is being expressed about the economic damage being done to city centres by the relocation of shopping areas to large industrial sites out of town. The dilemma for planners is to find ways in which commercial sites can be located in the community, while still retaining the privacy of residential areas. As with most things, it is a case of finding a solution that optimises the positive aspects of both. A special problem in urban areas is travel.

Design and travel

Traffic congestion in cities is becoming an ever increasing problem with so many negative side effects such as pollution, increased noise levels, increases in stress and aggression, and ultimately the number of accidents. It seems an almost impossible problem, with the continuous demand for bigger and better roads leading to more congestion during construction and the often discovered conclusion that even before it is complete the road is already insufficient to meet the demand. Traffic congestion reduces the efficiency of buses and in many cities the railways are unable to meet the demand. Attempts to reduce the use of cars have not really been very successful, though it does seem that it is the best target for intervention.

Innovations in public transport have not proved a resounding success as exemplified by the experience with BART in the USA. On the whole it seems that attempts to reduce the need to travel can be justified more effectively, on several counts. The evidence is that current road and rail systems are generally inadequate and in many cases expansion is not possible. Secondly travelling long distances to work is a major source of stress and disrupts the individual's social and family life (Cassidy, 1992). Thirdly the damage done to the environment through increased pollution and noise is already beyond reasonable limits and requires action to reduce it rather than increase it.

Box 39: Addicted to cars

One of the difficulties for city planners is in convincing car drivers to use public transport. One might argue that public transport is sometimes unreliable and overcrowded, and it is clear that car drivers do feel some sense of control even in todays congested streets (Cassidy, 1992). However Reser (1980) suggests that there may be more to the relationship between people and cars. He suggests that we may have become addicted to cars because they have become an important coping mechanism. He identifies five functions served by cars. They provide transportation, are part of our self-image, provide privacy and familiarity, provide a sense of freedom, and "a responsive micro-environment which allows a feeling of competence and mastery, avoiding the learned helplessness derived from the lack of control of the urban environment". The suggestion is that psychologists may need to devote more effort to releasing drivers from their addiction.

Reducing the need to travel

Attempts to reduce the need to travel involve such innovations as the neighbourhood work centre approach (Becker, 1984). This involves attempts to locate work centres in local communities and of course brings with it the problems discussed under mixed land use. However with some innovative planning it is likely that the positive effects will outweigh the negative. Another potential development is the increase in home work which is being enhanced by major developments in communication technology. While it is clear that not all occupations lend themselves to this approach studies have found that home work can have positive effects for individuals and employers. Atkinson (1985) found increased production, greater company loyalty, and less stress among home workers. Where travel to work is unavoidable, the stress of commuting can be reduced by allowing employees some flexibility in starting and finishing times, something that has acquired the term flexitime (Winett, Neale, & Williams, 1982).

Travel on the grand scale

Of course travel is not just a problem within cities. People are increasingly travelling between cities, nations and continents, for both business and pleasure. The congestion at airports and the levels of noise in areas near to airports is becoming a problem of increasing concern. Planners need to explore ways in which residential areas can be sited further from airports, or ways in which noise levels can be reduced. The design of airports themselves needs to be researched more fully in order to find ways of reducing congestion. Long distance travel involving large numbers of people at high speed by air, sea or land, brings the horror of major disasters as previously discussed. Psychology can contribute to design in two main areas, reducing the potential for accidents through better person–machine design, and providing more effective support services to those who have been involved in disasters.

Design and crime

The relationship between design and crime has two main dimensions. First of all there is evidence that levels of crime can be reduced through environmental design (Newman, 1972). Second, the design of environments contributes to fear of crime, which is sometimes more of a problem for people than actual levels of crime (Halpern, 1995; Heinzelmann, 1981). Perhaps the best known concept in this context is defensible space (Newman, 1972). The evidence as discussed in the last chapter is that enhancing territoriality in a neighbourhood reduces crime levels. A number of studies have found evidence that the provision of defensible space around homes is important in making it more difficult for criminals (Mergen, 1983; Newman, 1975; Rand, 1984). A term that has crept into the literature is target hardening which refers to interventions that make targets of crime more inaccessible to criminals. Combined with increased surveillance (Rand, 1984) and proactive policing (Moffatt, 1983) target hardening has been shown to produce substantial reductions in crime rates and fear of crime. Rand (1984) does warn of the dangers to individual freedom from overzealous use of such techniques. The use of defensible space in design can be described as a target hardening technique. Fear of crime on the other hand has been shown to bear little relationship either to actual levels of crime or previous experience of crime (Halpern, 1995). It is associated with low levels of social cohesion, social integration, and hence lack of community (Hunter & Baumer, 1982), size and homogeneity of the neighbourhood (Box, Hale & Andrews, 1988), the physical appearance of the neighbourhood in terms of vacant properties, graffiti, broken windows, etc. (i.e. physical incivilities) and the presence of gangs of youths, homeless people and poverty generally (i.e. social incivilities) (Box, Hale & Andrews, 1988; Maxfield, 1984). It is argued that people associate incivilities with a breakdown in social order and increased crime rates (Hunter, 1978). In order to combat fear of crime therefore, designers need to consider all the aspects of neighbourhood design.

Design conclusions

While the design process is likely to differ across the different aspects of the physical environment, some general conclusions can be drawn.

First of all, it is very clear that the participation of all interested parties, in particular the users, in the design process is essential if the end product is to fulfil its function satisfactorily. Participation not only ensures that the needs of users are more likely to be met, but also increases social cohesion and social support, and empowers the users. Across all the different areas discussed, satisfaction with the environment and the mental health of inhabitants was related to the way in which the design influenced levels of social support and perceived control, with environments that enhanced both providing better mental health. One of the major aspects of control was in terms of control over access to the self, or privacy. Buildings, homes, institutions, and neighbourhoods which provide the opportunity for interaction, but also allow the autonomy not to interact, provide most satisfaction and correlate with better mental health. Finding the necessary balance between social interaction and privacy in design should be a major target for designers. Other conflicts also appear which require optimisation. One is the balance between homogeneity and heterogeneity in neighbourhoods. Homogeneous neighbourhoods are more socially cohesive and provide better social support and hence better mental health. However completely homogeneous neighbourhoods create ghettos and exacerbate the already existing social division which are the source of prejudice and social conflicts. Another conflict exists between the separation of differential land use. Siting commercial and residential areas together increases traffic volume and presence of strangers leading to less social cohesion and increased fear of crime. Separating commercial and residential areas increases the need to commute with its increases in stress, aggression, pollution, and demand for overstretched transportation facilities. Again the solution seems to lie in some sort of balance between the two. Most studies have focused on the mental health and satisfaction effects, or the effects on crime or fear of crime, of environmental designs. While the issue of homogeneity of neighbourhoods raises the issue of design and social conflict, it seems to have been underresearched. It seems appropriate to suggest that as well as designing environments for better health, comfort and satisfaction, and less crime, we need to also consider designing for peace.

CHAPTER EIGHT

Using and abusing the world

Humans are one of the many species that inhabit this planet earth, and depend on it to sustain life. The tragedy of those species that have become extinct should be a constant reminder that it is not an infallible source. What we often forget is that the earth is also a living thing and that our survival depends on a satisfactory interaction which optimises the continued health of both parties. This health analogy is more appropriate than the economic one of supply and demand, since it is very clear that the earth's supply is not unlimited. The environment provides us with a vast range of resources, but these resources are not limitless and we cannot rely on finding alternatives when the resources run out. In fact some writers paint a very pessimistic picture of the future. Heilbroner (1974) argues that continued growth in demand by industrialised societies for a life style of the standard currently enjoyed will rapidly deplete resources to such an extent that it will be necessary for a vast decrease in population size to occur if any life is to continue. He predicted that this reduction would occur through large-scale war as a result of competition for scarce resources. Of course war and maintaining the resources to be able to engage in war are major factors which contribute to the depletion of those resources. We all witnessed the large scale destruction of oil wells during the Gulf War and the continued testing of nuclear bombs by some nations despite large-scale opposition. The problems brought about by the continued population growth have been a source of debate for some time, notably in the

203

writings of another pessimist from almost two centuries ago, Thomas Malthus (1798). However it isn't only the number of people on the earth that is the problem, it is how effectively they use and share the resources. There is much wasteful use of resources and damaging side effects which could be avoided. Sometimes people lack the knowledge of environmental problems, but more often it seems that we are not motivated to change. How people can be motivated to develop more positive environmental attitudes and behaviours is a central problem for environmental psychologists.

THE NATURAL WORLD AND BEHAVIOUR

The natural environment provides us with life, but we often take much more than we give back, leading to concerns about the future of our natural resources. In Stephen King's *Children of the Corn*, the horror theme presented involves the earth taking revenge for the way humans have exploited it without restoring the balance that is assumed to exist in nature. While this is an extreme example, to some extent the outcome of our exploitation of natural resources could have even more horrific results. Understanding the relationship between the natural environment and behaviour can contribute to this issue. There is clearly a need to conserve our natural resources and as I write this I am reminded of a very recent debate concerning the possible closure of one of Britain's most advanced recycling centres. The argument was that the centre was not making a profit and was actually costing money to run. One cannot but be disappointed at the short-sighted arguments from politicians which ignore the consequences for the future of our planet, something which is very difficult to put into economic terms. When Adam Smith wrote his *Wealth of Nations* in 1776 he presupposed that individual capitalism would automatically lead to a promotion of public interest and the good of all. As the example above and our general experience indicates, Smith was wrong. Thankfully the plant was not closed, although more recently it has again been threatened, this time because of a major fire at the plant which itself became an environmental hazard for a time. It would seem very important that governments should take a strong lead on the environment.

Environmental issues

Humans are impacting on the global environment in damaging ways on a number of fronts. Stern (1992) identifies five categories of damage which need to be addressed.

- Alterations to the earth's radiative balance thus altering its climate—the global warming effect.
- Causing species to become extinct at a rate 10,000 times as fast as in the period before the emergence of humans.
- Damaging the ozone layer that shields living things from ultraviolet radiation.
- Polluting the oceans with oil, heavy metals, fertilisers, and trash.
- Other alterations in the earth's life support systems, some known, some suspected, and probably others yet unrecognised.

The last identifies the fact that while much is known about what we are doing to our world, much is either speculation or even not yet contemplated. The speed and constancy of change contributes to this unpredictability. The earth evolved through different stages which took millions of years (for example the ice age), but more recent effects have taken much less time. The greenhouse effect or global warming which was first noticed in the 1980s was not present prior to 1930 (Houghton et al., 1990). In addition it takes quite a long time for any intervention to take effect. Even if we were to stop releasing pollutants into the atmosphere immediately, it would take many decades before the pollutants already released stop having an effect. These effects are global in that they tend not to be easily localised. However local effects also occur in terms of pollution of water and air supplies, the production of waste, and damage to the habitats of other species. For example the continued development of land for housing or agriculture reduces the amount available to wildlife. This loss of wilderness has localised effects but because it occurs in many different localities it contributes to the global problem of species extinction. When I was growing up I remember a bird called the corncrake which could be seen and heard in abundance in the late spring or early summer. The only place this bird can now be seen or heard in the British Isles is in a very small area of North Donegal in Ireland. The global and local effects are under human control, which clearly identifies an important role for psychology in the process. While other scientists may explore the use of different fuels or the modification of existing ones, in order to reduce damage to the environment, by far the greater effect is likely to occur through changes in attitudes and behaviours. This is not to suggest that psychology can solve the problem in isolation. Rather it requires an interdisciplinary effort across the behavioural and social sciences. It is little use creating a nation of people who prefer to walk or cycle, if political and economic structures make the use of cars a necessity. There is a need for analysis and change of factors at different levels if interventions are to be effective.

Identifying the problems

It is generally the case that most people know of a range of factors that damage the environment, such as the emission of carbon dioxide from car exhausts, the waste of products through lack of recycling, and so on, but they are generally unaware of the relative importance of the factors. For example a study by Gigliotti (1994) found that his sample of students considered all environmental issues to be of equal importance. The same seems to be true of social scientists, since the literature often does not discriminate between different issues. In order to apply psychology effectively Stern (1992) suggests that the first stage is to assess this relative effect. In other words if the effect of car fuel emissions is 50 times greater than the effect of use of fertilisers, we should focus more effort in trying to reduce the car fuel emissions. Stern calculates that fossil fuel use makes by far the greater contribution to global warming and that carbon dioxide, which is the product, is the greater culprit (61% compared to 12% for chlorofluorocarbons). In the USA 20% of carbon dioxide emissions comes from cars, and if fuel efficiency of cars were to double this would lead to a fall of 2.5% in carbon dioxide emission in global terms. According to Stern (1992) this is not only technically but politically possible. The point being made is that before we focus on changing behaviour we need to know which behaviours have the most damaging effects; otherwise we will have difficulty targeting the most effective interventions.

Attitudes towards the environment

Attitudes represent feelings about issues or objects, and it is difficult to believe that people actually feel positively about damaging the environment. Yet given that many people continue to drive fast, fuel guzzling cars, and to waste energy, a general assumption would be that this is the case. The evidence is that in fact many people do have positive attitudes in behaving towards the environment, but unfortunately do not translate their attitudes into behaviour. In fact evidence across the range from adults (Bloom, 1995) to college students (Larsen, 1995) and children (Kahn & Friedman, 1995) report positive attitudes towards environmental issues. This attitude–behaviour discrepancy is not surprising when we consider health attitudes and behaviours. Most people would agree that smoking, lack of exercise, and overeating is bad for health, yet many of the same people would engage in those behaviours.

Attitudes and behaviour

The evidence from research on the relationship between attitudes and behaviour is that attitudes only predict behaviour in certain circumstances. Attitudes often are good predictors of the intention to

---

Box 40: Perception, judgment, and risk

It is generally accepted that the ability to maintain a positive view of the world and ourselves is an important survival skill. In the area of depression it is argued that depressed people are not necessarily pessimistic, they are just not optimistic. In fact it could be argued that they have a more realistic view of events. In the area of attribution theory this is referred to as the self-serving bias. It is the ability to believe that bad things happen to others, not to us. The reverse of this is referred to as the just world hypothesis, which reflects the belief that ultimately the world is just, and therefore if bad things happen to people, they must have been bad people. In cases such as rape, this leads to blaming the victim for the crime. Given that we develop a distorted view of events which helps to protect us from reality, one would expect this to be very important in regard to environmental attitudes and behaviour. While a range of basic psychological research is relevant, as yet it doesn't appear to have been drawn on to any great extent in the area. Stern (1992) suggests that areas such as how experts make judgments and the potential for error and overconfidence, how the level of risk is communicated to the general population (Poumadere, 1995), how lay people judge the options and then combine those judgments into a decision, are all areas that have been researched. Perhaps we have identified an area where theory and practice do not communicate and are reminded of Lewin's view that theory and practice should be interdependent. Certainly there seems to be a need to use the knowledge base more effectively.

---

behave in the predicted way but often fail to translate into the actual behaviour. There is an extensive literature in social psychology on the relationship between attitudes and behaviour (Hogg & Vaughan, 1995). Ever since La Piere (1934) discovered that people may hold prejudices but may not actually discriminate against the objects of those prejudices, psychologists have attempted to discover the necessary conditions under which an attitude will be translated into behaviour. The problem is that attitudes coexist with beliefs and intentions within complex cognitive schemata or maps of the individual's world. Thus attitudes do not exist in isolation but form a complex system of interrelated and interdependent attitudes and beliefs. In fact they are the store of knowledge and feeling about the world that the person has accumulated over their lifetime. The interdependence of attitudes means that change in one attitude may necessitate changes in the whole system, and can help us to understand why some attitudes are so resistant to change. Some attitudes will be central to the individual's personal and social identity and will be very difficult to change. Attitudes will be of different strengths and different levels of complexity in terms of how they relate to behaviour. There will be social constraints on the expression of some attitudes, and social approval of others. All of these factors will be involved in decisions about actions that reflect our attitudes.

Factors that mediate the attitude-behaviour link

Probably the best-known theory or model of attitude–behaviour relationships is Ajzen and Fishbein's (1980) theory of reasoned action which was revised as the theory of planned behaviour (Ajzen, 1989; see Fig. 13). This provides us with a model of the process which we need to follow in order to understand whether an attitude is likely to be translated into behaviour. It identifies several important factors. Ultimately we need to know the direction and strength of the individual's intention to behave. To do this we need to get a more specific measure of the attitude. In fact what we need is a measure of the attitude towards the specific behaviour. In other words knowing that someone feels positively about saving the planet is much too general and not very useful in predicting whether someone will engage in recycling behaviour. What we need is a measure of how they feel about recycling

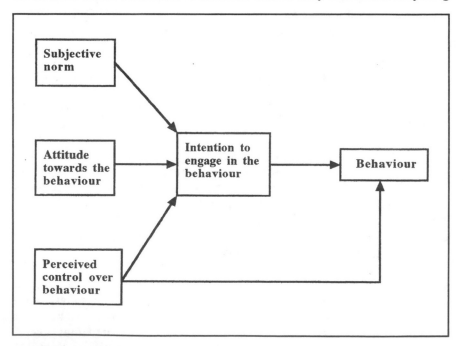

FIG. 13. The theory of planned behaviour and reasoned action (based on Ajzen & Fishbein, 1980; Ajzen, 1989).

waste material. The more specific we can be in measurement, the more likely we are to produce accurate predictions about behaviour. The model also considers the role of social influence in the process and predicts that we are more likely to engage in the behaviour if it is socially approved by others whose views we value, i.e. the subjective norm. In addition we must consider whether the person can actually engage in the behaviour, i.e. perceived behavioural control. For example someone working in an organisation which uses a lot of paper may have the intention to recycle waste paper, but if the company does not provide any facility for recycling it is unlikely that the recycling will occur. This sort of model can incorporate a range of important variables which need to be considered, such as habit, personality, degree of control, and so on. In a study of environmental attitudes and behaviours Stern and Oskamp (1987) concluded that attitudes are more predictive of behaviour when both are measured at the same level of specificity and when the behaviours are easier to perform. In fact they propose a causal chain of factors that lead to a behavioural outcome (see Fig. 14). Using this process, they argue, allows better prediction of behaviour. Stern's (1992) review identifies a range of evidence on factors that are related to environmentally relevant behaviour. These include personal norms, knowledge about the financial costs of different behaviours, perceived difficulty of engaging in behaviours, knowledge or skill in performing behaviours, knowledge of which actions have the greatest effect, issue involvement, issue salience, instrumentality to personal values, and the presence of intrinsic motives or satisfactions.

Essentially if the environmental issue is really important to us, if we have a detailed knowledge of it and know what to do about it, if we are not prohibited from engaging in action by physical, economic, social or political restraints, and if we will be socially rewarded for the action, we are more likely to take the action. Clearly the influence of others is very important in the process since our attitudes are socially constructed and acquired through observing and modelling others' behaviours. Thus not only are we influenced by social pressure at the time, but our beliefs and feelings about the environment are socially determined. Interestingly it appears that social cohesion among the target group has an important influence on environmental behaviours (Berk et al., 1980). There is evidence from research on group processes that individuals will be more committed to a course of action if the decision to pursue that course has been taken in a group setting (Brown, 1988). The relationship between a sense of community or a strong social identity and environmentally relevant behaviour has not been explored in any detail, but the above findings would indicate that it may be a useful future development. We will discuss this further below. Stern (1992) also highlights the need for

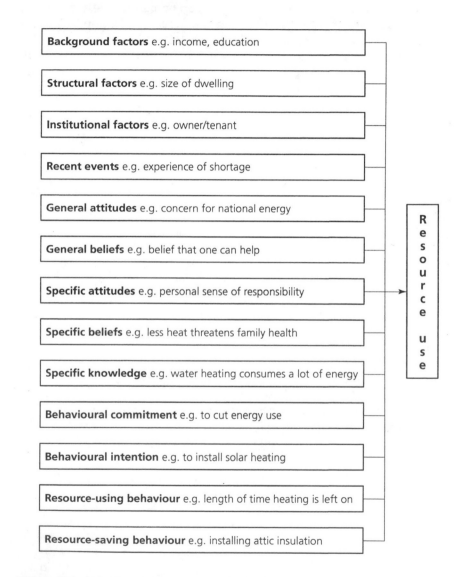

| Background factors e.g. income, education |
| Structural factors e.g. size of dwelling |
| Institutional factors e.g. owner/tenant |
| Recent events e.g. experience of shortage |
| General attitudes e.g. concern for national energy |
| General beliefs e.g. belief that one can help |
| Specific attitudes e.g. personal sense of responsibility |
| Specific beliefs e.g. less heat threatens family health |
| Specific knowledge e.g. water heating consumes a lot of energy |
| Behavioural commitment e.g. to cut energy use |
| Behavioural intention e.g. to install solar heating |
| Resource-using behaviour e.g. length of time heating is left on |
| Resource-saving behaviour e.g. installing attic insulation |

Resource use

FIG.14. The chain of contributing to an understanding of resource use (based on Stern, 1992).

multilevel, interdisciplinary and multimethod approaches. A wide range of factors including, education, income, family size, local weather conditions, economic incentives, government policy, and so on will all play an important role. Whatever the level of good intentions, people will not conserve energy if to do so means they are freezing to death, or if the alternatives are beyond their financial means. Psychological factors can only be considered within their political, economic, and social contexts.

The effect of behaviour on attitudes

Another perspective on the attitude–behaviour relationship considers the situation where attitudes and behaviours are in conflict. The cognitive dissonance theory first introduced by Festinger (1957) suggests that when there is dissonance between attitudes and behaviour individuals feel uncomfortable and are motivated to restore some sort of cognitive balance. For example if we feel strongly about environmental conservation but work in an environment where recycling is impossible, we will feel uncomfortable. We will try to restore comfort either by getting to a situation where recycling is possible (through actively pursuing a change in policy or leaving), or by rationalising the attitude. Cognitive dissonance theory leads us to the prediction that forcing someone to behave in environmentally friendly ways will change their attitude. There is some evidence that legislation that makes positive environmental behaviours the more accepted behaviour also leads to more general changes in attitudes in line with those behaviours (Kahle & Beatty, 1987).

Attitude expression and control

However we are not totally in control of the attitude–behaviour process, and often behavioural expression of an attitude will be obvious to the observer even when the person expressing the attitude attempts to hide it. Two very important ways in which this occurs are through "leaky" nonverbal cues and in the words we use. Though someone may use words that imply an unprejudiced view, the way they say it may actually convey a totally different message. On the other hand the words we use may themselves indicate an attitude which we do not wish to express. The best examples tend to come from sexist use of language as when we refer to a female as someone's wife as opposed to an individual in her own right. We are often aware that someone is sexist or racist without being aware of how we have reached that conclusion. It is important to recognise this lack of volition since it may convey a lack of commitment in the area of environmental attitudes, such as when a politician speaks on environmental issues.

Knowledge about the environment

One of the problems in the attitude–behaviour discrepancy issue is knowledge about environmental problems. As already stated most people have some awareness of the issues, but this is often very general, piecemeal and almost mythical in cases. Studies of US students tend to find that they are aware of very general issues such as the inadequate funding for environmental projects (Krause, 1993) but less knowledgeable about more specific factors. In fact there is some evidence that US students are less knowledgeable than students in other parts of the world (Benton & Funkhouser, 1994). The evidence from studies of children show that preschool children often have quite a substantial awareness of environmental issues (Cohen & Horm-Wingerd, 1993; Palmer, 1994). One obvious focus for raising environmental awareness is in the school. However it appears that education on environmental issues is less structured and effective than might be hoped. Studies tend to suggest that only small amounts of time are spent on environmental issues in school. This is not because teachers think that environmental issues are unimportant, rather it is because many teachers do not feel competent on these issues (Lane et al., 1994).

Why the continued abuse

The general literature on attitudes provides evidence which might give us some cause for optimism in that the behaviours we observe may not reflect attitudes. There is need for optimism given the evidence of the extent of our abuse of the resources we depend upon which leads us to explore more specific research which attempts to shed light on why we continue to engage in this abuse. The analogy often used in this context is that of the behaviour of traditional communities in regard to the commons, something generally referred to as the tragedy of the commons. The commons was the piece of commonly owned land surrounding the houses in traditional communities. They date back to feudal times when the majority of the land was in the hands of the lords and barons, who magnanimously granted the commons to their workers. The problem was that the land was everybody's and nobody's. In other words it was available to everyone in the community, but no one person in the community had overall control of it. The land was used to graze livestock, and as long as everyone used it fairly and equally, the animals and humans would prosper. However this was not what happened. Gradually individuals began to add more than their share of animals, following the philosophy that if I add one more cow or goat it won't really have an effect. However since most people acted on the same philosophy it did have a major effect. Ultimately there was insufficient land to feed all the animals and gradually the commons disappeared. The commons dilemma can be observed in many areas of human behaviour. As I write this two news items spring to mind. In one, two companies who rent punts on the River Cam at Cambridge are engaged in a dispute over mooring places. Up until recently both companies have used public moorings along the river, but one company has increased its number of punts thus overcrowding the commons. In the other news item, Members of Parliament have just voted themselves a 9% pay rise, as opposed to the 3% limit they have imposed on everyone else. It does seem rather like the behaviour of those who grazed more than their share of cows or goats on the commons of old. The global environment has become the commons of today, and one would hope that lessons are learned before it is too late. Attempts have been made to analyse this type of behaviour and provide some explanation for it. Platt (1973) identified what is called the social trap phenomenon which works against changes in attitudes and behaviour under certain circumstances. The social trap occurs when the behaviour in question has immediate reinforcing consequences, while the costs are in the distant future and to some extent hidden from immediate view. Such was the case with the commons, and is the case with depletion of natural resources and use of polluting and harmful materials. A fast and sporty car provides immediate gratification to the owner, while its exorbitant consumption of fuel will probably not directly effect the owner in his or her life time. However if everyone acts similarly the consequences will be extensive, but may still only affect future generations. This difference between short- and long-term consequences is a major factor according to Platt. In addition people appear to believe that the positive outcomes outweigh the bad. It is this tendency for individuals to opt more often for the selfish choice that is the problem. Platt (1973) suggests four ways in which we might escape the social trap.

1. Moving the future negative consequences closer to the present. It is the same principle as keeping a picture of an overweight person on the refrigerator or a picture of a damaged lung on a packet of cigarettes. A suggestion provided by Seamon and Kendrick (1992) is to have a bright red indicator which flashes when energy is being wasted either at home or in the car.

2. Reinforcing more desirable behaviours. An example might be making it more rewarding for people to use buses rather than cars, or using car pools where a number of people travel in one car. Providing more peak hour buses and special bus lanes which reduce the impedance to travel have been shown to be effective in encouraging more people to use them (Rose & Hinds, 1976).

3. Changing the nature of the long-term consequences. This involves a larger scale intervention where for example cars are designed to run on a less endangered fuel and to be more economical. Other examples are the use of alternative energy sources and the building of homes that are more efficient in terms of energy consumption. The important thing here is to consider the possible consequences of change. For example there is a debate about whether nuclear energy is really a safer alternative.

4. Use of social pressure. One of the reasons put forward to explain why people opt for the selfish choice is the diffusion of responsibility hypothesis (Latane & Darley, 1968) or the process of deindividuation (Zimbardo, 1969). Both these processes involve individuals not taking responsibility for their own actions because they are in a situation which allows them to assume that others can be blamed and that the finger won't point at them. Use of social pressure tackles just this issue by ensuring that the finger will point at specific individuals if people don't respond. An example might be where people are encouraged to make a public commitment, for example at a community meeting. It is much more difficult for people not to meet commitments if others know about them and are likely to be aware if the commitment was honoured.

To some extent the suggestions put forward by Platt reflect the ideas expressed by Skinner (1972) in his book *Beyond freedom and dignity*. In essence what Skinner proposed was that society should be designed around behavioural principles so that reinforcements operated to produce and maintain behaviours that would ultimately be for the good of all. Because it would involve control over people, even if the motivation was positive, the idea is controversial. It is useful to consider for yourself the ethics of behavioural control in all areas of psychological application.

SOCIAL AND COMMONS DILEMMAS

An interesting approach to large scale social issues such as depletion of natural resources is the analogy of the social dilemma (Dawes, 1980). This stems from laboratory research into cooperation and competition (Coombs, Dawes & Tversky, 1970). This work stemmed from research using a game called the *Prisoner's dilemma*, where players have to choose between benefiting themselves or the group. In essence it involves several prisoners who have to choose between confessing or not to a crime. If one confesses that prisoner goes free while the others get 10 years, if all confess they get five years each, and if no one confesses they all get one year on a minor charge. Numerous variations have been developed but all tend to have some common ground rules. Ultimately making a selfish choice is the most beneficial, but as a group the most benefit is achieved through not making selfish choices. In designs that best reflect social dilemmas, too many selfish choices will ultimately destroy the resource for everyone. While simulations like this cannot totally reflect real life behaviour they do allow psychologists some insight into the processes involved in light of the fact that field studies of these issues are almost impossible to set up and control. By varying the conditions, researchers may identify some of the contingencies which make cooperation more likely. Such research may help to identify ways in which physical and social environments might be manipulated to increase cooperation over scarce resources in the real world.

Theories of social dilemmas

A number of theories have developed in regard to social dilemmas, and Gifford (1987) discusses five such theories: tragic choice theory, game theory, social trap theory, equity theory, and limited processing theory. We have discussed Platt's (1973) social trap theory and we will now briefly review the other four. Tragic choice theory is based on the premise that some ideals such as freedom and equality are incompatible. In other words people have different abilities and motivations, and freedom means that some will do better than others, hence no equality. Equality therefore requires control, and lack of freedom. Another premise of the theory is that scarcity is consciously created in order to maintain economic stability and reflects the fact that while we may speak of equality, as a society we do not value everyone equally. This state of affairs then leads to people making self-interest choices. This reflects a societal level of analysis. A more individual level of analysis is presented in game theory which is based on a microanalysis of individual behaviour in games such as the *Prisoner's dilemma* (Gifford & Wells, 1991; Smith & Bell, 1992; Ward, 1993). It appears that the essential ingredient in determining whether people will cooperate or compete is the level of trust. When people trust others they are more likely to cooperate and therefore everyone gains equally. If they don't trust others they will make self-interest choices and ultimately destroy the resource. Equity theory is quite well known in other areas of psychology and has been used to explain levels of job satisfaction and satisfaction in relationships. It was first developed by Adams (1965) and is based on estimates of fairness. In essence we make rational evaluations of our own efforts and rewards against the efforts and rewards of others. Where we perceive that equity exists between ourselves and others we will be satisfied with the situation. However if we perceive inequity we will be motivated to change things. An interesting aspect of equity theory is that it predicts we will be dissatisfied if we feel we are getting too much as well as when we are getting too little. Furthermore it doesn't necessarily mean equality. We may perceive that someone else should get more for a variety of reasons ranging from their greater need or having expended more effort. Thus we will make self-interest choices if we perceive inequity. The problem is that we may actually distort the reality of the situation because judgments are made on perceptions of equity rather than any objective measure. In addition a preoccupation with immediate equity may distract us from the real issue, i.e. the ultimate destruction of the resource. Equity theory proposes a rational model of human behaviour, where people make conscious, evaluated choices. While providing a useful overview, it doesn't account for "mindless" or irrational behaviour where we behave unconsciously. We can usefully refer here to the stimulus screening ability of people in cities, where lack of helping behaviour may simply be the result of not being aware of the need for help. In a similar way we may not be aware of the consequences of our actions in the commons, or we may have a different view of events. This explanation suggests that we make self-interest choices because we are not consciously processing the information that would lead us to see the dangers and is referred to as limited processing theory. A common theme across these theories is that being informed about the consequences of our actions is the first necessary condition for action. Whether we are rationally judging the equity of the situation or whether we trust others, or if it is that we are only processing a limited amount of information, it is important that we have the facts, in as much as they are facts.

Social identity and social dilemmas

As mentioned in the section on attitude–behaviour discrepancies, there is some evidence that attitudes shared by a community and instrumental in attaining shared goals are more likely to be acted upon. This has been linked to social identity theory by some recent research (Brewer & Schneider, 1990). It is based on the argument by Turner et al. (1987) that when the self is depersonalised, as occurs when people act in terms of social (or group) identity, so too is self-interest. When a particular social identity is salient our behaviour is better explained in terms of the goals of the relevant social group than in terms of our individual goals, hence we are no longer acting in terms of our personal interest. It is likely that we will perceive the group interest as one and the same as our personal interest, but our behaviour will benefit the group. It is this distinction between behaviour in terms of self-interest and behaviour in terms of group interest that needs to be explained in social dilemmas. Social identity theory would therefore predict that when the group sharing the commons have a strong sense of social identity (community) they will be more likely to cooperate. The social identity effect was confirmed in a laboratory study by Parker et al. (1983). In this study size of group and salience of social identity were both manipulated. The overall effect was a significant reduction in self-interest choices when social identity was salient for both small and large groups. It would appear then that social identity theory provides a very useful theoretical framework for explaining behaviour in social dilemmas and for altering that behaviour through manipulating social identity. Herein lies the problem. If it is to be effective the salient social identity must be shared by all. This means that for local issues people must be motivated in terms of a community identity, and in terms of global issues they must behave in terms of a shared global identity. As we shall see, our world and our communities are more likely to be made up of several social categories and when opposing social identities are salient, the outcome is more likely to be conflict rather than cooperation.

Conflict and collective action

Clearly in societies that have created the demand for resources which deplete or damage the environment, there will be conflicts of interest between those who benefit from a continuation of current behaviours and those who recognise and support the need for change. In addition, within any community there will be already existing social categories whether in terms of race, social class, religion or simply which football team one supports. The evidence from the vast literature on social identity theory shows that our behaviour is to some degree at the mercy of whatever social identity happens to be salient at the time. Thus any benefit of shared social identity discussed before will be lost in terms of intergroup conflict. Research on social conflict suggests that an important factor in the reduction of conflict is the provision of superordinate goals (Allport, 1954; Brown, 1996; Sherif et al., 1961). In other words where a particular goal transcends the goals of different groups and requires joint action by the groups in order to attain it, inter-group conflict will be reduced. This can be explained in terms of a new social identity defined by this new shared goal. One would expect that conservation of the global environment would be a superordinate goal for human society. However as we have seen from the discussion of social traps, many do not recognise the threat as having any immediate impact. One overriding goal of environmental psychology should be to create an environmental ethic, or to turn environmental concern into a superordinate goal. In addition it might be useful to consider environmental attitudes and behaviour within the context of social conflict resolution. An understanding of the goals and interests of different groups and the ways in which conflicts of interest make group identity salient can help us gain a much deeper understanding of when and why collective social action is unlikely to occur in regard to environmental issues. It forces us to question assumptions which generalise our own interests to others. Highlighting the threat of skin cancer as a result of ozone depletion will tend only to work with fair skinned people since they are most endangered (Stern, 1992). Global warming may have positive effects, through longer hotter summers for example, in some areas of the world. In one study Polish workers felt that driving a car was more environmentally friendly than using public transport (Meseke, 1994). The issue of differential threat must be recognised in education programmes so that factors can be identified which make the issues ones that are valued by everyone. The essential issue is to move from a position of competition between groups to a cooperative effort to preserve the earth for all.

Individual differences and environmental behaviour

Studies have shown some evidence of individual differences in two areas, attitudes towards the environment and in cooperation versus self-interest choices. It is suggested that older, more educated and higher status individuals report more positive attitudes towards the environment (Veitch & Arkkelin, 1995). However when specific issues are identified it is found that there is a less consistent age effect. For example younger homeowners were quicker to adopt energy-saving actions than older homeowners. The relationship between age and ability to cooperate tends to show a developmental effect with very young children being more self-centred and cooperative behaviour increasing between the ages of about 3 and 16 (Gifford, 1982). Cooperation tends to drop significantly between ages 16–20 and no real evidence of what happens beyond this. In regard to sex differences Schahn and Holzer (1990) suggest that men know more about environmental problems while women report higher levels of environmental concern in regard to issues connected with the home. In regard to cooperation there is conflicting evidence on sex with some studies finding that females are more cooperative (Vinacke et al., 1974) and others finding no difference (Caldwell, 1976). Meux (1973) postulated a cooperative personality trait and suggests that when this is considered sex differences are not found. Given that environmental attitudes are influenced by socialisation and that the evidence is that males and females are socialised differently (Siann, 1994) one might expect that difference would be more to do with gender than biological sex. However this hasn't been investigated. It is clear from the work of people like McKechnie (1974) that some environmental psychologists assume a link between personality and environmental attitudes. In fact the ERI has two dimensions which reflect this, pastoralism (the tendency to oppose land development, etc.) and environmental adaptation (the tendency to favour altering the environment to suit human needs). In addition the Environmental Preference Questionnaire (Kaplan, 1975) would intuitively seem to be related to environmental attitudes. Yet this avenue has not been really explored. While it is clear that personality can only be considered in the context of social, political, and economic factors, it seems a rather neglected area of research.

Changing attitudes and behaviour

The major aim of psychology in the area of use and abuse of the environment is to change attitudes and behaviours in the direction of a more positive approach to environmental issues. This could be described as the development of an environmental ethic (Veitch & Arkkelin, 1995). While the creation of a superordinate social identity provides us with an overall framework, a useful approach to identifying the problems and designing interventions is Lewin's (1951) force field model, originally used in the field of organisational change. Lewin argued that equilibrium in any system is maintained by the opposition of restraining and driving forces. In the area of attitudes and behaviours towards the environment, current attitudes and behaviours can be similarly conceptualised. In any society there will be (driving) forces towards positive change (e.g. environmental activists, individuals attitudes, local legislation, etc.), and (restraining) forces which oppose these changes (e.g. multinational fuel companies, government policies, individual attitudes). In line with Stern's (1992) analysis, we can begin to identify factors at all levels which contribute to the driving or restraining forces. It is then a matter of designing interventions that reduce the restraining forces and enhance the driving forces. This is of course a gross simplification since the driving and restraining forces are many and complex, but it serves a useful guiding role. The driving and restraining forces will include all the factors identified above as determining the likelihood that attitudes will predict behaviour.

Driving and restraining forces

Stern (1992) identifies four major areas of research on attempts to change environmentally destructive behaviour:

- Information feedback and persuasive communications;
- altering rewards and costs;
- regulation and technological development;
- behaviour change in institutional settings.

Communicating information

The reasons why conservation is not a superordinate goal begin with issues of knowledge and information. There is still a great lack of knowledge about environmental issues and often the knowledge that is available is partial or inaccurate. The information available doesn't always clarify the issues and may lack conviction. Simply providing information has been shown to be ineffective (Stern, 1992). For information to be effective the communication must be persuasive. Research on attitude change generally shows that to be persuasive the message must attract and sustain attention, it must be perceived as credible which means that the source must be seen as knowledgeable and believable. The evidence is that environmental information which is clear, vividly presented, appropriately aimed, providing realistic recommendations, and from a credible source is most effective (Stern, 1986; 1992). As mentioned above, politicians who espouse environmental issues at election times may be let down by nonverbal cues or by the words they use. Lack of credibility may lead to a lack of attention to future information. Two strategies which stand out in the literature as being effective are the use of clear and regular feedback about the success of changes in behaviour, and providing effective models. It seems clear that the way in which the information is conveyed is an important factor in the process of changing attitudes and behaviours in regard to environmental issues and may be one reason why some educational programmes are ineffective (Cantrill, 1992). Cantrill argues that people use self-interest in selectively attending to parts of communications and that this needs to be considered in designing communications. More effective use of psychological evidence on effective communication strategies is indicated.

Rewards and costs

The evidence from social dilemmas is that cooperation will be enhanced when rewards are immediate and valued and when costs are minimised for the individual. An equity theory analysis would suggest that ultimately this sort of economic evaluation will be an important factor in determining behaviour. The preferred approach to environmental behaviour change has often been applied behavioural analysis. This approach stems from the highly scientific behaviourism of the 1950s and 60s and focuses on a thorough analysis of the behaviour in question, its antecedent circumstances, and its consequences. The intensive analysis allows interventions which attempt to alter the antecedents and the consequences so that people are less likely to engage in the behaviour

---

Box 41: Too frightened to act

One aspect of persuasive communications which has been used both effectively and ineffectively is fear. It is widely recognised among attitude researchers that use of fear is a double-edged sword. In terms of environmental issues we need to fear the consequences of environmentally destructive behaviours somewhat in order to be motivated to act. However overuse of fear can lead to denial and a sense of learned helplessness (Rakoczy, 1987). It is useful at this point to refer to the study by Bluhm (1992), discussed in a previous chapter, which raised the issue of the mood-depressing effect of observing the stark images of death and destruction in the aftermath of an oil spill. It is important to recognise that while many may be able to screen out information about the damage we are doing to our world, others may be very sensitive to these issues already. For those people overuse of fear may lead to a withdrawal from action rather than the desired goal of increased action. This is a dilemma that does need to be addressed in communicating information about environmental issues.

---

in future. This approach and its application is covered in detail by Geller, Winett, and Everett (1982). Though often criticised for its omission of cognitive factors, applied behavioural analysis provides a structured method for analysing environmental behaviour and some useful ideas for intervention. In the literature on social dilemmas, it is quite clear that if people are to escape the social trap, the costs of environmentally destructive behaviours must be seen to be immediate and important, while the benefits must also be seen to be valued and individual. One problem with this approach has been the tendency to be less rigorous in identifying the actual rewards and costs. It seems to have been assumed that environmentally positive behaviours will be seen as rewards and environmentally destructive ones as costs. Unfortunately it is not quite so simple, and what is rewarding for one person or group may be a cost to others. Global warming may be seen as a reward to those in northern climes who experience its consequences as longer and hotter summers. It is this aspect of identifying rewards and costs that will be effective that needs more careful attention. Rewards and costs not only apply to individuals, but must also be considered in terms of groups. Herein lies another problem with the applied behavioural approach. It tends to focus exclusively on an individual level of analysis. As we have seen from the discussion of social identity theory, perhaps we need to focus on discovering the rewards and costs that will enhance large-scale group cooperation.

Legislation

While increased control of behaviour by governments may not be the most favoured of suggestions, it is clear that on environmental issues it is sometimes both necessary and effective. Legislation on lead pollution from car exhausts in the UK and on fuel economy of cars in the USA has had a positive effect. In addition laws are generally enacted for the public good and the lack of legislation on environmental issues does attest to the low priority they are given. Governments can also legislate in regard to the development of new technologies which benefit the environment (Stern, 1992). Work needs to be done on activating societies and communities towards more effective environmental legislation. In addition people often fail to comply with legislation, something that could also be more effectively explored.

A focus on institutions

Stern also identifies attempts to change environmental behaviour by focusing on institutions such as apartment buildings or college dormitories. In many ways this relates to legislation, in that governments (local and national) can become more involved in the design of buildings which enhance the environment and by offering incentives for schools, factories, and other institutions enable them to become more environmentally friendly. In fact all those involved in the design process discussed in the previous chapter could include this as an aspect of the design process.

Stern suggests that the most effective findings have been in terms of attempts which combine several different techniques, although the larger and more complex the intervention, the more expensive it becomes.

Monitoring and evaluating the process

As with environmental design it is important that any intervention to reduce environmentally damaging attitudes and behaviour must be followed through. Lewin in his force field analysis identified the process of planned organisational change in terms of three stages, unfreezing–change–refreezing. This is also very relevant to the area of changing environmental attitudes and behaviours since it highlights the need to treat the process as developmental. In other words we need to monitor the process from the initial stages of investigation through the actual intervention to the follow-up evaluation. This is even more clearly illustrated in Lewin's action research approach (Fig. 15). This identifies the four important major stages of diagnosis, planning, action and evaluation, with each having several substages and with feedback between various stages which allow modification if effects turn out not

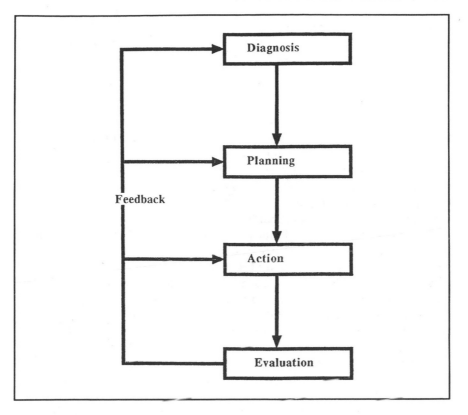

FIG. 15. Lewin's action research model.

to be as predicted. Environmental strategies are often of the "wind it up and let it go" variety with no attempt to monitor, evaluate, or modify. Particular problems do occur in evaluating the effectiveness of an environmental intervention, not least because any intervention now is likely only to begin to show effect in decades or even centuries hence. The multiple-level approach which incorporates sociological, political, economic, and technological factors as well as psychological factors in intervention, also requires that all these factors are controlled for, and assessed in evaluation. The problems of cost, time, and assessment strategies need to be overcome. In addition, as Stern (1992) points out, there are swings and roundabouts. For example a policy which makes cars more fuel efficient, means that they become cheaper to run, and some people may then decide to purchase bigger cars. The overall effect may mean stability rather than reduction in carbon monoxide emissions. More fuel-efficient heating and insulated homes leads to greater thermal comfort, but the fuel efficiency may encourage people to turn up the heat or leave it on for longer periods. As Stern (1992) suggests it is difficult to evaluate an intervention which only stabilises fuel use, but increases well-being.

Advocacy and activation

Another target for attitude and behaviour change is in increasing the likelihood that people will take action to change government policies, to influence decisions made by organisations or communities, and to change attitudes generally on environmental issues: in other words, a focus on what factors make people environmental activists. This area has largely been neglected by environmental psychologists in exchange for a focus on changing attitudes directly. In a way it is a bit like giving psychology away, in that an understanding of what makes people take action may then allow psychology to be shared so that those actions may be more effective. Some ideas can be gleaned from political psychology and sociology on factors that mobilise social action. In essence the basis of environmental activism lies in individual attitudes towards the environment, but it is more complex than that since many people who hold positive attitudes may not translate them into behaviour, and of those who do only a small number become active campaigners on environmental issues. There is evidence that activists score higher on measures of environmental concern than non-activists, that they have had greater exposure to the problems on which they become active, are generally more politically minded or have had more contact with other activists, have more knowledge of the issues and how to take effective action, and have a stronger sense of control or autonomy in regard to political issues. (Stern, 1992). Stern suggests that the latter two are of most importance, with attitudes determining the direction of political interest but knowledge and autonomy determining the level of activity. It is not really surprising that perceived powerlessness leads to inaction in regard to environmental issues and one must conclude that empowerment is an effective strategy in this area as well as in the areas of mental health discussed in the last chapter. Empowerment depends on social support, social identity, and a strong sense of social cohesion. Just as these factors make it more likely that attitudes will be reflected in behaviours, they may also lead those concerned to engage in political activity to promote their concerns.

A focus on children

We have already indicated that preschool children often have quite an advanced awareness of environmental issues, but that this awareness is not very effectively developed within the education process. Clearly there is a need to provide more effective environmental education which produces adults who have an accurate and realistic knowledge of the issues and how they may be tackled. On the other hand many children would appear to have an impoverished view of the natural world. There is little evidence on the differential effects in regard to environmental knowledge and attitudes between those growing up in different environments, for example the impoverished inner-city high rise environment compared to the rural or village setting. Kahn and Friedman (1995) did look at the environmental views of children from an inner city and found that they were quite sensitive to issues such as pollution. However they did not have a comparison group. A rather depressing note is sounded in a study by Hicks and Holden (1994) in the UK. They found that, while older children expressed concern about environmental issues, 50% felt there would be little they could do to make the world a better place. One of the ways in which children learn is through play, and again there is little evidence on how different types of play or play areas affect environmental attitudes. Planners and others involved in the design or allocation of play areas might consider how environmental awareness might be enhanced through this medium (Freeman, 1995).

Box 42: Population control:
The unacceptable face of environmentalism

While environmental problems are mainly a result of human inability to share and use resources sensibly, one cannot avoid the thorny issue of population. The massive increase in population size of the human species over the past few centuries has created the excessive demand which makes environmental conservation such an urgent issue. As already mentioned some theorists see war as the ultimate population control mechanism (Heilbroner, 1980), which raises the emotive issues promoted by the sociobiological perspective. Just as control over access to mates and territory among animals is ensured through aggression, sociobiologists argue that a major evolutionary function of aggression in humans is to achieve the same goal. In other words we are born with the instinct to aggress and ultimately the strong will survive while the weak will perish. Rather than allow such a pessimistic view to prevail it would appear that psychologists should consider how population control can be achieved through other means. The recent dying rooms tragedy reported from China, where baby girls are left to die in terrible conditions while boys are nurtured, raises the horrific spectre of government control of populations. This is an area of importance, but one where serious ethical issues are raised. It is important that social scientists do not ignore or avoid the issue.

SUMMARY

There is little doubt that humans are facing a crisis in terms of what we are doing to our world. We do need to recognise the dangers and to take action. Environmental psychologists have a worthwhile contribution to make and we have reviewed research which helps us to understand why we do abuse our world and what we might do to change our behaviour. Clearly there is much more that could be and needs to be done. There is a lot not yet understood and there is also a lot of theoretical evidence in the social psychological literature which has not been drawn on as yet. While the problems that are faced may be quite daunting, the knowledge that behaviour can be changed and that many avenues have not really been tried should be a cause for optimism and should inspire environmental psychologists to renewed efforts. An additional note of optimism may be generated by the studies of preschool children which show that they were aware of both environmental issues and what can be done about them even before school had had any influence on them.

CHAPTER NINE

Environmental psychology looking forward

We have covered quite a bit of ground, some of it not in as much depth or detail as we might have liked, and it is hoped that the reader will be inspired to follow up various areas of interest in other texts. I have tried to identify the major areas of contemporary environmental psychology and in so doing there have been many suggestions for future research. As a young field it has spawned many interesting ideas on the transaction between people and environments, and produced some conclusions that might guide future research and application. It is clear that it is the world inside the head, or the phenomic world which is individually constructed through interaction, that best explains behaviour and experience. In maintaining a healthy and happy relationship with ourselves and our world it is also clear that control and social support are important. We need to be empowered and supported by our environments and in this process the physical and social world are inseparable. In that we do have some control, autonomy and freedom to choose, we need to make wise choices in terms of the physical resources that we depend upon. There is much yet to be done in the field of environmental psychology, and in order to advance there is a need to be clear about the principles that guide our research and practice. Before going on to consider the potential future of the field it is important therefore to reconsider these basic principles which were introduced briefly in Chapter 1.

AN INTERACTIONAL PERSPECTIVE

The interactional or person-in-context perspective is central to environmental psychology as the title of this text suggests. It reflects a very basic assumption in environmental psychology that reciprocal relations of causality exist between the person and the environment. The person–situation debate, highlighted by Walter Mischel (1968) and hotly debated in the early 1970s, identifies the importance of this approach in concluding that behaviour cannot be explained in terms of either person variables or situational variables alone but rather in terms of an interaction between the two. What is often misunderstood, however, is the distinction between the additive effects of person and situation factors and their interaction. In other words research is more often a matter of assessing person factors and situational variables separately and then attempting to calculate their summative effect. What this type of research is lacking is an understanding of the process of interaction which Lewin was very concerned with. This element of interaction is captured to some extent in Barker and Wright's (1955) concept of behaviour setting and more so in David Cantor's (1977) concept of place, both of which were discussed in more detail in earlier chapters.

Research and practice—a reciprocal relationship

The fundamental interdependence of research and application is also central to the philosophy of Kurt Lewin who advocated action research whereby research is a problem-solving exercise focusing on real world problems, and where results inform both knowledge and practice. Lewin was particularly concerned by the separation that existed between academic psychology which took place in the universities, and the practice of psychology which took place in the real world. Environmental psychology adopts the approach that theory and practice are necessarily interrelated.

Levels of analysis

In understanding behaviour we may look for explanations at a number of levels: individual level, group level, and societal or organisational level. Psychology has traditionally sought individual-level explanations for behaviour and tended to ignore the larger scale environment. For example the five traditional perspectives in psychology, behaviourism, cognitive psychology, humanistic psychology, biological psychology, and psychodynamics, all focus on the individual in seeking causes for behaviour. Thus studies generally oversimplified environments (generally laboratories) and used a micro-level analysis. While these perspectives all contribute to an understanding of behaviour and experience, it is clear that no one perspective provides a complete explanation. In addition they tend to ignore factors at a more molar level, such as the influence of groups and social and cultural factors. These areas were traditionally the focus of other disciplines such as sociology and anthropology. However in applied psychology this is no longer the case. The need to include variables at all levels was a lesson learned through experience. For example, in work and organisational psychology, instigating change at the individual level is generally ineffective, unless changes in the attitudes of management and group factors are also part of the equation.

Environmental psychology moves towards a molar level of analysis by trying to understand the individual in her/his natural habitat. It is clear, for example, that an analysis of the experience of commuting must include consideration of economic and political factors that influence current transport policy and systems, especially at the level of trying to improve those systems.

Multiple methods and full-cycle research

Methodological issues are central to applied psychology because it is through the choice of method that the range of application will be limited or enhanced. With the growth in modern applications of psychology the limitations of conclusions based on laboratory research, which only samples a small part of behaviour in an artificial environment, become immediately apparent. This problem of ecological validity has led environmental psychologists to locate their research in real world settings. A good example was the work of Barker and Wright (1955) on behaviour settings, discussed in an earlier chapter. It must be acknowledged however that carrying out research in the real world is extremely difficult because of the large number of variables one has to deal with, the fact that one cannot control variables as is the case in laboratory research, and because the researcher is always in danger of influencing what happens simply by studying it, and of producing a Hawthorne effect. Because of these difficulties environmental psychology research sometimes doesn't reach the ideal level of ecological validity. This can to some extent be overcome by the use of a multimethod approach or a full-cycle model of research.

In environmental psychology a multimethod approach is used. In essence this reflects a philosophy of problem-centred research where the problem being investigated determines the method rather than the other way round. In experimental psychology it is often the case that topics which are not accessible by experimental methods are ignored. For example, the study of mental processes was rejected by early behaviourists. A preoccupation with methodology which over rides a concern to research important issues was described by Tajfel as analogous to packing one's bags for a journey never taken (Brown, 1988). A wide range of methods are available in psychology and are covered in introductory texts on research methods in psychology such as Breakwell, Hammond, and Fife-Schaw (1995). For the purposes of introducing students to the different methods they tend to be presented separately in introductory texts. However, in applied psychology methods often have to be combined or modified. In fact methodological issues are currently a topic of debate in psychology as is evidenced by recent publications in the area (Haworth, 1995; Smith, Harré, & van Langenhove, 1995). It is useful to think of the methods as a set of tools and, just like any other tools, they can be used in combination with each other and often for purposes other than that for which they were designed. As long as we all know and follow ethical guidelines and are aware of the reliability and validity of our methods we can be inventive in their application to applied problems. In this brief introduction to environmental psychology we have encountered a range of different methods and you will see how in combination they provide us with more valuable information.

The ideal model of research in environmental psychology is one which employs multiple methods and allows analysis at multiple levels. However this is not often the case in practice and often knowledge in an area is accumulated by integrating research carried out by different researchers, each using a single method. For example in the area of environmental perception, we draw on experimental work (Gibson, 1979), participant observations (Turnbull, 1961), attitude research using questionnaire and survey methods, and the work of Kelly (1955) which was based on clinical interviews and the role construct repertory grid. It should be fairly obvious why not many researchers actually use a multimethod approach. It is mainly because of the time and expense of such a large-scale project. However one can see at the same time that a more complete understanding is achieved when data from all sorts of sources and methods are collated.

Related to the issue of multiple methods is what is referred to as the full-cycle model of research where a variety of laboratory and field studies are combined to validate each other and provide a more complete understanding. In this approach a problem would be identified in the real world in the first instance. This might lead to a field study using either observational methods, surveys, interviews, diary methods, or a combination of the above. Because of the complexity of the data generated from a field study, it might be appropriate to design a laboratory study to test some of the initial conclusions. The outcome of the laboratory studies would then be retested in the real world. This cyclical process helps to clarify the problem and identify possible interventions for the applied psychologist and reflects a very healthy approach to research. Environmental psychology was the first applied approach to advocate both a multimethod approach and a full-cycle model.

Freewill, determinism, and the active or passive person

The whole process of research and application in any area of psychology is dependent on the assumptions which the researcher holds about people and these assumptions are inextricably bound up with the researcher's position on major philosophical questions. In some areas it is easier to avoid philosophical issues, such as freewill, than others. The issue of whether or not an individual has autonomy or freewill in determining their own actions is a source of some tension in psychology. Traditional perspectives have assumed that individuals have no autonomy and the only perspective that clearly acknowledges the person as having a role to play in determining their own actions is the humanistic perspective. The cognitive approach presents a model of the person as being active in the process of learning (for example Piaget's theory of development). However, although by implication an active role appears to involve some exercise of autonomy, the issue is not really explicitly dealt with in cognitive psychology. The issue becomes more pressing when we come to apply psychology. Related to the freewill issue is the question of whether the person plays an active or a passive role in behaviour. A basic assumption of environmental psychology is that the person is engaged in reciprocal relations of causality with the environment so that as well as being influenced by the environment they play an active role in modifying it. In doing so they exercise some degree of autonomy. Part of the process involves the person constructing their own view of the world so that reality is not so much what exists out there, but what exists within the person. Thus the model of the person in environmental psychology is one of an active person who exercises a degree of autonomy in their interactions with their environment and who constructs their own internal reality through giving meaning to their experience. It is useful to consider the ideas of George Kelly (1955) in regard to this issue of freewill–determinism.

The original model of the scientist

Kelly proposed a model of the person as a scientist who develops hypotheses about the world based on their experience of it and who continually tests and modifies these hypotheses as a result of new experiences. Despite the fact that this is suspiciously similar to the model of the person proposed by current cognitive psychology, where these hypotheses are the cognitive schemata or maps which guide behaviour and are developed and modified by experience (as in Neisser's and Gregory's models), Kelly is not given a central role in cognitive psychology. Kelly devised a very structured theory with a fundamental postulate and a number of related corollaries and a method for measuring constructs (the role construct repertory grid—rep grid for short) which has had widespread application in applied psychology.

Kelly, freewill, and cognitive psychology
According to Kelly the person develops constructs, cognitive schemata or cognitive maps, based on their experience within their physical and social environment and these cognitive maps or constructs determine how they attend to and process information from their environment. If the information doesn't match the construct or map, the construct or map is altered or modified. According to Kelly, constructs must be open to change and problems occur when an individual is unable to change a rigid construct despite the fact that it no longer fits with their current experience. Cognitive psychologists also focus on inappropriate cognitive schemata (Beck, 1976), or cognitive styles (Abramson, Seligman and Teasdale, 1978; Nezu, Nezu, & Perri, 1989), in explaining problem behaviour.

One of the main differences between Kelly and mainstream cognitive psychologists lies in dealing with the freewill (autonomy)–determinism issue. While the constructivist or top-down theories above tend to present cognition as adding an active dimension enabling the person to act on the information received, they tend not to go beyond this to the thorny issue of freewill versus determinism. Interpreting information and constructing images of reality imply some autonomy but the implication is often unsatisfactory. In employing scientific methods to seek out causes for behaviour, we assume that causes exist, therefore behaviour is determined. However an ambiguity exists between the psychologist and her/his subject matter. As Bannister and Fransella (1986) state:

> How many scientists, who say they are determinists, sound like determinists when they are describing the glory of scientific method? (p.6).

They talk of manipulating variables (freely chosen from any number of possible alternatives), choosing subjects, and choosing among alternative explanations the one that best fits the data. If all behaviour is determined where does the psychologist acquire choice? Some psychologists may deny their subjects the facility of being able to reflect on their behaviour, but I doubt if any would deny themselves the same ability. Kelly argues that the psychologist is fundamentally a person and inextricably bound up in the behaviour he or she aims to explain or predict. It is generally true that one can see links between the biography of a theorist and the types of theory they espouse. Psychology has effectively demonstrated that all persons are influenced by their developmental socialisation and psychologists are not excluded. This doesn't mean that we are necessarily victims of our own biography. Kelly argued that we may, however, enslave ourselves to it by believing in an unalterable determinism.

Bannister and Fransella (1986) argue that in Kelly's theory freewill–determined are simply two ends of a construct which we use to discriminate between acts and are only useful for this purpose. In other words we will construe some acts as determined and some as free. In fact it is probably more useful to see them as two ends of a continuum where no act is totally either free or determined. Stevens (1984) argues that at least an element of freewill or autonomy is available to the individual in reflexivity, i.e. their ability to reflect on their own experience. In reflecting on the causes for our behaviour we acquire some (albeit often limited) choice between alternative responses. Thus from a philosophy of constructive alternativism we gain some optimism in the existence of some element of autonomy in a largely determined world. In this sense Kelly's theory goes beyond the cognitive theories of perception of Neisser and Gregory, in that it postulates that the person not only interprets and constructs a phenomic world, but they do so at least partially by making choices. What Brunswick saw as a probabilistic process is more optimistically explained in terms of choices between alternatives.

An interdisciplinary approach

Related to the issue of levels of analysis and the advocacy of research and practice based in the real world is the need for an interdisciplinary approach. The traditional compartmentalising of disciplines in the academic world often leads to situations where several disciplines are covering some common areas. The most obvious examples are psychology and sociology. In understanding and modifying behaviour in the environment several disciplines make a contribution. For example those with backgrounds in architecture, environmental studies, social geography, urban studies, and anthropology will all have a contribution to make. In addition, to be effective in practice, environmental psychologists will need to take account of factors that fall within the domains of the other specialists just listed and more, since this is not an exhaustive list. This may be done through working with other specialists, or in some cases the environmental psychologist may have had training in some of the other disciplines. Interdisciplinary work is necessary in all areas of applied psychology and how well the interdisciplinary principle is put into practice is a determinant of the effectiveness of the approach. In this regard it is important to emphasise the need for environmental designers, and architects, to incorporate psychological research in the process of their work.

A holistic approach

Environmental psychology reflects a holistic rather than a reductionist philosophy in which it is recognised that reductionism is often necessary because of the complexity of the subject matter but where it can only be useful within a holistic framework. This is related to the levels of analysis discussed above, in particular the molar versus micro perspective. However, since the issue is an important one in both research and practice and has far-reaching implications for the philosophy of science applied to psychology, it is important to highlight it. Science has traditionally adopted a reductionist philosophy in which it is assumed that anything can be understood by breaking it down to its basic components. The objection to this comes from those who argue that "the whole is greater than the sum of its parts", and in psychology is represented by the Gestalt theorists (Wertheimer, 1944). The ultimate in reductionism is the assumption that everything in the universe will eventually be explained in terms of physics. However even in physics, reductionism is being challenged as a sound basis for science. As Stephen Hawking says in his book, *A brief history of time*:

> If everything in the universe depends on everything else in a fundamental way, it might be impossible to get close to a full solution by investigating parts of the problem in isolation (p.11).

Certainly in psychology it is widely accepted that events and experiences are interrelated (and interdependent) in fundamental ways which should make us wary of what can be gleaned from partial analysis. In environmental psychology reductionist approaches are seen as limited and would only be used in the context of a holistic model.

Multivariate methods

To meet the requirements of a holistic approach, methods used need to be mulivariate (i.e. using a large number of independent and dependent variables) rather than the more limited traditional univariate approach (one independent variable, one dependent variable). For example, in a study of commuter stress Novaco et al. (1990) produced an ecological model which located the person within their total environment and considered a wide range of both person and environmental variables. The model is presented in Fig. 1. This type of model allows for univariate research on aspects of the model which can then be related to the overall perspective. For example research on the sources of stress in the work domain may be carried out as a separate activity, but can only be fully interpreted with regard to the effects of other domains such as home, commuting, and leisure. It is easy to see once such a model is used how limited a reductionist, univariate approach is in the real world.

Systems models

Finally. a principle which is becoming more a part of applied psychology is the adoption of a systems model of the person and their world. The concept originated in biology where it describes not only the interrelatedness, but also the interdependence of biological processes.

In environmental psychology it is recognised that the person and their world operate in a similar fashion. The importance of a model like this becomes most obvious in application where change is being made in some aspect of the person–environment relationship. Instigating change in this way without recognising the possible unintended consequences can be disastrous. For instance, at present there is a new debate in the press and in government about the ill-effects of high rise housing. A simple, economic solution to housing may ignore very serious effects of that environment on individual and group behaviour. Now even government ministers are recognising that deteriorating mental health, family breakdown, and serious crimes are all likely results of not clearly considering the whole system in making a person- or environment-oriented intervention. Adopting a systems model allows the practitioner or the researcher to recognise important links and to avoid as far as possible the negative consequences of an intervention. The concept is inextricably bound up with the issues of reductionism and levels of analysis. Using a reductionist approach or a micro-level of analysis is likely to ignore the interdependence of parts.

These basic principles reflect the ways in which environmental psychologists currently approach research and practice. They are all logically interrelated. For example a systems model implies a molar level of analysis and a holistic philosophy. Not all text books will present the principles in the same format, but the basic ideas covered will generally be the same. An understanding of the principles enables us to better understand how environmental psychology relates to psychology in general and gives an insight into the approach adopted by the environmental psychologist.

Definitions revisited

Having considered some of the basic principles which unite those who participate in the discipline of environmental psychology we can see the narrowness of our previous definitions. While they provide an initial summary of what environmental psychology is, they are also rather uninformative. Incorporating the basic principles gives us a much broader understanding of the discipline. Veitch & Arkkelin (1995) recognise this in the definition they provide:

> a multidisciplinary behavioural science, both basic and applied in orientation, whose foci are the systematic interrelationships between the physical and social environments and individual human behaviour and experience.

From this discussion of definitions you will hopefully have gained some sense of what distinguishes environmental psychology as a discipline. However, it is hoped you will also have gained an understanding of the problems and limitations involved in defining a relatively new and developing area. It is a cause for optimism to recognise that psychology is a living discipline, alive with debates about theory, method, and application. As such it has changed and will continue to change. Change requires us to be flexible and therefore definitions will need to be changed as new topic areas evolve and greater understanding is gained about the causes for human behaviour and experience and about improved methods of intervention.

FUTURE DIRECTIONS

In each chapter I have identified areas where more research is needed and where current research indicates a potential direction for future productivity in the field. Let us now consider some common themes that have evolved.

Social identity and the environment

Social identity theory and the process of self-categorisation has evolved in social psychology as a reaction against individual level explanations for social behaviour and represents a higher order level of analysis incorporating group-level factors (Tajfel & Turner, 1979). It has been widely applied to the area of intergroup behaviour, but its potential in environmental psychology has not yet been tapped. There are at least three areas of environmental psychology wherein social identity theory offers a promising way forward.

Social identity, cohesion, and community

First of all there is the issue of how the physical environment enhances or restricts the development of social identities. People strive for a positive social identity and the physical environment will reflect and be reflected in the identity developed. For example economically deprived inner-city areas enhance the development of street gangs, each with a particular identity and territory. Territories marked with graffiti contribute to the incivilities discussed by Halpern (1995) which are important in perpetuating fear of crime. The levels of social cohesion and sense of community have been shown to be extremely important in satisfaction with one's neighbourhood and ultimately a determinant of both mental and physical health. The mechanism proposed is social support. Social cohesion is central to a sense of shared identity, and many of the aspects of neighbouring and community can be better understood in the context of social identity. It would appear that the re-establishment of a positive social identity in communities after moving to new towns is central to the healthy development of the new community and to other factors such as the fear of crime and use of facilities in the new neighbourhood.

Social identity and neighbourhood design

Designers of new neighbourhoods are faced with a dilemma in terms of whether they should be socially homogeneous or socially heterogeneous. Again social identity theory provides a useful framework. Homogeneous neighbourhoods tend to have a strong sense of common identity which provides social support and better health, but may strengthen the conflict with other neighbourhoods along the lines of already established social divisions such as race, religion, or social class. Heterogeneous neighbourhoods dilute the quality and quantity of social support through an exacerbation of different social identities and intergroup hostility. Hence a neighbourhood with a mixture of racial or religious groups tends to result in increased levels of both mental illness and fear of crime. Considering this problem in terms of how it influences social identity looks like being a very useful way forward.

Social identity and social dilemmas

Social identity theory allows us to understand conflict on the grand scale since identity varies between groups of different size. Our behaviour at various times may be in terms of small groups such as our immediate work group, or very large groups such as our nation. Thus we can conceptualise conflicts of interest which restrict collective social action on environmental issues in terms of different social identities. Using this approach we can begin to explore ways in which collective action might be enhanced by manipulating social identity.

An integration of psychological perspectives

It might be useful to consider the development of psychology within the framework of social identity theory. A range of different fields of study have developed which all set out their territories and defend them with some determination. Yet it should be clear from what we have covered that the boundaries are artificial and no longer useful. We have seen in most areas how people's transactions with the environment vary across the lifespan. The transaction is an ongoing process from childhood, with the environment enhancing or restricting development and with behaviour and experience being influenced differently in childhood, adulthood, old age, and so on. Some researchers have talked of developmental environmental psychology as a subdiscipline. In addition it is clear that health, community and clinical psychology intermingle with environmental psychology in areas such as environmental stress, effects of environments on mental health, and relationships within communities. We have covered the relationship between the environment and crime, or fear of crime, an area sometimes referred to as criminological environmental psychology. Without labouring the point too much, it seems that a future development in the field must be closer and more productive collaboration between the different fields.

The technological environment

Technological development over the past 30 years has outstripped anything that early inventors might have imagined. Communications, transport, and work have developed to a stage where everything can be done faster and on a grander scale. The negative side has been the increased demand on human abilities both to operate the technology and to cope with the stress generated, and ultimately the increased risk of large-scale accidents and disasters. The area of accident prevention, risk reduction, and dealing with disasters is likely to become a growth area. In addition technological advance has changed aspects of how we work and play. More people use computers, people communicate without ever meeting, working from home has been made possible for many, and we often play in a world of virtual reality. The effect of the technological environment on human behaviour and experience has only begun to be understood.

Language and the environment

The relationship between language and meaning has been hotly debated over the years. It is argued that since the written or spoken word is the only mechanism we have to describe the world, we can only think about things that we have language to describe (Sapir, 1947). Hence if we tell someone that we love them, the meaning of love is tied up with the words we use. Some of you may have realised that there are situations where the feeling or meaning that we want to express cannot be adequately captured in the words we have available. In so far as this is the case we can argue that meaning can transcend language. Whether meaning and thought are totally subject to language, or if it is that language is the servant of meaning, clearly the two are closely interrelated. The study of language has led some to argue that language is a form of negotiation in discourse and that attitudes and feelings are constructed through that discourse (Harré, 1995). For example the meaning we give to issues such as global warming and the attitudes we hold towards such issues would in this perspective only be understood through an analysis of discourse. In its extreme form discourse analysis is offered as a critique of traditional psychology and is suggested as a replacement for it. While not endorsing the extreme view it does seem that there is a need to explore the use of language in regard to environmental issues as part of an overall attempt to understand and change environmentally destructive behaviours.

Becoming an environmental psychologist

In a chapter in her book, *Psychology in perspective*, Hayes (1995) argues for the development of an ecopsychology with a focus on the ecology of behaviour. The suggestion is that all psychologists have a responsibility to their world to become active in preserving it. In this way every psychologist should be to some extent an environmental psychologist. However, as a profession, environmental psychology has been slow to develop. Becoming an environmental psychologist involves either completing one of the few MSc courses in environmental psychology offered at universities in the UK, or completing a research degree (PhD/DPhil) in an area of environmental research. It is then usual to go into either teaching or full-time research and to become involved in consultancy on a part-time basis. Many of those with a background in environmental psychology use it in other areas such as community psychology or criminological psychology. The most famous example is David Cantor who has moved from being one of the leading British environmental psyhologists to his current position as the leading British criminological or investigative psychologist. A similar process seems to be the norm in other countries.

What do environmental psychologists do?

The critical mass of environmental psychologists tend to be academics, teaching, carrying out research, and building a knowledge base. This is because there is no currently recognised profession of environmental psychologist in the way there is for other fields such as clinical or occupational psychology. There are postgraduate courses in environmental psychology leading to both masters and doctoral qualifications, but these are relatively few in comparison with some other fields. The most common route to a career in environmental psychology is through a postgraduate research degree. On completion individuals go into teaching, research, or a combination of the two.

Individuals who work as applied environmental psychologists tend to concentrate on consultancy regarding the behavioural aspects of building and other physical environmental structure design. Thus they might be consulted on any aspect of the process beginning with working out what the building is supposed to do (e.g. enhancing interaction in a home for the elderly), how the building might be designed to meet its aims, and assessing how effectively it does its job once it has been built and occupied. The opportunities for consultancy would appear to be increasing with the development of community psychology and the recognition of the social or people element in environmental psychology.

Throughout the text I have indicated areas for future research and application, and I have briefly outlined a few emergent themes. The research discussed in previous chapters should indicate the great need to understand more fully the transaction between people and environments and to translate that knowledge into practice in improving the human condition. It is hoped you will have gained some sense of the immediate relevance of psychology to understanding and improving the quality of everyday life. In addition you may have recognised the living quality of psychology in the fact that as a discipline it is continuously developing. Much has been done, but much is yet to be done. Before closing it might be useful to provide a definition of the field which reflects the approach taken in this book. Environmental psychology is:

> the application of psychological knowledge and method to understanding the process and implications of the human–environment transaction and applying the insight attained to improving the quality of the experience.

As Halpern (1995) suggests in the subtitle of his text, the environment is more than just bricks and mortar. It has provided a context for behaviour and experience and it deserves to be more fully understood if it is to continue to do so effectively.

References

Abe, K. (1982). *Introduction to disaster psychology.* Tokyo: Science Publications.

Abey-Wickerama, I., Brook, M.F., Gattoni, F.E.G., & Herridge, C.F. (1969). Mental hospital admission and aircraft noise, *Lancet, 2*(7633), 1275–1277.

Abrams, D., & Hogg, M.A. (1990). *Social identity theory: Constructive and critical advances.* London: Harvester/Wheatsheaf.

Abramson, L.Y., Seligman, M.E.P., & Teasdale, J.D. (1978). Learned helplessness in humans: A critique and reformulation. *Journal of Abnormal Psychology, 87,* 49–74.

Adams, J.S. (1965). Inequity in social exchange. In L. Berkowitz (Ed.), *Advances in experimental social psychology.* New York: Academic Press.

Ahrentzen, S.B. (1989). A place of peace, prospect and … a PC: The home as office. *Journal of Architectural and Planning Research, 6*(4), 271–288.

Aiello, J.R., Nicosla, G., & Thompson, D.E. (1979). Physiological, social and behavioural consequences of crowding on children and adolescents. *Child Development, 50,* 195–202.

Ainsworth, R.A., Simpson, L.E., & Cassell, D. (1993). Effects of three colours in an office interior on mood and performance. *Perceptual and Motor Skills, 76*(1), 235–241.

Ajzen. I. (1989). Attitude structure and behaviour. In A.R. Pratkanis, S.J. Breckler, & A.G. Greenwald (Eds.), *Attitude structure and function.* Hillsdale, NJ: Lawrence Erlbaum Associates Inc.

Ajzen, I., & Fishbein, M. (1980). *Understanding attitudes and predicting social behaviour.* Englewood Cliffs, NJ: Prentice-Hall.

Alington, D.E., Leaf, R.C., & Monaghan, J.R. (1992). Effects of stimulus colour, pattern and practice on sex differences in mental rotation task performance. *Journal of Psychology, 126*(5), 539–553.

241

Allport, F.H. (1955). *Theories of perception and the concept of structure*. New York: Wiley

Allport, G.W. (1954). *The nature of prejudice*. Reading, MA: Addison-Wesley.

Allport, G.W., & Pettigrew, T.F. (1957). Cultural influence on the perception of movement: The trapezoid illusion among Zulus. *Journal of Abnormal and Social Psychology, 55*, 104–113.

Alpert, G.P., & Crouch, B.M. (1991). Cross-gender supervision, personal privacy, and institutional security: Perceptions of jail inmates and staff. *Criminal Justice and Behaviour, 18*(3), 304–317.

Altman, I. (1975). *The environment and social behaviour: Privacy, personal space, territoriality and crowding*. Monterey, CA: Brooks/Cole.

Altman, I. (1976). Environmental psychology and social psychology. *Personality and Social Psychology Bulletin, 2*, 96–113.

Altman, I. (1986). *Theoretical issues in environmental psychology*. Paper presented to the 21st IAAP Congress, Jerusalem.

Altman, I., & Chemers, M. (1980). *Culture and environment*. Monterey, CA: Brooks/Cole.

Altman, I., Nelson, P.A., & Lett, E.E. (1972). *The ecology of home environments: Catalogue of selected documents in psychology*. Washington DC: APA.

Altman, I., & Stokols, D. (1987). *Handbook of environmental psychology*. New York: Wiley.

American Psychiatric Association (1980). *Diagnostic and Statistical Manual of Mental Disorders* (3rd ed.) (DSM–III). Washinghton DC.

Ames, A. (1955). *An interpretative manual: The nature of our perceptions, comprehensions and behaviour*. Princeton: Princeton University Press.

Andereck, K.L., & Becker, R.H. (1993). Perceptions of carry-over crowding in recreation environments. *Leisure Sciences, 15*(1), 25–35.

Anderson, C.A. (1989). Temperature and aggression: Ubiquitous effects of heat on occurrence of human violence. *Psychological Bulletin, 106*(1), 74–96.

Anderson, C.A., & Anderson, D.C. (1984). Ambient temperature and violent crime: Tests of the linear and curvilinear hypothesis. *Journal of Personality and Social Psychology, 46*, 91–97.

Anderson, E.A., & Spruill, J.W. (1993). The dual-career commuter family: A lifestyle on the move. *Marriage and Family Review, 19*(1–2), 131–147.

Anson, R.H., & Hancock, B.W. (1992). Crowding, proximity, inmate violence and the Eighth Amendment. *Journal of Offender Rehabilitation, 17*(3–4), 123–132.

Ardrey, R. (1966). *The territorial imperative*. New York: Atheneum.

Argyle, M., & Dean, J. (1965). Eye contact, distance and affiliation. *Sociometry, 28*, 289–304

Atkinson, W. (1985). Home/Work. *Personnel Journal, 64*(11), 104–109.

Aucliems, A. (1972). Some observed relationships between the atmospheric environment and mental health. *Environmental Research, 5*, 217–240.

Ayllon, T., & Azrin, N.H. (1968). *The token economy: A motivational system for therapy and rehabilitation*. New York: Appleton-Century-Crofts.

Baghurst, K.I., Baghurst, P.A., & Record, S.J. (1992). Public perceptions of the role of dietary and other environmental factors in cancer causation or prevention. *Journal of Epidemiology and Community Health, 46*(2), 120–126.

Baker, A., Davis, R., & Silvadon, P. (1960). *Psychiatric services and architecture*. Geneva: World Health Organisation.

Baker, S.P., Lamb, M.W., Li, G., & Dodd, R.S. (1993). Human factors in crashes of commuter airplanes. *Aviation, Space and Environmental Medicine, 64*(1), 63–68.

Bandura, A. (1977). *Social learning theory*. Englewood Cliffs, NJ: Prentice-Hall.

Bannister, D., & Fransella, F. (1986). *Inquiring man: The psychology of personal constructs* (3rd ed.). London: Routledge.

Barker, R.G. (1968). *Ecological psychology: Concepts and methods for studying the environment of human behaviour*. Stanford, CA: Stanford University Press.

Barker, R.G., & Wright, H. (1955). *Midwest and its children*. New York: Row and Petersen.

Barnard, J.D., Christophersen, E.R., & Wolf, M.M. (1977). Teaching children appropriate shopping behaviour through parent training in the supermarket setting. *Journal of Applied Behaviour Analysis, 10*(1), 49–59.

Barnes, B.L. (1992). Stress adjustments of railway personnel. *Journal of Personality and Clinical Studies, 8*(1–2), 57–61.

Baron, R.A. (1972). Aggression as a function of ambient temperature and prior anger arousal. *Journal of Personality and Social Psychology, 21*, 183–189.

Baron, R.A. (1978a). Aggression and heat: The "long hot summer" revisited. In A. Baum, S. Valins, & J.E. Singer (Eds.), *Advances in environmental research* (Vol.1, pp.186–207). Hillsdale, NJ: Lawrence Erlbaum Associates Inc.

Baron, R.A. (1978b). Invasions of personal space and helping: Mediating effects of invader's apparent need. *Journal of Experimental Social Psychology, 14*, 304–312.

Baron, R.A. (1983). Sweet smell of success? The impact of pleasant artificial scents on evaluations of job applicants. *Journal of Applied Psychology, 68*, 709–713.

Baron, R.A. (1987). Effects of negative ions on cognitive performance. *Journal of Applied Psychology, 72*(1), 131–137.

Baron, R.A., & Bell, P.A. (1975). Aggression and heat: Mediating effects of prior provocation and exposure to an aggressive model. *Journal of Personality and Social Psychology, 31*, 825–832.

Baron, R.A., Russell, G.W., & Arms, R.L. (1985). Negative ions and behaviour: Impact on mood, memory and aggression among Type A and Type B persons. *Journal of Personality and Social Psychology, 48*, 746–754.

Bauer, R.M., Greve, K.W., Besch, E.L., & Schramke, C.J. (1992). The role of psychological factors in the report of building related symptoms in sick building syndrome. *Journal of Consulting and Clinical Psychology, 60*(2), 213–219.

Baum, A., Aiello, J., & Davies, G. (1979). *Neighbourhood determinants of stress symptom perception*. Paper presented to the American Psychological Association Meeting, New York.

Beck, A.T. (1976). *Cognitive theory and the emotional disorders*. New York: International Universities Press.

Becker, F.D. (1984). Loosely-coupled settings: A strategy for computer-aided work decentralization. In B. Staw & L.L. Cummings (Eds.), *Research in organisational behaviour*. Greenwich, CT: JAI Press.

Becker, F.D., & Poe, D.B. (1980). The effects of user generated design modifications in a general hospital. *Journal of Nonverbal Behaviour, 4*, 195–218.

Becker, F.D., Sommer, R., Bee, J., & Oxley, B. (1973). College classroom ecology. *Sociometry, 36*, 514–525.

Bell, P.A., & Baron, R.A. (1976). Aggression and heat: The mediating role of negative affect. *Journal of Applied Social Psychology, 6*, 18–30.

Bell, P.A., & Fusco, M.E. (1989). Heat and violence in the Dallas field data: Linearity, curvilinearity and heteroscedasticity. *Journal of Applied Social Psychology, 19*(17), 1479–1482.

Bellizzi, J.A., Crowley, A.E., & Hasty, R.W. (1983). The effects of colour in store design. *Journal of Retailing, 59*(1), 21–45.

Bennett, C.P., Hague, A., & Perkins, C. (1991). The use of Baker–Miller pink in police operational and University experimental situations in Britain. *Internatiional Journal of Biosocial and Medical Research, 13*(1), 118–217.

Benton, R., & Funkhouser, G.R. (1994). Environmental attitudes and knowledge: An international comparison among business students. *Journal of Managerial Issues, 6*(3), 366–381.

Berg, M., & Medrich, E.A. (1980). Children in four neighbourhoods: The physical environment and its effect on play and play patterns. *Environment and Behaviour, 12*(3), 320–348.

Berk, R.A., Berk, S.F., Newton, P.J., & Loseke, D.R. (1980). Cops on call: Summoning the police to the scene of spousal violence. *Law and Society Review, 18*(3), 479–498.

Berkowitz, L. (1993). *Aggression: Its causes, consequences and control*. New York: McGraw-Hill.

Berkowitz, L., & LePage, A. (1967). Weapons as aggression-eliciting stimuli. *Journal of Personality and Social Psychology, 7*, 202–207.

Berlyne, D.E. (1960). *Conflict, arousal and curiosity*. New York: McGraw-Hill.

Bhattacharya, S.K., Tripathi, S.R., & Kashyap, S.K. (1989). The combined effects of noise and illumination on the performance efficiency of visual search and neuromotor task components. *Journal of Human Ergology, 18*(1), 41–51.

Biassoni-de-Serra, E.C. (1990). Effects of sonic contamination on the comprehension of oral speech by school children. *Revista Interamericana de Psicologia, 24*(2), 173–187.

Biner,, P.M., Butler, D.L., Lovegrove, T.E., & Burns, R.L. (1993). Windowlessness in the workplace: A re-examination of the compensation hypothesis. *Environment and Behaviour, 25*(2), 205–227.

Birley, J.L. (1987). Psychogeriatrics: The smell of success or the odour of chronicity? *International Journal of Geriatric Psychiatry, 2*(2), 131–134.

Blake, R.R., Rhead, C.C., Wedge, B., & Mouton, J.S. (1956). Housing architecture and social interaction. *Sociometry, 19*, 133–139.

Bloom, D.E. (1995). International public opinion on the environment. *Science, 269*(5222), 354–358.

Bluhm, C. (1992). Where otters exist as utters: Beauty, love and truth in the postmodern world. *Theory and Psychology, 2*(3), 391–396.

Bonnes, M., Bonaiuto, M., & Ercolani, A.P. (1991). Crowding and residential satisfaction in the urban environment: A contextual approach. *Environment and Behaviour, 23*(5), 531–552.

Bonnes, M., & Secchiaroli, G. (1995). *Environmental psychology: A psycho-social introduction*. London: Sage.

Borger, J.B., Lo, C.L., Oh, S.S., & Walberg, H.J. (1985). Effective schools: A quantitative synthesis of constructs. *Journal of Classroom Interaction, 20*(2), 12–17.

Box, S., Hale, C., & Andrews, G. (1988). Explaining fear of crime. *British Journal of Criminology, 28*(3), 340–356.

Boyatzis, C.J., & Varghese, R. (1994). Children's emotional associations with colours. *Journal of Genetic Psychology, 155*(1), 77–85.

Branthwaite, A., & Trueman, M. (1989). Explaining the effects of unemployment. In J. Hartley & A. Branthwaite (Eds.), *The applied psychologist*. Milton Keynes, UK: Open University Press.

Breakwell, G.M., Hammond, S., & Fife-Schaw, C. (Eds.) (1995). *Research methods in psychology*. London: Sage.

Breckler, S.J., & Fried, H.S. (1993). On knowing what you like and liking what you smell: Attitudes depend on the form in which the object is represented. *Personality and Social Psychology Bulletin, 19*(2), 228–240.

Brewer, M.B., & Schneider, S.K. (1990). Social identity and social dilemmas: A double-edged sword. In D. Abrams & M.A. Hogg (Eds.), *Social identity theory: Constructive and critical advances*. London: Harvester/Wheatsheaf.

Bronfenbrenner, U. (1977). The ecology of human development in retrospect and prospect. In H. McGurk (Ed.), *Ecological factors in human development*. Amsterdam: North-Holland.

Bronfenbrenner, U. (1979). *The ecology of human development*. Cambridge, MA: Harvard University Press.

Brooks, K.L., Mulaik, J.S., Gilead, M.P., & Daniels, B.S. (1994). Patient overcrowding in psychiatric hospital units: Effects on seclusion and restraint. *Administration and Policy in Mental Health, 22*(2), 133–144.

Brown, D., Sijpkes, P., & MacLean, M. (1986). The community role of public indoor space. *Journal of Architectural and Planning Research, 3*(2), 161–172.

Brown, G.W., & Harris, T.O. (1978). *The Bedford College Life Events and Difficulty Schedule: Directory of contextual threat ratings of events*. London: Bedford College, University of London.

Brown, G.W., & Harris, T.O. (Eds.) (1989). *Life events and illness*. London: Unwin-Hyman.

Brown, I.D. (1994). Driver fatigue. *Human Factors, 36*(2), 298–314.

Brown, R. (1988). *Group Processes*. Oxford: Blackwell.

Brown, R. (1996). *Prejudice*. Oxford: Blackwell.

Brunetti, F.A. (1972). Noise, distraction and privacy in conventional and open school environments. In W.J. Mitchell (Ed.), *Environmental design: Research and practice*. LA: University of California Press.

Brunswick, E. (1947). *Systematic and representative design of psychological experiments*. LA: University of California Press.

Brunswick, E. (1957). Scope and aspects of cognitive problems. In J. Bruner et al. (Eds.), *Contemporary approaches to cognition*. Cambridge, MA: Harvard University Press.

Bull, A.J., Burbage, S.E., Crandall, J.E., Fletcher, C.I., Lloyd, J.T., Ravenberg, R.L., & Rockett, S.L. (1972). Effects of noise and intolerance of ambiguity upon attraction for similar and dissimilar others. *Journal of Social Psychology, 88*, 151–152.

Bull, R., & Brooking, J. (1985). Does marriage influence whether a facially disfigured person is considered physically unattractive? *Journal of Psychology, 119*(2), 163–167.

Bull, R., & Stevens, J. (1981). The effects of facial disfigurement on helping behaviour. *Italian Journal of Psychology, 8*(1), 25–33.

Bullinger, M. (1989). Psychological effects of air pollution on healthy residents: A time series approach. *Journal of Environmental Psychology, 9*(2), 103–118.

Bunker-Hellmich, L.A. (1987). A case study of space use and visiting policy in a neonatal intensive care unit. *Children's Environments Quarterly, 4*(3), 25–32.

Burns, T. (1964). Nonverbal communication. *Discovery,* 31–35.

Burroughs, W.J. (1989). Applied environmental psychology. In W.L. Gregory & W.J. Burroughs (Eds.), *Introduction to applied psychology.* London: Scott, Foresman and Company.

Bushnell, F.K.L., & Deforge, V. (1994). Seasonal affective disorder. *Perspectives in Psychiatric Care, 30*(4), 21–25.

Byerley, W.F., Brown, J., & Lebeque, B. (1987). Treatment of seasonal affective disorder with morning light. *Journal of Clinical Psychiatry, 48,* 447–448.

Cairns, E. (1988a). *Caught in the crossfire: Children of the troubles.* Belfast: Appletree.

Cairns, E. (1988b). Social class, psychological well-being and minority status in Northern Ireland. *International Journal of Social Psychiatry, 35*(3), 231–236.

Caldwell, M.D. (1976). Communication and sex effects in a five-person prisoner's dilemma game. *Journal of Personality and Social Psychology, 33,* 273–280.

Calhoun, J.B. (1962). Population density and social pathology. *Scientific American, 206,* 136–148.

Calhoun, J.B. (1973). Death squared: The explosive growth and demise of a mouse population *Proceedings of the Royal Society of Medicine, 66,* 80–88.

Cameron, P., Robertson, D., & Zaks, J. (1972). Sound pollution, noise pollution and health: Community parameters. *Journal of Applied Psychology, 56,* 67–74.

Cangelosi, V.E., & Lemoine, L.F. (1988). Effects of open versus closed physical environment on employee perception and attitude. *Social Behaviour and Personality, 16*(1), 71–77.

Cantor, D. (1968). *The measurement of meaning in architecture.* Unpublished manuscript. Glascow Building Performance Research Unit.

Cantor, D. (1969). An intergroup comparison of connotative dimensions. *Environment and Behaviour, 1,* 37–48.

Cantor, D. (1970). *Architectural psychology.* London: Royal Institute of British Architects.

Cantor, D. (1977). *The psychology of place.* London: Architectural Press.

Cantor, D. (1983). The purposive evaluation of places: A facet approach. *Environment and Behaviour, 15,* 659–698.

Cantor, D. (1986). Putting situations in their place: Foundations for a bridge between social and environmental psychology. In A. Furnham (Ed.), *Social behaviour in context.* London: Allyn and Bacon.

Cantor, D., & Thorne, R. (1972). Attitudes to housing: A cross cultural comparison. *Environment and Behaviour, 4,* 3–32.

Cantril, H. (1950). *The "why" of man's experience.* New York: Macmillan.

Cantrill, J.G. (1992). Understanding environmental advocacy: Interdisciplinary research and the role of cognition. *Journal of Environmental Education, 24*(1), 35–42.

Carlsmith, J.M., & Anderson, C.A. (1979). Ambient temperature and the occurrence of collective violence: A new analysis. *Journal of Personality and Social Psychology, 37,* 337–344.

Carron, A.V., Brawley, L.R., & Widmeyer, W.N. (1990). The impact of group size in an exercise setting. *Journal of Sport and Exercise Psychology, 12*(4), 376–387.

Cassidy, T. (1992). Commuting-related stress: Consequences and implications. *Employee Counselling Today, 4*(2), 15–21.

Cassidy, T. (1994a). Current psychological perspectives on stress: A brief guided tour. *Management Bibliographies and Reviews, 20*(3), 2–12.

Cassidy, T. (1994b). *Cognitive appraisal and vulnerability to stress in the development of healthiness.* Paper presented to the BPS Annual Conference.

Cassidy, T. (1996). All work and no play: A focus on leisure time as a means for promoting health. *Counselling Psychology Quarterly, 9*(1), 77–90.

Cassidy, T., & Lynn, R. (1991). Achievement motivation, educational attainment, cycles of disadvantage and social competence. *British Journal of Educational Psychology, 61,* 1–12.

Chapman, D., & Thomas, G. (1944). Lighting in dwellings. *Post War Building Studies 12.*

Chattopadhyay, P.K., Som, B., & Biswas, D. (1993). Air pollution and health hazards: An exploratory study. *Indian Journal of Clinical Psychology, 20*(1), 25–30.

Cherpitel, C.J. (1992). The epidemiology of alcohol-related trauma. *Alcohol Health and Research World, 16*(3), 191–196.

Cherpitel, C.J. (1994). Cause of casualty and drinking patterns: An emergency room study of unintentional injuries. *Drug and Alcohol Dependence, 35*(1), 61–67.

Cherulnik, P.D. (1993). *Applications of environment-behaviour research: Case studies and analysis.* New York: Cambridge University Press.

Christensen, K. (1989). Home-based clerical work: No simple truth; no single reality. In E. Boris & C. Daniels (Eds.), *Homework.* Urbana, IL: University of Illinois Press.

Christensen, K. (1993). Eliminating the journey to work. In C. Katz & J. Monk (Eds.), *Full circles: Geographies of women over the life course.* London: Routledge.

Cialdini, R.B. (1980). Full cycle social psychology. In L. Bickman (Ed.), *Applied Social Psychology Annual* (Vol.1). Beverly Hills, CA: Sage.

Classen, C. (1990), Sweet colours, fragrant songs: Sensory models of the Andes and the Amazon. *American Ethologist, 17*(4), 722–735.

Cocchi, A. (1989). The reality of utopia: Elimination of the psychiatric hospital—Utopia or reality? *Rivista Sperimentale di Freniatria e Medicina Legale delle Aliena zioni Mentali, 109*(6), 1352–1354.

Cochrane, J.J., & Freeman, S.J. (1989). Working in Arctic and sub-Arctic conditions: Mental health issues. *Canadian Journal of Psychiatry, 34*(9), 884–890.

Cochrane, R. (1983). *The social creation of mental illness.* London: Longman.

Cohen, H., Moss, S., & Zube, E. (1979). Pedestrians and wind in the urban environment. *Environmental Design Research Association, 10,* 71–82.

Cohen, S. (1978). Environmental load and the allocation of attention. In A. Baum, J.E. Singer, & S. Valins (Eds.), *Advances in environmental psychology* (Vol.1). Hillsdale, NJ: Lawrence Erlbaum Associates Inc.

Cohen, S., Glass, D.C., & Singer, J.E. (1973). Apartment noise, auditory discrimination and reading ability in children. *Journal of Experimental Social Psychology, 9,* 407–422.

Cohen, S., & Horm-Wingerd, D.M. (1993). Children and the environment: Ecological awareness among preschool children. *Environment and Behaviour, 25*(1), 103–120.

Cohen, S., & Trostle, S.L. (1990). Young children's preferences for school-related physical-environmental setting characteristics. *Environment and Behaviour, 22*(6), 753–766.

Cohen, S., & Weinstein, N. (1981). Non-auditory effects of noise on behaviour and health. *Journal of Social Issues, 37,* 36–70.

Cohn, E.G. (1993). The prediction of police calls for service: The influence of weather and temporal variables on rape and domestic violence. *Journal of Environmental Psychology, 13*(1), 71–83.

Collett, D. (1971). Training Englishmen in the nonverbal behaviour of Arabs. *International Journal of Psychology, 6,* 209–215.

Collins-Eiland, K., Dansereau, D.F., Brooks, L.W., & Holley, C.D. (1986). Effects of conversational noise, locus of control and field dependence/independence on the performance of academic tasks. *Contemporary Educational Psychology, 11*(2), 139–149.

Conan, M. (1987). Dwellers' involvement in housing design: A developmental perspective. *Journal of Architectural and Planning Research, 4*(4), 301–309.

Cook, M. (1970). Experiments in orientation and proxemics. *Human Relations, 23,* 61–76.

Coolican, H. (1994). *Research methods and statistics in psychology* (2nd ed.). London: Hodder & Stoughton.

Coombs, C.H., Dawes, R.M., & Tversky, A. (1970). *Mathematical psychology: An elementary introduction.* Englewood Cliffs, NJ: Prentice Hall.

Cooper, I. (1985). Teachers' assessments of primary school buildings: The role of the physical environment in education. *British Educational Research Journal, 11*(3), 253–269.

Coren, S., & Halpern, D.F. (1991). Left-handedness: A marker for decreased survival fitness. *Psychological Bulletin, 109*(1), 90–106.

Coren, S., Porac, C., & Ward, L.M. (1984). *Sensation and perception.* Toronto: Academic Press.

Corwin, J., Loury, M., & Gilbert, A.N. (1995). Workplace, age and sex as mediators of olfactory function: Data from the National Geographic Smell Survey. *Journals of Gerontology—Series B: Psychological Sciences and Social Sciences, 50b*(4), 179–186.

Costa, G., Pickup, L., & Di-Martino, V. (1988). Commuting—a further stress factor for working people: Evidence from the European Community, Part ii, An empirical study. *International Archives of Occupational and Environmental Health, 60*(5), 377–385.

Cover, J.D. (1995). The effects of social contact on prejudice. *Journal of Social Psychology, 135*(3), 403–405.

Craik, K.H. (1976). The personality research paradigm in environmental psychology. In S. Wapner, S.B. Cohen, & B. Kaplan (Eds.), *Experiencing the environment.* New York: Plenum.

Crockford, G.W. (1967). Heat problems and protective clothing in iron and steel works. In C.N. Davies, P.R. Davis, & F.H. Tyler (Eds.), *The effects of abnormal physical conditions at work.* London: Livingstone.

Crowell, B.A., George, L.K., Blazer, D., & Landerman, R. (1986). Psychosocial risk factors and urban-rural differences in the prevalence of major depression. *British Journal of Psychiatry, 149,* 307.

Curley, M.D., & Hawkins, R.N. (1983). Cognitive performance during a heat acclimatisation regimen. *Aviation, Space and Environmental Medicine, 54*(8), 709–713.

Cytowic, R.E. (1993). *The man who tasted shapes*. New York: Putnam.

Dahl, R. (1957). The concept of power. *Behavioural Scientist, 2*, 201–215.

Dahrendorf, R. (1959). *Class and class conflict in industrial society*. Stanford: Stanford University Press.

Davey, G.C.L. (1994). Worrying, social problem-solving abilities and social problem-solving confidence. *Behaviour Research and Therapy, 32*(3), 327–330.

David, A.S., & Wessely, S.C. (1995). The legend of Camelford: Medical consequences of a water pollution accident. *Journal of Psychosomatic Research, 39*(1), 1–9.

Davies, D.R., Lang, L., & Shackleton, V.J. (1973). The effect of music and task difficulty on performance of a visual vigilance task. *British Journal of Psychology, 64*, 383–389.

Dawes, R.M. (1980). Social dilemmas. *Annual Review of Psychology*.

Dean, K., & James, H. (1984). Depression and schizophrenia in an English city. In H. Freeman (Ed.), *Mental health and the environment*. London: Churchill Livingstone.

DeJoy, D.M. (1984). The non-auditory effects of noise: Review and perspectives for research. *Journal of Auditory Research, 24*(2), 123–150.

Deregowski, J.B. (1980). *Illusions, patterns and pictures: A cross-cultural perspective*. London: Academic Press.

Desor, J.A. (1972). Toward a psychological theory of crowding. *Journal of Personality and Social Psychology, 21*, 79–89.

Devlin, A.S. (1992). Psychiatric ward renovation: Staff perception and patient behaviour. *Environment and Behaviour, 24*(1), 66–84.

Devlin, K., & Nasar, J.L. (1989). The beauty and the beast: Some preliminary comparisons of "high" versus "popular" residential architecture and some public versus architect judgments of same. *Journal of Environmental Psychology, 9*, 333–344.

Dewey, J., & Bentley, A. (1949). *Knowing and known*. Boston: Beacon Press.

Dorn, L., & Matthews, G. (1992). Two further studies of personality correlates of driver stress. *Personality and Individual Differences, 13*(8), 949–951.

Doty, R.L. (1981). Olfactory communication in humans. *Chemical Senses, 6*(4), 351–376.

Doty, R.L., Applebaum, S., Zusho, H., & Settle, R.G. (1985). Sex differences in odour identification ability: A cross-cultural analysis. *Neuropsychologia, 23*(5), 667–672.

Doty, R.L., Green, P.A., Applebaum, S., Ram, C., & Yankell, S.L. (1984). Smell identification ability: Changes with age. *Science, 226*(4681), 1441–1443.

Doty, R.L., Green, P.A., Ram, C., & Yankell, S.L. (1982). Communication of gender from human breath odours: Relationship to perceived intensity and pleasantness. *Hormones and Behaviour, 16*(1), 13–22.

Downs, R.M., & Meyer, J.T. (1978). Geography and the mind: An exploration of perceptual geography. *American Behavioural Scientist, 22*, 59–78.

Dubos, R. (1965). *Man adapting*. New Haven, CT: Yale University Press.

Dumont, J. (1989). Validity of multidimensional scaling in the context of structured conceptualization. Special issue. Concept mapping for evaluation and planning. *Evaluation and Program Planning, 12*(1), 81–86.

Dwyer, W.O., Leeming, F.C., Cobern, M.K., Porter, B.E. (1993). Critical review of behavioural interventions to preserve the environment: Research since 1980. *Environment and Behaviour, 25*(3), 275–321.

Edney, J.J. (1972). Property, possession and permanence: A field study in human territoriality. *Journal of Applied Social Psychology, 2*, 275–282.

Edwards, J.N., Fuller, T.D., Sermsri, S., & Vorakitphokatorn, S. (1992). Household crowding and reproductive behaviour. *Social Biology, 39*(3–4), 212–230.

Edwards, J.N., Fuller, T.D., Sermsri, S., & Vorakitphokatorn, S. (1994). Why people feel crowded: An examination of objective and subjective crowding. *Population and Environment, 16*(2), 149–173.

Endler, N.S. (1982). Interactionism comes of age. In M.P. Zanna, E.T. Higgins, & C.P. Herman (Eds.), *Consistency in social behaviour: The Ontario Symposium* (Vol.2). Hillsdale, NJ: Lawrence Erlbaum Associates Inc.

Endler, N.S. (1983). Interactionism: A personality model but not yet a theory. In M.M. Page (Ed.), *Personality: Current theory and research: 1982 Nebraska Symposium on Motivation*. Lincoln, NE: University of Nebraska Press.

Engen, T. (1987). Remembering odours and their names. *American Scientist, 75*(5), 497–503.

Epstein, Y.M. (1982). Crowding stress and human behaviour. In G.W. Evans (Ed.), *Environmental stress*. Cambridge: Cambridge University Press.

Epstein, Y.M., Woolfolk, R.L., & Lehrer, P.M. (1981). Physiological, cognitive and nonverbal responses to repeated exposure to crowding. *Journal of Applied Social Psychology, 11*, 1–13.

Essa, E.L., Hilton, J.M., & Murray, C.I. (1990). The relationship between weather and preschoolers' behaviour. *Children's Environments Quarterly, 7*(3), 32–36.

Evans, G.W. (1979). Crowding and human performance. *Journal of Applied Social Psychology, 9*, 27–46.

Evans, G.W., & Lepore, S.J. (1993). Household crowding and social support: A quasiexperimental analysis. *Journal of Personality and Social Psychology, 65*(2), 308–316.

Evans, G.W., & Lovell, B. (1979). Design modification in an open-plan school. *Journal of Educational Psychology, 71*, 41–49.

Evans, G.W., Palsane, M.N., Lepore, S.J., & Martin, J. (1989). Residential density and psychological health: The mediating effects of social support. *Journal of Personality and Social Psychology, 57*(6), 994–999.

Fedoroff, I.C., Stoner, S.A., Anderson, A.E., Doty, R.L. (1995). Olfactory dysfunction in anorexia and bulimia nervosa. *International Journal of Eating Disorders, 18*(1), 71–77.

Ferrari, J.R., & Baldwin, C.H. (1989). From cars to carts: Increasing safety belt usage in shopping carts. *Behaviour Modification, 13*(1), 51–64.

Festinger, L. (1954). A theory of social comparison processes. *Human Relations, 7*, 117–140.

Festinger, L., Schachter, S., & Back, K. (1950). *Social pressure in informal groups*. Stanford: Stanford University Press.

Festinger, L.A. (1957). *A theory of cognitive dissonance*. Evanston, IL: Row-Peterson.

Field, S. (1992). The effect of temperature on crime. *British Journal of Criminology, 32*(3), 340–351.

Firestone, I.J., Lichtman, C.M., & Evans, J.R. (1980). Privacy and solidarity: Effects of nursing home accommodation on environmental perception and sociability preferences. *International Journal of Aging and Human Development, 11*(3), 229–241.

Fischer, C.S. (1976). *The urban experience*. New York: Harcourt Brace Jovanovich.

Fisher, J.D., & Byrne, D. (1975). Too close for comfort: Sex differences in response to invasions of personal space. *Journal of Personality and Social Psychology, 32*(1), 15–21.

Fisher, S., & Reason, J. (1988) (Eds.). *Handbook of life stress, cognition and health*. Chichester, UK: Wiley.

Fleming, J.W., Holmes, S., & Barton, L. (1988). Differences in colour preferences of school-age children in varying stages of health: A preliminary study. *Maternal Child Nursing Journal, 17*(3), 173–189.

Folkins, C., O'Reilly, C., Roberts, K., & Miller, S. (1977). Physical environment and job satisfaction in a community mental health centre. *Community Mental Health Journal, 13*(1), 24–30.

Fowler, E.P. (1987). Street management and city design. *Social Forces, 66*(2), 365–389.

Freeman, C. (1995). Planning and play: Creating greener environments. *Children's Environments, 12*(3), 381–388.

Freeman, H.F. (1986). Environmental stress and psychiatric disorder. *Stress Medicine, 2*, 291–299.

Fried, M. (1963). Grieving for a lost home. In L.J. Duhl (Ed.), *The urban condition*. New York: Basic Books.

Fuller, T.D., Edwards, J.N., Sermsri, S., & Vorakitphokatorn, S. (1993a). Housing, stress, and physical well-being: Evidence from Thailand. *Social Science and Medicine, 36*(11), 1417–1428.

Fuller, T.D., Edwards, J.N., Vorakitphokatorn, S., & Sermsri, S. (1993b). Household crowding and family relations in Bangkok. *Social Problems, 40*(3), 410–430.

Gabe, J., & Williams, P. (1987). Women, housing and mental health. *International Journal of Health Services, 17*(4), 667–679.

Gallagher, R.M., Marbach, J.J., Raphael, K.G., Handte, J., et al. (1995). Myofascial face pain: Seasonal variability in pain intensity and demoralisation. *Pain, 61*(1), 113–120.

Galle, O.R., Gove, W.R., & McPherson, J.M. (1972). Population density and pathology: What are the relationships for man? *Science, 176*, 23–30.

Garcia-Carretero, L.I., Liorca-Romon, G., Villoria-Medina, M.J., Blazquez, J.M. (1989). Relationship between psychiatric emergencies and meteorological factors. *Actas Luso Espanolas de Neurologia, Psiquitria y Ciencias Afines, 14*,(2), 85–94.

Geen, R.G., McCown, E.J., & Broyles, J.W. (1985). Effects of noise on sensitivity of introverts and extraverts to signals in a vigilance task. *Personality and Individual Differences, 6*(2), 237–241.

Geen, R.G., & O'Neal, E.C. (1969). Activation of cue-elicited aggression by general arousal. *Journal of Personality and Social Psychology, 11*, 289–292.

Gehlbach, R.D., & Partridge, M.J. (1984). Physical environmental regulation of verbal behaviour during play. *Instructional Science, 13*(3), 225–242.

Geller, E.S., Winett, R.A., & Everett, P.B. (1982). *Preserving the environment: New strategies for behaviour change*. Elmsford, NY: Pergamon Press.

Genhart, M.J., Kelly, K.A., Coursey, R.D., & Datiles, M. (1993). Effects of bright light on mood in normal elderly women. *Psychiatry Research, 47*(1), 87–97.

Gibson, E.J., & Walk, R. (1960). The "visual cliff". *Scientific American, 202*, 64–71.

Gibson, J.J. (1950). *The perception of the physical world*. Boston: Houghton Mifflin.

Gibson, J.J. (1979). *The ecological approach to visual perception*. Boston: Houghton Mifflin.

Gifford, R. (1982). Projected interpersonal distance and orientation choice: Personality, sex and social situations. *Social Psychology Quarterly, 45*, 145–152.

Gifford, R. (1987). *Environmental psychology: principles and practice*. Boston: Allyn & Bacon.

Gifford, R., & Peacock, J. (1979). Crowding: More fearsome than crime-provoking? Comparison of an Asian city and a North American city. *Psychologia, 22*, 79–83.

Gifford, R., & Wells, J. (1991). FISH: A commons dilemma simulation. *Behaviour Research Methods, Instruments and Computers, 23*(3), 437–441.

Gigliotti, L.M. (1994). Environmental issues: Cornell students' willingness to take action, 1990. *Journal of Environmental Education, 26*(1), 34–42.

Gill, W.M. (1977). A look at the change to open-plan schools in New Zealand. *New Zealand Journal of Educational Studies, 12*, 3–16.

Gilliam, J.E. (1991). The effects of Baker–Miller pink on physiological and cognitive behaviour of emotionally disturbed and regular education students. *Behavioural Disorders, 17*(1), 47–55.

Gilliam, J.E., & Unruh, D. (1988). The effects of Baker–Miller pink on biological, physical and cognitive behaviour. *Journal of Orthomolecular Medicine, 3*(4), 202–206.

Gist, R., & Lubin, B. (1989). *Psychosocial aspects of disasters*. Chichester: Wiley.

Glass, D.C., & Singer, J.E. (1972). *Urban stress*. New York: Academic Press.

Glendon, A.I., Dorn, L., Matthews, G., Gulian, E., Davies, D.R., & Debney, L.M. (1993). Reliability of the Driving Behaviour Inventory. *Ergonomics, 36*(6), 719–726.

Goduka, I.N., Poole, D.A., & Aotaki-Phenice, L. (1992). A comparative study of black South African children from three different contexts. *Child Development, 63*(3), 509–525.

Goffman, E. (1959). *The presentation of self in everyday life*. New York: Doubleday.

Gold, J.R. (1980). *An introduction to behavioural geography*. Oxford: Oxford University Press.

Gold, S.M. (1977). Neighbourhood parks: The nonuse phenomenon. *Evaluations Quarterly, 1*(2), 319–328.

Gove, W.R., & Hughes, M. (1983). *Overcrowding in the household*. New York: Academic Press.

Greenberg, R.A., Strecher, V.J., Bauman, K.E., & Boat, B.W., et al. (1994). Evaluation of a home based intervention programme to reduce infant passive smoking and lower respiratory illness. *Journal of Behavioural Medicine, 17*(3), 273–290.

Greene, B.F., Bailey, J.S., & Barber, F. (1981). An analysis and reduction of disruptive behaviour on school buses. *Journal of Applied Behaviour Analysis, 14*(2), 177–192.

Greene, K., Parrott, R., & Serovich, J.M. (1993). Privacy, HIV testing, and AIDS: College students' versus parents' perspectives. *Health Communication, 5*(1), 59–74.

Greening, L., & Dollinger, S.J. (1992). Illusions (and shattered illusions) of invulnerability: Adolescents in natural disaster. *Journal of Traumatic Stress, 5*(1), 63–75.

Gregory, R.L. (1966). *Eye and brain.* New York: McGraw-Hill.

Gregory, R.L. (1973). The confounded eye: In R.L. Gregory & E.H. Gombrich (Eds.), *Illusions in nature and art.* London: Duckworth.

Groat, L. (Ed.) (1985). *Readings in environmental psychology: Giving places meaning.* London: Academic Press.

Grobe, R.P., Pettibone, T.J., & Martin, D.W. (1973). Effects of lecturer pace on noise level in a university classroom. *Journal of Educational Research, 67*(2), 73–75.

Grosjean, L., Lodi, R., & Rabinowitz, J. (1976). Noise and pedagogic efficiency in school activities. *Experientia, 32*(5), 575–576.

Guardo, C.J., & Meisels, M. (1971). Child-parent spatial patterns under praise and reproof. *Developmental Psychology, 5*, 365.

Gulian, E., Glendon, A.I., Matthews, G., Davies, D.R., & Debney, L.M. (1990). The stress of driving: A diary study. *Work and Stress, 4*(1), 7–16.

Gulian, E., Matthews, G., Glendon, A.I. & Davies, D.R. (1989). Dimensions of driver stress. *Ergonomics, 32*(6), 555–560

Guski, R., Wichmann, U., Rohrmann, B., & Finke, H.O. (1981). Construction and application of a questionnaire for social scientific study of the effects of environmental noise. *Zeitschrift fur Sozialpsychologie, 9*(1), 50–65.

Gutheil, I.A. (1992). Considering the physical environment: An essential component of good practice. *Social Work, 37*(5), 391–396.

Gutkowski, S., & Guttman, F. (1992). Programme and process: Designing the physical space of a day hospital. *Israel Journal of Psychiatry and Related Sciences, 29*(3), 167–173.

Hall, E.T. (1959). *The silent language.* New York: Doubleday.

Hall, E.T. (1966). *The hidden dimension.* Garden City, NY: Doubleday.

Halmiova, O., & Potasova, A. (1994). The effects of environmental neurotoxins on performances of children in sensorimotor tasks. *Studia Psychologica, 36*(2), 103–111.

Halpern, D.S. (1987). Architectural preference and mere exposure effects: The role of recognition in attitudinal enhancement by exposure: Cited in D. Halpern (1995), *Mental health and the built environment.* London: Taylor & Francis.

Halpern, D.S. (1993). Minorities and mental health. *Social Science and Medicine, 36*(5), 597–607.

Halpern, D. (1995). *Mental health and the built environment.* London: Taylor & Francis.

Hamid, P.N., & Newport, A.G. (1989). Effect of colour on physical strength and mood in children. *Perceptual and Motor Skills, 69*(1), 179–185.

Hancock, P.A. (1986). Sustained attention under thermal stress. *Psychological Bulletin, 99*(2), 263–281.

Hansard. (1943). House of Commons rebuilding. *Parliamentary debates: House of Commons, 393* (114). London: HMSO.

Hare, E.N., & Shaw, G.K. (1965). Mental health on a new housing estate. *Maudsley Monograph, 12*. Oxford: Oxford University Press.

Harré, R. (1995). Discursive psychology. In J.A. Smith, R. Harré, & L. van Langenhove, *Rethinking psychology*. London: Sage.

Harrell, G., Hutt, M., & Anderson, J. (1980). Path analysis of buyer behaviour under conditions of crowding. *Journal of Marketing Research*.

Hartman, C. (1963). Social values and housing orientations. *Journal of Social Issues, 19*(2), 155–168.

Hathaway, W.E. (1995). Effects of school lighting on physical development and school performance. *Journal of Educational Research, 88*(4), 228–242.

Hawking, S. (1992). *A brief history of time*. London: Transworld.

Haworth, J. (Ed) (1996). *Psychological research: Innovative methods and strategies*. London: Routledge.

Hayduk, L.A. (1983). Personal space: Where we now stand. *Psychological Bulletin, 94*, 293–335.

Hayes, N. (1995). *Psychology in perspective*. London: Macmillan.

Hayward, D., Rothenberg, M., & Beasley, R.R. (1974). Children's play and urban playground environments: A comparison of traditional, contemporary and adventure playground types. *Environment and Behaviour, 6*(2), 131–168.

Heilbroner, R.L. (1974). *An inquiry into the human prospect*. New York: W.W. Norton.

Heinzelmann, F. (1981). Reactions to crime: Impacts of crime: Crime prevention and the physical environment. *Sage Criminal Justice System Annuals, 16*, 87–101.

Heller, J.F., Groff, B.D., & Solomon, S.H. (1977). Toward an understanding of crowding: The role of physical interaction. *Journal of Personality and Social Psychology, 35*, 183–190.

Helmreich, R.L. (1994). Anatomy of a system accident: The crash of Avianca flight 052. *International Journal of Aviation Psychology, 4*(3), 265–284.

Helsen, H. (1964). *Adaptation-level theory*. New York: Harper & Row.

Hepper, P. (1992). Smoking, passive smoking and smell. *Medical Science Research, 20*(7), 265–266.

Herridge, C.F. (1974). Aircraft noise and mental health. *Journal of Psychomotor Research, 18*, 239–243.

Hershberger, R.G. (1968). A study of meaning and architecture. *Man and his Environment, 1*(6), 6–7.

Hicks, D., & Holden, C. (1994). Tomorrow's world: Children's hopes and fears for the future. *Educational and Child Psychology, 11*(4), 63–70.

Higgins, P.M. (1984). Stress at Thamesmead. In H. Freeman (Ed.), *Mental health and the environment*. London: Churchill Livingstone.

Hodgkinson, P.E., & Stewart, M. (1991). *Coping with catastrophe: A handbook of disaster management*. London: Routledge.

Hogg, M.A., & Vaughan, G.M. (1995). *Social psychology*. London: Prentice-Hall.

Hohnsbein, J., Piekarski, C., Kampman, B., & Noack, T. (1984). Effects of heat on visual acuity. *Ergonomics, 27*(12), 1239–1246.

Holahan, C.J. (1976). Environmental change in a psychiatric setting: A social systems analysis. *Human Relations, 29*, 153–166.

Holahan, C.J., & Saegert, S. (1973). Behavioural and attitudinal effects of large scale variation in the physical environment of a psychiatric ward. *Journal of Abnormal Psychology, 82*, 454–462.

Holley, H.L., & Arboleda-Florez, J.E. (1988). Hypernomia and self-destructiveness in penal settings. *International Journal of Law and Psychiatry, 11*(2), 167–178.

Holmes, T.S., & Rahe, R. (1967). The social readjustment rating scale. *Journal of Psychosomatic Research, 11*, 213–218.

Homma, M. (1990). A Japanese perspective on crowding: How well have the Japanese adapted to high density? *Psychologia: An International Journal of Psychology in the Orient, 33*(2), 128–137.

Hopkins, J. (1994). Orchestrating an indoor city: Ambient noise inside a megamall. *Environment and Behaviour, 26*, 785–812.

Hopkins, N. (1992). *Paper presented to the BPS London Conference.*

Houghton, S., Wheldall, K., Jukes, R., & Sharpe, A. (1990). The effects of limited private reprimands and increased private praise on classroom behaviour in four British secondary school classes. *British Journal of Educational Psychology, 60*(3), 255–265.

Huang, X., Huang, W., & Li, X. (1991). The symbolic implication of colours to the Chinese. *Psychological Science. China, 6*, 1–7.

Hui, M.K., & Bateson, J.E. (1991). Perceived control and the effects of crowding and consumer choice on the service experience. *Journal of Consumer Research, 18*(2), 174–184.

Hunter, A. (1978). Symbols of incivility. Paper presented to the American Society of Criminology, Dallas, Texas. Cited in D. Halpern (1995), *Mental health and the built environment*. London: Taylor & Francis.

Hunter, A., & Baumer, T.L. (1982). Street traffic, social interaction and fear of crime. *Sociological Inquiry, 52*(2), 122–131.

Irlen, H. (1983). Quoted in G. Stanley (1990), Rose-coloured spectacles: A cure for dyslexia? *Australian Psychologist, 25*(2), 65–76.

Irvine, S., Cawood, F., Richardson, D., MacDonald, E., & Aitken, J. (1996). Evidence of deteriorating semen quality in the United Kingdom: Birth Cohort Study in 577 men in Scotland over 11 years. *British Medical Journal, 7029*(312), 467–471.

Ittelson, W.H. (1960). *Some factors influencing the design and functions of psychiatric facilities*. Brooklin College Progress Report.

Ittelson, W.H. (1961). The constancies in perceptual theory. *Psychological Review, 58*, 285–294.

Ittelson, W.H. (Ed.) (1973). *Environment and cognition*. New York: Holt, Rinehart & Winston.

Izumi, K. (1957). An analysis of the design of hospital quarters for the neuropsychiatric patient. *Mental Hospitals, 8*, 31–32.

Jacobs, K.W., & Blandino, S.E. (1992). Effects of colour of paper on which the Profile of Mood States is printed on the psychological states it measures. *Perceptual and Motor Skills, 75*(1), 267–271.

Jain, U. (1993). Effects of density: The role of moderators for the consequences of crowding. *Psychologia, 36*(3), 133–139.

James, W. (1890). *Principles of psychology*. New York: Holt.

Janis, I.L. (1967). Effects of fear arousal on attitude change: Recent developments in theory and experimental research. In L. Berkowitz (Ed.), *Advances in experimental social psychology* (Vol. 3). New York: Academic Press.

Janis I.L., & Feshback, S. (1953), Effects of fear-arousing communications. *Journal of Abnormal and Social Psychology, 48*, 78–92.

Jarvis, M.J., Foulds, J., & Feyerabend, C. (1992). Exposure to passive smoking among bar staff. *British Journal of Addiction, 87*(1), 111–113.

Johnson, J.G. (1993). Associations between family relationships and psychiatric symptomatology in undergraduate students. *Journal of College Student Psychotherapy, 7*(3), 79–95.

Jones, K., & Poletti, A. (1986). The Italian experience in mental health care. *Hospital and Community Psychiatry, 37*(8), 795–802.

Kagehiro, D.K., Taylor, R.B., & Harland, A.T. (1991). Reasonable expectation of privacy and third party consent searches. *Law and Human Behaviour, 15*(2), 121–138.

Kahle, L.R., & Beatty, S.E. (1987). The task situation and habit in the attitude-behaviour relationship: A social adaptation view. *Journal of Social Behaviour and Personality, 2*(2), 219–232.

Kahn, P.H., & Friedman, B. (1995). Environmental views and values of children in an inner city Black community. *Child Development, 66*(5), 1403–1417.

Kahn, R., & Antonucci, T. (1980). Convoys over the life course: Attachments, roles and social support. In P. Baltes & O. Brim (Eds.), *Lifespan development and behaviour* (Vol. 3). New York: Academic Press.

Kaitz, M., & Eidelman, A.I. (1992). Smell recognition of newborns by women who are not mothers. *Chemical Senses, 17*(2), 225–229.

Kamal, P., & Gupta, I.D. (1988). Feeling of crowding and psychiatric disorders. *Indian Journal of Psychiatry, 30*(1), 85–89.

Kanner, A.D., Coyne, J.C., Schaefer, C., & Lazarus, R.S. (1981). Comparisons of two modes of Stress Management: Daily Hassles and Uplifts versus Major Life Events. *Journal of Behavioural Medicine, 10*, 19–31.

Kaplan, R. (1980). Citizen participation in the design and evaluation of a park. *Environment and Behaviour, 12*, 494–507.

Kaplan, S. (1973). Cognitive maps in perception and thought. In R. Downs & D. Stea (Eds.), *Image and Environment: Cognitive mapping and spatial behaviour*. Chicago: Aldine.

Kaplan, S. (1975). An informal model for the prediction of preference. In E.H. Zube, R.O. Brush, & J.G. Fabos (Eds.), *Landscape assessment*. Stroudsburg, PA: Dowden, Hutchinson & Ross.

Kaplan, S. (1979). Perception and landscape: Conceptions and misconceptions. In G. Elsner & R. Smardon, *USDA Forest Service Report PSW-35*. Berkeley, CA.

Kaplan, S. (1987). Aesthetics, affect and cognition: Environmental preference from an evolutionary perspective. *Environment and Behaviour, 19*, 3–32.

Kaplan, S., & Kaplan, R. (1978). *Humanscape: Environments for people*. North Scituate, MA: Duxbury.

Kaplan, S., & Kaplan, R. (1982). *Cognition and environment: Functioning in an uncertain world*. New York: Praeger.

Karlin, R.A., Epstein, Y., & Aiello, J. (1978). Strategies for the investigation of crowding. In A. Esser & B. Greenbie (Eds.), *Design for community and privacy*. New York: Plenum.

Kasl, S.V. (1974). Effects of housing on mental and physical health. *Man–Environment Systems, 4*, 207–226.

Kaye, S.M. (1975). Psychology in relation to design: An overview. *Canadian Psychological Review, 16*, 104–110.

Kelly, A.D., & Kanas, N. (1992). Crewmember communication in space: A survey of astronauts and cosmonauts. *Aviation, Space and Environmental Medicine, 63*(8), 721–726.

Kelly, G.A. (1955). *The psychology of personal constructs*. New York: Norton.

Kendrick, D.T., & McFarlane, S.W. (1986). Ambient temperature and horn honking: A field study of the heat/aggression relationship. *Environment and Behaviour, 18*(2), 179–191.

Kilpatrick, F.P. (1954). Two processes of perceptual learning. *Journal of Experimental Psychology, 47*, 362–370.

Kilpatrick, F.P. (1961). *Explorations in transactional psychology*. New York, NY: University Press.

King, M.G. (1966). Interpersonal relations in preschool children and average approach distance. *Journal of Genetic Psychology, 109*, 109–116.

King, N., & Anderson, N. (1995). *Innovation and change in organisations*. London: Routledge.

Kinkade, P., Leone, M., & Semond, S. (1995). The consequences of jail crowding. *Crime and Delinquency, 41*(1), 150–161.

Kira, A. (1976). *The bathroom*. New York: Viking.

Kleck, R. (1969). Physical stigma and task oriented interaction. *Human Relations, 22*, 53–60.

Kline, N.A., & Rausch, J.L. (1985). Olfactory precipitants of flashbacks in post traumatic stress disorder: Case reports. *Journal of Clinical Psychiatry, 46*(9), 383–384.

Kluckholn, C.M., & Murray, H.A. (1953). Personality formation: Its determinants. In C.M. Kluckholn & H.A. Murray (Eds.), *Personality in nature, society and culture* (2nd ed.). New York: Knopf.

Knowles, E.S. (1983). Social physics and the effects of others: Tests of the effects of audience size and distance on social judgments and behaviour. *Journal of Personality and Social Psychology, 45*, 1263–1279.

Kobayashi, S. (1961). *An introduction to architectural psychology*. Tokyo: Shokokusha Publishing.

Kobrick, J.L., & Sleeper, L.A. (1986). Effect of wearing chemical protective clothing in the heat on signal detection over the visual field. *Aviation, Space and Environmental Medicine, 57*(2), 144–148.

Koehler, R.J., & Lindner, C. (1992). Alternative incarceration: An inevitable response to institutional overcrowding. *Federal Probation, 56*(3), 12–18.

Koelega, H.S. (1994). Sex differences in olfactory sensitivity and the problem of the generality of smell acuity. *Perceptual and Motor Skills, 78*(1), 203–213.

Koffka, K. (1935). *Principles of Gestalt psychology*. New York: Harcourt, Brace and World.

Köhler, W. (1929). *Gestalt psychology*. New York: Liveright.

Köhler, W. (1940). *Dynamics in psychology*. New York: Liveright.

Konecni, V. (1975). The mediation of aggressive behaviour: Arousal level vs anger and cognitive labelling. *Journal of Personality and Social Psychology, 32*, 706–712.

Konecni, V.J., Libuser, L., Morton, H., & Ebbesen, E.B. (1975). Effects of a violation of personal space on escape and helping response. *Journal of Experimental Social Psychology, 11*, 288–299.

Kopala, L.C., Good, K., Goldner, E.M., & Birmingham, C.L. (1995). Olfactory identification ability in anorexia nervosa. *Journal of Psychiatry and Neuroscience, 20*(4), 283–286.

Korte, C., & Kerr, N. (1975). Responses to altruistic opportunities under urban and rural conditions. *Journal of Social Psychology, 95*, 183–184.

Koslowsky, M., & Krausz, M. (1993). On the relationship between commuting, stress symptoms, and attitudinal measures: A LISREL application. *Journal of Applied Behavioural Medicine, 29*(4), 485–492.

Kovrigin, S.D., & Mikheyev, A.P. (1965). The effect of noise level on working efficiency. *Report N65-28297*. Washington DC: Joint Publications Research Service.

Krause, D. (1993). Environmental consciousness: An empirical study. *Environment and Behaviour, 25*(1), 126–142.

Kryter, K.D. (1970). *The effects of noise on man*. New York: Academic Press.

Kuentzel, W.F., & Heberlein, T.A. (1992). Cognitive and behavioural adaptations to perceived crowding: A panel study of coping and displacement. *Journal of Leisure Research, 24*(4), 377–393.

Kuller, R., & Lindsten, C. (1992). Health of behaviour of children in classrooms with and without windows. *Journal of Environmental Psychology, 12*(4), 305–317.

Kwallek, N., & Lewis, C.M. (1990). Effects of environmental colour on males and females: A red or white or green office. *Applied Ergonomics, 21*(4), 275–278.

Lam, R.W., Goldner, E.M., Solyom, L., & Remick, R.A. (1994). A controlled study of light therapy for bulimia nervosa. *American Journal of Psychiatry, 151*(5), 744–750.

Lambert, J.F., & Olivereau, J.M. (1980). Single trial passive avoidance learning by rats treated with ionized air. *Psychological Reports, 47*, 1323–1330

Lane, J., Wilke, R., Champeau, R., & Sivek, D. (1994). Environmental education in Wisconsin: A teacher survey. *Journal of Environmental Education, 25*(4), 9–17.

Lanza, M.L., Kayne, H.L., Hicks, C., & Milner, J. (1994). Environmental characteristics related to patient assault. *Issues in Mental Health Nursing, 15*(3), 319–335.

La Piere, R.T. (1934). Attitudes vs actions. *Social Forces, 13*, 113–120.

Larsen, K.S. (1995). Environmental waste: Recycling attitudes and correlates. *Journal of Social Psychology, 135*(1), 83–88.

Latane, B., & Darley, J.M. (1968). Group inhibition of bystander intervention in emergencies. *Journal of Personality and Social Psychology, 10*, 215–221.

Latane, B., & Nida, S. (1981). Ten years of research on group size and helping. *Psychological Bulletin, 89*(2), 308–324.

Laudenslager, M.L., & Reite, M.L. (1984). Losses and separations: Immunological consequences and health implications. *Review of Personality and Social Psychology, 5*, 285–312.

Lawrence, R.J. (1984). Transition spaces and dwelling design. *Journal of Architectural and Planning Research, 1*(4), 261–271.

Lawton, M.P., Fulcomer, M., & Kleban, M.H. (1984). Architecture for the mentally impaired elderly. *Environment and Behaviour, 16*, 730–757.

Lazarus, R.S., & Folkman, S. (1984). *Stress, appraisal and coping*. New York: Springer.

Lee, T. (1976). *Psychology and the environment*. London: Methuen.

Lee, T. (1984). *Environmental effects on behaviour.* Talk given to the annual congress of psychology students in Ireland. Coleraine: University of Ulster.

Lefebvre, P. (1984). Hygiene mentale et grands ensembles en europe occidentale. *Societe Medico-Psychologique*, 527–542.

Lepore, S.J., Evans, G.W., & Palsane, M.N. (1991). Social hassles and psychological health in the context of chronic crowding. *Journal of Health and Social Behaviour, 32*(4), 357–367.

Lepore, S.J., Evans, G.W., & Schneider, M.L. (1991). Dynamic role of social support in the link between chronic stress and psychological distress. *Journal of Personality and Social Psychology, 61*(6), 899–909.

Lepore, S.J., Evans, G.W., & Schneider, M.L. (1992). Role of control and social support in explaining the stress of hassles and crowding. *Environment and Behaviour, 24*(6), 795–811.

Lester, D. (1991). The etiology of suicide and homicide in urban and rural America. *Journal of Rural Community Psychology, 12*(1), 15–27.

Levine, M.E., Duffy, L.K., & Bowyer, R.T. (1994). Fatigue, sleep and seasonal hormone levels: Implications for drinking behaviour in northern climates. *Drugs and Society, 8*(2), 61–70.

Levy, L., & Rowitz, L. (1973). *The ecology of mental disorder*. New York: Behavioral Publications.

Levy-Leboyer, C. (1982). *Psychology and environment*. London: Sage.

Lewin, K. (1951). *Field theory in social science*. New York: Harper.

Lewy, A.J., Sack, R.L., Miller, L.S., & Hoban, T.M. (1987). Antidepressant and circardian phase-shifting effects of light. *Science, 235*(4786), 352–354.

Lifton, R.J. (1967). *Life in death*. New York: Simon & Schuster.

Little, K.B. (1965). Personal space. *Journal of Experimental Social Psychology*, 237–247.

Lorenz, K. (1958). The evolution of behaviour. *Scientific American, 199*(6), 67–78.

Lorenz, K. (1966). *On aggression*. New York: Harcourt Brace Jovanovich.

Luchins, A.S. (1988). The rise and decline of the American asylum movement in the 19th century. *Journal of Psychology, 122*, 471–486.

Lynch, K. (1960). *The image of the city*. Cambridge, MA: MIT Press.

MacNiven, E. (1994). Increased prevalence of left-handedness in victims of head trauma. *Brain Injury, 8*(5), 457–462.

Magenau, E. (Ed.) (1959). *Research for architecture*. Washington DC: American Institute of Architects.

Malthus, T. (1798). Malthus' Law: An essay on the principles of population. In J.F.C. Harrison (Ed.) (1965), *British society and politics*. London: Harper & Row.

Marascuilo, L.A., & Penfield, D.A. (1972). Learning to listen: A study of auditory perception. *California Journal of Educational Research, 23*(1), 4–16.

Martin, F.M., Brotherston, J.H.F., & Chave, S.P.W. (1957). Incidence of neurosis in a new housing estate. *British Journal of Preventative Social Medicine, 11*, 196–202.

Mascie-Taylor, C.N. (1991). Biosocial influences on stature: A review. *Journal of Biosocial Sciences, 23*(1), 113–128.

Matheny, A.P. (1986). Injuries among toddlers: Contributions from child, mother and family. *Journal of Pediatric Psychology, 11*(2), 163–176.

Matheny, A.P. (1987). Psychological characteristics of childhood accidents: Children's injuries: Prevention and public policy. *Journal of Social Issues, 43*(2), 45–60.

Matthews, G., Dorn, L., & Glendon, A.I. (1991). Personality correlates of driver stress. *Personality and Individual Differences, 12*(6), 535–549.

Maxfield, M.G. (1984). The limits of vulnerability in explaining fear of crime: A comparative neighbourhood analysis. *Research in Crime and Delinquency, 21*(3) 233–250.

May, J., & Brackett, D. (1987). Adapting the classroom environment. *Hearing Rehabilitation Quarterly, 12*(2).

Mayo, E. (1933). *The human problems of an industrial civilization.* New York: Macmillan.

McGuire, W.J. (1969). The nature of attitudes and attitude change. In G. Lindsay & E. Aronson (Eds.), *Handbook of social psychology* (2nd. ed., Vol. 3). Reading, MA: Addison Wesley

McIntosh, N.A., Clark, N.M., & Howatt, W.F. (1994). Reducing tobacco smoke in the environment of the child with asthma: A cotinine-assisted, minimal contact intervention. *Journal of Asthma, 31*(6), 453–462.

McKechnie, G.E. (1974). *ERI Manual: Environmental Response Inventory.* Berkeley, CA: Consulting Psychologists Press.

McKenna, J.J. (1990). Evolution and sudden infant death syndrome (SIDS): 1. Infant responsivity to parental contact. *Human Nature, 1*(2), 145–177.

McKenzie, D.L., & Piquero, A. (1994). The impact of shock incarceration programs on prison crowding. *Crime and Delinquency, 40*(2), 222–249.

Meerum-Terwogt, M., & Hoeksma, J.B. (1995). Colors and emotions: Preferences and combinations. *Journal of General Psychology, 122*(1), 5–17.

Meese, G.B., Lewis, M.I., Wyon, D.P., & Kok, R. (1984). A laboratory study of the effects of moderate thermal stress on the performance of factory workers. *Ergonomics, 27*(1), 19–43.

Mehrabrian, A. (1976). *Public places and private spaces.* New York: Basic Books.

Mehrabrian, A., & Russell, J.A. (1974). *An approach to environmental psychology.* Cambridge, MA: MIT Press.

Meltzer, S.B., Hovell, M.F., Meltzer, E.O., Atkins, C.J. (1993). Reduction of secondary smoke exposure in asthmatic children: Parent counselling. *Journal of Asthma, 30*(5), 391–400.

Mercer, G.W., & Benjamin, M.L. (1980). Spatial behaviour of university undergraduates in double occupancy residence rooms: An inventory of effects. *Journal of Applied Social Psychology, 10*, 32–44.

Mergen, A. (1983). Urban security. *Revue Internationale de Criminologie et de Police Technique, 36*(4), 42–50.

Meseke, C. (1994). Understanding the environment: A comparison of workers in Germany and Poland. *Psychology: A Journal of Human Behaviour, 31*(2), 1–8.

Meux, E.P. (1973). Concern for the common good in an N-person game. *Journal of Personality and Social Psychology, 28*, 414–418.

Milford, H.S. (1934). *The poetical works of William Cowper* (4th ed.). Oxford: Oxford University Press.

Miller, G. (1969). Psychology in the promotion of human welfare. *Presidential address to the American Psychological Association.*

Mills, C. (1956). *The power elite.* New York: Oxford University Press.

Minckley, B. (1968). A study of noise and its relationship to patient discomfort in the recovery room. *Nursing Research, 17*, 247–250.

Mischel, W. (1968). *Personality and assessment*. New York: Wiley.

Mitchell, R. (1971). Some social implications of high density housing. *American Sociological Review, 36*, 18–29.

Moch, A. (1984). Type A and Type B behaviour patterns, task type and sensitivity to noise. *Psychological Medicine, 14*(3), 643–646.

Moffatt, R.E. (1983). Crime prevention through environmental design: A management perspective. *Canadian Journal of Criminology, 25*(1), 19–31.

Molhave, L. (1992). Design considerations for experiments at exposure levels below TLVs. Special issue: Behavioural effects of contaminated air: Applying psychology in neurotoxicology. *Applied Psychology: An International Review, 41*(3), 229–238.

Molnar, G., & Pinchoff, D.M. (1993). Factors in patient elopements from an urban state hospital and strategies for prevention. *Hospital and Community Psychiatry, 44*(8), 791–792.

Montello, D.R. (1988). Classroom seating location and its effect on course achievement, participation and attitudes. *Journal of Environmental Psychology, 8*, 149–157.

Moore, E.O. (1989). Prison environments and their impact on older citizens: Special issue: Older offenders: Current trends. *Journal of Offender Counseling, Services and Rehabilitation, 13*(2), 175–191.

Morin, M. (1989). Applied social psychology and noise in work situations. *Cahiers Internationaux de Psychologie Sociale*, March, No.1, 31–51.

Moscovici, S. (1984). The phenomenon of social representations. In R. Farr & S. Moscovici (Eds.), *Social representations*. Cambridge: Cambridge University Press.

Moser, G. (1988). Urban stress and helping behaviour: Effects of environmental overload and noise on behaviour. *Journal of Environmental Psychology, 8*(4), 287–298.

Mowrer, O.H. (1960). *Learning theory and behaviour*. New York: Wiley.

Murray, H.A. (1938). *Explorations in personality*. New York: Oxford University Press.

Nagy, E., Yasunaga, S., & Kose, S. (1995). Japanese office employees' psychological reactions to their underground and above ground offices. *Journal of Environmental Psychology, 15*(2), 123–134

Nakajima, M. (1986). Review of traffic safety research. *Japanese Journal of Psychology, 57*(2), 100–114.

Nayh, S., Vaisanen, E., & Hassi, J. (1994). Season and mental illness in an arctic area of northern Finland. *Acta Psychiatrica Scandinavica, 89*, 46–49.

Neisser, U. (1976). *Cognition and reality: Principles and implications of cognitive psychology*. San Francisco: W.H. Freeman.

Neisser, U. (Ed.) (1987). *Concepts and conceptual development: Ecological and intellectual factors in categorization*. Cambridge: CUP.

Newman, O. (1972). *Defensible space*. New York: Macmillan.

Newman, O. (1975). Reactions to the "defensible space" study and some further findings. *International Journal of Mental Health, 4*(3), 48–70.

Nezu, A.M., Nezu, C.M., & Perri, M.G. (1989). *Problem-solving therapy for depression: Theory, research and guidelines*. New York: Wiley.

Ng, S. (1980). *The social psychology of power*. London: Academic Press.

Norback, D., Michel, I., & Widstrom, J. (1990). Indoor air quality and personal factors related to the sick building syndrome. *Scandinavian Journal of Work, Environment and Health, 16*(2), 121–128.

Nosulenko, V.N. (1991). Psychological peculiarities and acoustical environment changes: The psychological dimension of global change. *International Journal of Psychology, 26*(5), 623–632.

Novaco, R.W., Kliewer, W., & Broquet, A. (1991). Home environmental consequences of commute travel impedance. *American Journal of Community Psychology, 19*(6), 881–909.

Novaco, R.W., Stokols, D., & Milanesi, L. (1990). Objective and subjective dimensions of travel impedance as determinants of commuting stress. *American Journal of Community Psychology, 18*(2), 231–257.

Noweir, M.H. (1984). Noise exposure as related to productivity, disciplinary actions, absenteeism, and accidents among textile workers. *Journal of Safety Research, 15*(4), 163–174.

Odera, P., & Hasan, Q. (1993). Assessment of difficulties of foreign students in India. *Journal of Personality and Clinical Studies, 9*(1–2), 25–30.

Ohrstrom, E., Bjorkman, M., & Rylander, R. (1988). Noise annoyance with regard to neuropsychological sensitivity, subjective noise sensitivity and personality variables. *Psychological Medicine, 18*, 605–613.

Olsen, R. (1978). *The effect of the hospital environment*. Doctoral dissertation, City University of New York.

O'Mahony, M. (1978). Smell illusions and suggestion: Reports of smells contingent on tones played on television and radio. *Chemical Senses and Flavor, 3*(2), 183–189.

O'Neal, E.C., Brunault, M.S., Carifio, M.S., Troutwine, R., & Epstein, J. (1980). Effect of insult upon personal space preferences. *Journal of Nonverbal Behaviour, 5*, 56–62.

Orford, J. (1992). *Community psychology*. Chichester: Wiley.

Osmond, H. (1957). Function as the basis of psychiatric ward design. *Mental Hospitals, 8*, 23–30.

Otto, D., Molhave, L., Rose, G., Hudnell, H.K. (1990). Neurobehavioural and sensory irritant effects of controlled exposure to a complex mixture of volatile organic compounds. *Neurotoxicology and Teratology, 12*(6), 649–652.

Page, R.A. (1977). Noise and helping behaviour. *Environment and Behaviour, 9*, 559–572.

Palinkas, L.A., Petterson, J.S., Russell, J., & Downs, M.A. (1993). Community patterns of psychiatric disorders after the Exxon Valdez oil spill. *American Journal of Psychiatry, 150*(10), 1517–1523.

Palmer, J.A. (1994). Acquisition of environmental subject knowledge in preschool children: An international study. *Children's Environments, 11*(3), 204–211.

Palmstierna, T., Huitfeldt, B., & Wistedt, B. (1991). The relationship of crowding and aggressive behaviour on a psychiatric intensive care unit. *Hospital and Community Psychiatry, 42*(12), 1237–1240.

Panin, L.Y., & Sokolov, V.P. (1988). Psychological and biochemical factors in the development of coronary heart disease and arterial hypertension in a non-resident population of the Asiatic North. *Journal of Psychosomatic Research, 24*(1), 39–44.

Paptheodorou, G., & Kutcher, S. (1995). The effect of adjunctive light therapy on ameliorating breakthrough depressive symptoms in adolescent-onset bipolar disorder. *Journal of Psychiatry and Neuroscience, 20*(3), 226–232.

Parke, R.D., & Sawin, D.B. (1979). Children's privacy in the home: Developmental, ecological, and child-rearing determinants. *Environment and Behaviour, 11*(1), 87–104.

Parker, D.A., Kaelber, C., Harford, T.C., & Brody, J.A. (1983). Alcohol problems among employed men and women in metropolitan Detroit. *Journal of Studies on Alcohol, 44*(6), 1026–1039.

Parsons, H.M. (1972). The bedroom. *Human Factors, 14*, 421–450.

Partonen, T. (1994). Pharmacotherapy of winter seasonal affective disorder: A review. *Psychiatrica Fennica, 25*, 67–72.

Partonen, T., Partinen, M., & Lonnqvist, J. (1993). Frequencies of seasonal major depressive symptoms at high latitudes. *European Archives of Psychiatry and Clinical Neuroscience, 243*(3–4), 189–192.

Paulus, P.B. (1988). *Prison crowding: A psychological perspective*. New York: Springer-Verlag.

Paulus, P., Cox, V., McCain, G,. & Chandler, J. (1975). Some effects of crowding in a prison environment. *Journal of Applied Social Psychology, 5*(1), 86–91.

Pedersen, D.M. (1982). Personality correlates of privacy. *Journal of Psychology, 112*, 11–14.

Pennartz, P.J. (1986). Atmosphere at home: A qualitative approach. *Journal of Environmental Psychology, 6*(2), 135–153.

Pervin, L.A. (1995). *The science of personality*. New York: Wiley.

Phillips, K.A., Coates, T.J., Everley, R.B., & Catania, J. (1995). Who plans to be tested for HIV or would get tested if no one could find out the result? *American Journal of Preventive Medicine, 11*(3), 156–162.

Platt, J. (1973). Social traps. *American Psychologist, 28*, 641–651.

Plutchik, R. (1995). *The psychology and biology of emotion*. New York: Harper Collins.

Pomerleau, A., Bolduc, D., Malcuit, G., & Cossette, L. (1990). Pink or blue: Environmental gender stereotypes in the first two years of life. *Sex Roles, 22*(5–6), 359–367.

Pontell, H.N., & Welsh, W.N. (1994). Incarceration as a deviant form of social control: Jail overcrowding in California. *Crime and Delinquency, 40*(1), 18–36.

Porter, H. (1996). Lone rangers. *The Guardian: G2 Society*, Wednesday 27th March.

Potasova, A. (1992). Serial position effect: Indicator of environment-toxic injury? *Studia Psychologica, 34*(2), 127–135.

Potasova, A., & Arochova, O. (1994). Effects of toxic agents in the environment on mental functions in children: Some methodological approaches and findings. *Ceskoslovensha Psychologie, 38*(2), 131–142.

Potasova, A., Kovac, D., & Arochova, O. (1993). Children's cognition burned by environmental neurotoxins. *Studia Psychologica, 35*(4–5), 336–340.

Potts, R., & Sanchez, D. (1994). Television viewing and depression: No news is good news. *Journal of Broadcasting and Electronic Media, 38*(1), 79–90.

Poulton, E.C., Hunt, F.C.R., Mumford, J.C., & Poulton, J. (1975). Mechanical disturbance produced by steady and gusty winds of moderate strength: Skilled performance and semantic assessment. *Ergonomics, 18*, 651–673.

Poumadere, M. (1995). Issues in communication with the public on health and environmental risk. *European Review of Applied Psychology, 45*(1), 7–16.

Powell, L. (1990). Factors associated with the under-representation of African Americans in mathematics and science. *Journal of Negro Education, 59*(3), 292–298.

Powell-Cope, G.M. (1995). The experiences of gay couples affected by HIV infection. *Qualitative Health Research, 5*(1), 36–62.

Poyner, B. (1983). *Design against crime: Beyond defensible space*. London: Butterworths.

Profusek, P.J., & Rainey, D.W. (1987). Effects of Baker–Miller pink and red on state anxiety, grip strength and motor precision. *Perceptual and Motor Skills, 65*(3), 941–942.

Propst, D.B., & Kurtzz, M.E. (1989). Perceived control/reactance: A framework for understanding leisure behaviour in natural settings. *Leisure Studies, 8*(3), 241–248.

Proshansky, H.M., Fabian, A.K., & Kaminoff, R. (1983). Place identity: Physical world socialization of the self. *Journal of Environmental Psychology, 3*, 57–83.

Proshansky, H.M., Fabian, A.K., & Kaminoff, R. (1985). Place identity: Physical world socialisation of the self. *Journal of Environmental Psychology, 3*, 57–83.

Proshansky, H.M., Ittelson, W.H., & Rivlin, L.G. (Eds.) (1976). *Environmental psychology* (2nd ed.). New York: Holt, Rinehart & Winston.

Raab, G.M., Thompson, G.O., Boyd, L., Fulton, M. (1990). Blood lead levels, reaction time, inspection time and ability in Edinburgh children. *British Journal of Developmental Psychology, 8*(2), 101–118.

Rakoczy, G. (1987). Mental images of towns: How they arise and a research method. *Przeglad Psychologiczny, 28*(4), 1043–1050.

Ramsey, J.D., Burford, C.L., Beshir, M.Y., & Jensen, R.C. (1983). Effects of workplace thermal conditions on safe work behaviour. *Journal of Safety Research, 14*(3), 105–114.

Rand, G. (1984). Crime and environment: A review of the literature and its implications for urban architecture and planning. *Journal of Architectural and Planning Research, 1*(1), 3–19.

Raphael, B., Singh, B., Bradbury, L., & Lambert, F. (1984). Who helps the helpers? The effects of a disaster on the rescue workers. *Omega Journal of Death and Dying, 14*(1), 9–20.

Raymond, M.W., & Moser, R. (1995). Aviators at risk. *Aviation, Space and Environmental Medicine, 66*(1), 35–39.

Reicher, S.D. (1984). The St Paul's riots: An explanation of the limits of crowd action in terms of a social identity model. *European Journal of Social Psychology, 14*, 1–21.

Reser, J.P. (1980). Automobile addiction: Real or imagined? *Man–Environment Systems, 10*, 279–287.

Richardson, G.S., Miner, J.D., & Cziesler, C.A. (1990). Impaired driving performance in shift workers: The role of the circadian system in a multifactorial model. *Alcohol, Drugs and Driving, 5*(4) & 6(1), 265–273.

Riley, M.W., & Cochran, D.J. (1984). Dexterity performance and reduced ambient temperature. *Human Factors, 26*(2), 207–214.

Rim, Y. (1975). Psychological test performance of different personality types on Sharav days in artificial air ionization. *International Journal of Biometeorology, 21*, 337–340.

Rivlin, L.G., & Rothenberg, M. (1976). The use of space in open classrooms. In H.M. Proshansky, W.H. Ittelson, & L.G. Rivlin (Eds.), *Environmental psychology: People and their physical settings*. New York: Holt, Rinehart & Winston.

Rizzini, I., & Lusk, M.W. (1995). Children in the streets: Latin-America's lost generation. *Children and Youth Services Review, 17*(3), 391–400.

Rodrigo, E.K., & Williams, P. (1986). Frequency of self-reported "anxiolytic withdrawal" symptoms in a group of female students experiencing anxiety. *Psychological Medicine, 16*(2), 467–472.

Roethlisberger, F.J., & Dickson, W.J. (1939). *Management and the worker*. Cambridge, MA: Harvard University Press.

Rohe, W. (1985). Urban planning and mental health. *Prevention in Human Sciences, 4*, 79–110.

Romelsjo, A., Alberts, K.A., & Andersson, R. (1993). The Stockholm County programme for accident and alcohol prevention and injury surveillance: Initial experiences. *Addiction, 88*(7), 1013–1016.

Rose, H.S., & Hinds, D.H. (1976). South Dixie contraflow bus and car-pool lane demonstration project. *Transportation Research Record, 606*, 18–22.

Rosen, S. (1985). The weather: Windy and grouchy. *The Catholic Digest*, 94–97.

Rosen, S., Bergman, M., Plestor, D., El-Mofty, A., & Satti, M. (1962). Presbycosis study of a relatively noise-free population in Sudan. *Annals of Ontology, Rhinology and Laryngology, 71*, 727–743.

Rosenhan, D.L. (1973). On being sane in insane places. *Science, 179*, 250–258.

Rotter, J.B. (1966). Generalised expectancies for internal versus external control of reinforcement. *Psychological Monographs, 80*, 1–28.

Rotton, J. (1990). Stress. In C.E. Kimble, *Social psychology*. Iowa: W C Brown.

Rotton, J., & Frey, J. (1985). Air pollution, weather and violent crimes: Concomitant time-series analysis of archival data. *Journal of Personality and Social Psychology, 49*, 1207–1220.

Ruback, R.B., & Pandey, J. (1992). Very hot and really crowded: Quasi-experimental investigations of Indian "Tempos". *Environment and Behaviour, 24*(4), 527–554.

Ruback, R.B., & Patnaik, R. (1989). Crowding, perceived control and the destruction of property. *Psychological Studies, 34*(1), 1–14.

Ruback, R.B., & Riad, J.K. (1994). The more (men), the less merry: Social density, social burden and social support. *Sex Roles, 30*(11–12), 743–763.

Rubin, Z., & Shenker, S. (1977). Friendship, proximity, and self-disclosure. *Journal of Personality, 46*, 1–22.

Rumsay, N., & Bull, R. (1986). The effects of facial disfigurement on social interaction. *Human Learning Journal of Practical Research and Application, 5*(4), 203–208.

Rumsay, N., Bull, R., & Gahagan, D. (1982). The effect of facial disfigurement on the proxemic behaviour of the general public. *Journal of Applied Social Psychology, 12*(2), 137–150.

Rumsay, N., Bull, R., & Gahagan, D. (1986). A developmental study of children's stereotyping of facially deformed adults. *British Journal of Psychology, 77*(2), 269–274.

Russell, J.A., & Ward, L.M. (1982). Environmental psychology. *Annual Review of Psychology, 33*, 651–682.

Russell, M., Mendelson, T., & Peeke, H.V. (1983). Mothers' identification of their infant's odours. *Ethology and Sociobiology, 4*(1), 29–31.

Ryan, C.M., & Morrow, L.A. (1992). Dysfunctional buildings or dysfunctional people: An examination of the sick building syndrome and allied disorders. *Journal of Consulting and Clinical Psychology, 80*(2), 220–224.

Sack, R.L., Lewy, A.J., White, D.M., & Singer, C.M. (1990). Morning versus evening light treatment for winter depression: Evidence that the therapeutic effects of light are mediated by circadian phase shifts. *Archives of General Psychiatry, 47*(4), 343–351.

Saito, M. (1994). A cross cultural study on colour preference in three Asian cities: Comparison between Tokyo, Taipei and Tianjin. *Japanese Psychological Research, 36*(4), 219–232.

Salame, P., & Baddeley, A.D. (1989). Effects of background music on phonological short term memory. *Quarterly Journal of Experimental Psychology, 41*, 107–122.

San-Gil-Martin, J., Gonzalez-de-Rivera, J.L., & Gonzalez-Gonzalez, J. (1988). Weather and psychiatry: Meteorotropism and psychopathology. *Psiquis Revista de Psiquiatria, Psicologia y Psicosomatica, 9*(6–7), 11–18.

Sapir, E. (1947). *Selected writings in language, culture and personality.* Los Angeles: UCP.

Scala, A. (1990). Buildings for mental patients; From the architecture of isolation towards architecture of social integration. *Zhurnal Nevropatologii i Psikhiatrii imeni S. S. Korsakova, 90*(11), 90–92.

Scarr, S. (1994). Ethical problems in research on risky behaviours and risky populations. Special issue: Reporting and referring child and adolescent research participants. *Ethics and Behaviour, 4*(2), 147–155.

Schab, F.R. (1990). Odors and the remembrance of things past. *Journal of Experimental Psychology, Learning, Memory and Cognition, 16*(4), 648–655.

Schachter, S. (1964). The interaction of cognitive and physiological determinants of emotional state. In L. Berkowitz (Ed.), *Advances in experimental social psychology.* New York: Academic Press.

Schachter, S., & Singer, J.E. (1962). Cognitive, social and physiological determinants of emotional states. *Psychological Review, 69*, 379–399.

Schaeffer, M.A., Baum, A., Paulus, P.B., & Gaes, G.G. (1988). Architecturally mediated effects of social density in prison. *Environment and Behaviour, 20*(1), 3–19.

Schahn, J., & Holzer, E. (1990). Studies of individual environmental concern: The role of knowledge, gender, and background variables. *Environment and Behaviour, 22*(6), 767–786.

Schauss, A.G. (1985). The physiological effect of colour on the suppression of human aggression: Research on Baker–Miller pink. *International Journal of Biosocial Research, 7*(2), 55–64.

Schuler, H.J. (1981). Grocery shopping choices: Individual preferences based on store attractiveness and distance. *Environment and Behaviour, 13*(3), 331–347.

Seamon, J.G., & Kendrick, D.T. (1992). *Psychology.* Englewood Cliffs, NJ: Prentice-Hall.

Segall, M.H., Campbell, D.T., & Herskovits, M.J. (1966). *The influence of culture on visual perception.* Indianapolis: Bobbs-Merrill.

Seidler, T.L. (1995). Effects of different coloured test environments on selected physiological and psychological responses during maximal graded treadmill tests. *Perceptual and Motor Skills, 80*(1), 225–226.

Seligman, M.E.P. (1975). *Helplessness: On depression, development and death*. San Francisco: W.H. Freeman.

Severy, L.J., Forsyth, D.R., & Wagner, P.J. (1979). A multi-method assessment of personal space development in female and male, black and white children. *Journal of Nonverbal Behaviour, 4*, 68–86.

Seyle, H. (1956). *The stress of life*. New York: McGraw-Hill.

Sherif, M., Harvey, O.J., White, B.J., Hood, W.R., & Sherif, C.W. (1961). *Intergroup conflict and cooperation: The robber's cave experiment*. Oklahoma: University of Oklahoma Press.

Ship, J.A., & Weiffenbach, J.M. (1993). Age, gender, medical treatment and medication effects on smell identification. *Journal of Gerontology, 48*(1), 26–32.

Shumaker, S.A., & Taylor, R.B. (1983). Towards a clarification of people–place relationships: A mode of attachment to place. In N.R. Feimer & E.S. Geller (Eds.), *Environmental psychology: Directions and perspectives*. New York: Praeger.

Siann, G. (1994). *Gender, sex and sexuality*. London: Taylor & Francis.

Sime, J.D. (1986). Creating places or designing spaces? *Journal of Environmental Psychology, 6*(1), 49–63.

Sinclair, R.C., Mark, M.M., & Clore, G.L. (1994). Mood-related persuasion depends on (mis)attributions. *Social Cognition, 12*(4), 309–326.

Sinha, S.P., Nayyar, P., & Mukherjee, N. (1995). Perception of crowding among children and adolescents. *Journal of Social Psychology, 135*(2), 263–268.

Sinha, S.P., & Sinha, S.P. (1991). Personal space and density as factors in task performance and feeling of crowding. *Journal of Social Psychology, 131*(6), 831–837.

Skinner, B.F. (1938). *The behavior of organisms: An experimental analysis*. New York: Appleton.

Skinner, B.F. (1953). *Science and human behaviour* New York: Macmillan.

Skinner, B.F. (1972). *Beyond freedom and dignity*. Harmondsworth, UK: Penguin.

Skinner, E. (1995). *Perceived control, motivation and coping*. London: Sage.

Skov, P., Valbjorn, O., & Pedersen, B.V. (1989). Influence of personal characteristics, job-related factors and psychosocial factors on the sick building syndrome. *Scandinavian Journal of Work, Environment and Health, 15*(4), 288–295.

Skov, P., Valbjorn, O., Pedersen, B.V., & Gravensen, S. (1990). The influence of indoor climate on the sick building syndrome in an office environment. *Scandinavian Journal of Work, Environment and Health, 16*(5), 363–371.

Smith, A.P. (1985). The effects of different types of noise on semantic processing and syntactic reasoning. *Acta Psychologica, 58*(3), 275–285.

Smith, H.W. (1981). Territorial spacing on a beach revisited: A cross-national exploration. *Social Psychology Quarterly, 44*, 132–137.

Smith, J.A., Harré, R., & van Langenhove, L. (1995). *Rethinking psychology*. London: Sage.

Smith, J.M., & Bell, P.A. (1992). Environmental concern and cooperative–competitive behaviour in a simulated commons dilemma. *Journal of Social Psychology, 132*(4), 461–468.

Smith, P.B., & Bond, M.H. (1993). *Social psychology across cultures: Analysis and perspectives*. London: Harvester/Wheatsheaf.

Sommer, R. (1959). Studies in personal space. *Sociometry, 22,* 247–60.

Sommer, R. (1969). *Personal space.* Englewood Cliffs, NJ: Prentice-Hall.

Sommer, R. (1976). *The end of imprisonment.* New York: Oxford University Press.

Sommer, R., & Ross, H. (1958). Social interaction on a geriatric ward. *International Journal of Social Psychiatry, 4,* 128–133.

Sommers, P., & Moos, R. (1976). The weather and human behaviour. In R.H. Moos (Ed.), *The human context: Environmental determinants of behaviour.* New York: Wiley.

Soyka, F., & Edmonds, A. (1978). *The ion effect.* New York: Bantam.

Spielberger, C.D., & Frank, R.G. (1992). Injury control: A promising field for psychologists. *American Psychologist, 47*(8), 1029–1030.

Spittle, B. (1994). Psychopharmacology of fluoride: A review. *International Clinical Psychopharmacology, 9*(2), 79–82.

Spreckelmeyer, K.F. (1993). Office relocation and environmental change: A case study. *Environment and Behaviour, 25*(2), 181–204.

Spreckelmeyer, K.F. (1995). Places for a work ethic: An appraisal of American workplace design and research. *Journal of Architectural and Planning Research, 12*(2), 104–120.

Stamps, A.E. (1994). All buildings great and small: Design review from high rise to houses. *Environment and Behaviour, 26*(3), 402–420.

Stanley, G. (1990). Rose-coloured spectacles: A cure for dyslexia? *Australian Psychologist, 25*(2), 65–76.

Stansfeld, S.A., Clark, C.R., Jenkins, L.M., & Tarnopolsky, A. (1985). Sensitivity to noise in a community sample. *Psychological Medicine, 15*(2), 243–263.

Stave, A.M. (1977). The effects of cockpit environment on long-term pilot performance. *Human Factors, 19*(5), 503–514.

Steidl, R.E. (1972). Difficult factors in homemaking tasks: Implications for environmental design. *Human Factors, 14,* 472–482.

Steinheider, B., & Winneke, G. (1993). Industrial odours as environmental stressors: Exposure–annoyance associations and their modification by coping, age, and perceived health. *Journal of Environmental Psychology, 13*(4), 353–363.

Stellman, J.M., Klitzman, S., Gordon, G.C., & Snow, B.R. (1987). Work environment and the well-being of clerical and VDT workers. *Journal of Occupational Behaviour, 8*(2), 95–114.

Steptoe, A., & Appels, A. (Eds.) (1989). *Stress, personal control, and health.* Chichester, UK: Wiley.

Stern, P.C. (1986). Blind spots in policy analysis: What economics doesn't say about energy use. *Journal of Policy Analysis Management, 5,* 200–227.

Stern, P.C. (1992). Psychological dimensions of global environmental change. *Annual Review of Psychology, 43,* 269–302.

Stern, P.C., & Oskamp, S. (1987). Managing scarce environmental resources. In D. Stokols & I. Altman (Eds.), *Handbook of environmental psychology.* New York: Wiley.

Stevens, J.C., Bartoshuk. L.M., & Cain. W.S. (1984). Chemical senses and aging: Taste versus smell. *Chemical Senses, 9*(2), 167–179.

Stevens, R. (1984). A note on assumptions of autonomy and determinism in social psychology. In R. Stevens et al. (Eds.), *Metablock: Social sciences: A third level course: Social psychology.* Milton Keynes, UK: Open University Press.

Stires, L. (1980). Classroom seating location, student grades and attitudes: Environment or selection? *Environment and Behaviour, 12*, 241–254.

Stokols, D. (1972). On the distinction between density and crowding: Some implications for future research. *Psychological Review, 79*, 275–277.

Stokols, D. (1978). A typology of crowding experiences. In A. Baum & Y. Epstein (Eds.), *Human response to crowding*. Hillsdale, NJ: Lawrence Erlbaum Associates Inc.

Stokols, D., Novaco, R.W., Stokols, J., & Campbell, J. (1978). Traffic congestion, Type A behaviour and stress. *Journal of Applied Psychology, 63*(4), 467–480.

Stokols, D., & Shumaker, S. (1981). People in place: A transactional view of settings. In J. Harvey (Ed.), *Cognition, social behaviour and the environment*. Hillsdale, NJ: Lawrence Erlbaum Associates Inc.

Stone, N.J., & Irvine, J.M. (1993). Performance, mood, satisfaction, and task type in various work environments: A preliminary study. *Journal of General Psychology, 120*(4), 489–497.

Suedfeld, P. (1980). *Restricted environmental stimulation: Research and clinical applications*. New York: Wiley.

Sundstrom, E., Bell, P.A., Busby, P.L., & Asmus, C. (1996). Environmental psychology, 1989–1994. *Annual Review of Psychology, 47*, 485–512.

Sundstrom, E., Burt, R., & Kamp, D. (1980). Privacy at work: Architectural correlates of job satisfaction and job performance. *Academy of Management Journal, 23*, 101–117.

Sundstrom, E., Herbert, R.K., & Brown, D.W. (1982). Privacy and communnication in an open-plan office. *Environment and Behaviour, 14*, 543–559.

Synnott, A. (1991). A sociology of smell. *Canadian Review of Sociology and Anthropology, 28*(4), 437–459.

Tajfel, H., & Turner, J.C. (1979). An integrative theory of intergroup conflict. In S. Worchel, & W.G. Austin (Eds.), *The social psychology of intergroup relations*. Monterey, CA: Brooks-Cole.

Tajfel, H., & Turner, J.C. (1986). The social identity theory of intergroup behaviour. In S. Worchel & W.G. Austin (Eds.), *Psychology of intergroup relations*. Chicago,IL: Nelson.

Tarnopolsky, A., & Morton-Williams, J. (1980). *Aircraft noise and prevalence of psychiatric disorders*. London Social and Community Planning Research.

Tarnopolsky, A., Watkin, G., & Hand, D.J. (1980). Aircraft noise and mental health: Prevalence of individual symptoms. *Psychological Medicine, 10*, 683–698.

Taylor, S. (1938). Suburban neurosis. *Lancet, 1*, 759–761.

Taylor, S., & Chave, S. (1964). *Mental health and the environment*. London: Longman.

Tchernitchin, A.N., & Tchernitchin, N. (1992). Imprinting of paths of heterodifferentiation by prenatal or neonatal exposure to hormones, pharmaceuticals, pollutants and other agents and conditions. *Medical Science Research, 20*(11), 391–397.

Tedesco, J.F., & Fromme, D.K. (1974). Cooperation, competition and personal space. *Sociometry, 37*, 116–121.

Thellier, F., Cordier, A., & Monchoux, F. (1994). The analysis of thermal comfort requirements through the simulation of an occupied building. *Ergonomics, 37*(5), 817–825.

Thompson, G.O., Raab, G.M., Hepburn, W.S., Hunter, R. (1989). Blood lead levels and children's behaviour: Results from the Edinburgh Lead Study. *Journal of Child Psychology and Psychiatry and Allied Disciplines, 30*(4). 515–528.

Thompson, R.A. (1990). Vulnerability in research: A developmental perspective on research risk. *Child Development, 61*(1), 1–16.

Thompson, T.J., & Gerhardt, D.L. (1985). The limited effects of room colour on the aggressive behaviour of a retarded person during time-out procedures. *International Journal of Biosocial Research, 7*(2), 65–74.

Thurman, Q., Jackson, S., & Zhao, J. (1993). Drunk-driving research and innovation: A factorial survey study of decisions to drink and drive. *Social Science Research, 22*(3), 245–264.

Tickell, N. (1966). Orimulsion. *Wildlife*, May issue.

Tinbergen, N. (1951). *The study of instincts*. Oxford: Oxford University Press.

Topf, M. (1989). Sensitivity to noise, personality hardiness and noise induced stress in critical care nurses. *Environment and Behaviour, 21*(6), 717–733.

Tosca, T.F. (1994). Dreams of light for the city. *Color Research and Applications, 19*(3), 155–170.

Truscott, J.C., Parmelee, P., & Werner, C. (1977). Plate touching in restaurants: Preliminary observations of a food related marking behavior in humans. *Personality and Social Psychology Bulletin, 3*, 425–428.

Turnbull, C. (1961). Some observations regarding the experiences of the Bambuti pygmies. *American Journal of Psychology, 74*, 304–308.

Turner, J.C., Hogg, M.A., Oakes, P.J., Reicher, S.D., & Wethrell, M.S. (1987). *Rediscovering the social group: A self-categorisation theory*. Oxford: Blackwell.

Turrisi, R., & Jaccard, J. (1991). Judgment processes relevant to drunk driving. *Journal of Applied Social Psychology, 21*(2), 89–118.

Valdez, P., & Mehrabian, A. (1994). Effects of colour on emotions. *Journal of Experimental Psychology: General, 124*(4), 394–409.

Van-der-Voordt, D.J.M. (1993). Spatial orientation in nursing homes: A review of the literature. *Tijdschrift voor Gerontologie en Geriatrie, 24*(6), 220–227.

Veitch, R., & Arkkelin, D. (1995). *Environmental psychology: An interdisciplinary perspective*. Englewood Cliffs, NJ: Prentice-Hall.

Velle, W. (1987). Sex differences in sensory functions. *Perspectives in Biology and Medicine, 30*(4), 490–522.

Vinacke, W.E., Mogy, R., Powers, W., Langan, C., & Beck, R. (1974). Accommodative strategy and communication in a three person matrix game. *Journal of Personality and Social Psychology, 29*, 509–525.

Wachs, T.D., Uzgiris, J.C., & McHunt, J. (1971). Cognitive development in infants of different age levels and from different environmental backgrounds. *Merrill-Palmer Quarterly of Behavior Development, 17*, 288–317.

Wagenaar, W.A., Hudson, P.T., & Reason, J.T. (1990). Cognitive failures and accidents: Special issue: Applying cognitive psychology in the 1990s. *Applied Cognitive Psychology, 4*(4), 273–294.

Wagenaar, W.A., & Reason, J.T. (1990). Types and tokens in road accident causation. *Ergonomics, 33*(10–11), 1365–1375.

Walden, T.A., Nelson, P.A., & Smith, D.E. (1981). Crowding, privacy and coping. *Environment and Behaviour, 13*(2), 205–224.

Ward, A. (1993). Resistance or reaction? The cultural politics of design. *Architecture and Comportement: Architecture and Behaviour, 9*(1), 39–67.

Warr, P. (1987). *Work, unemployment and mental health*. Oxford: Clarendon.

Webb, W.M., & Worchel, S. (1993). Prior experience and expectation in the context of crowding. *Journal of Personality and Social Psychology, 65*(3). 512–521.

Wechsler, H., & Pugh, T.F. (1967). Fit of individual and community characteristics and rates of psychiatric hospitalisation. *American Journal of Sociology, 73*, 331–338.

Weinstein, C.S. (1977). Modifying student behaviour in an open classroom through changes in the physical design. *American Education Research Journal, 14*, 249–262.

Weinstein, C.S., & Pinciotti, P. (1988). Changing a schoolyard: Intentions, design decisions and behavioural outcomes. *Environment and Behaviour, 20*(3), 345–371.

Wertheimer, M. (1944). *Productive thinking*. New York: Harper.

Westerberg, U. (1994). Climatic planning: Physics or symbolism? Special issue: Climatic factors in urban design. *Architecture and Comportement: Architecture and Behaviour, 10*(1), 49–71.

Whitehead, C.C., Polsky, R.H., Crookshank, C., & Fik, E. (1984). Objective and subjective evaluation of psychiatric ward redesign. *American Journal of Psychiatry, 141*(5), 639–644.

Wicker, A.W. (1987). Behavioural settings reconsidered: Temporal stages, resources, internal dynamics and context. In D. Stokols & I. Altman (Eds.), *Handbook of Environmental Psychology, Vol.1*. New York: Wiley.

Widmayer, S.M., Petersen, L.M., Larner, M., Carnahan, S. (1990). Predictors of Haitian-American infant development at twelve months. *Child Development, 61*(2), 410–415.

Willmott, P. (1963). *The evolution of a community*. London: Routledge & Kegan Paul.

Wilson, E.O. (1975). *Sociobiology: The new synthesis*, Cambridge, MA: Harvard University Press.

Wilson, S. (1972). Intensive care delirium. *Archive of Internal Medicine, 130*, 225.

Windley, P.G., & Scheidt, R.J. (1982). An ecological model of mental health among small town rural elderly. *Journal of Gerontology, 37*, 235–242.

Winett, R.A., Neale, M.S., & Williams, K. (1982). The effects of flexible work schedules on urban families with young children: Quasi-experimental ecological studies. *American Journal of Community Psychology, 10*(1), 49–64.

Winkel, G.H., & Holahan, C.J. (1986). The environmental psychology of the hospital: Is the cure worse than the illness? Special issue: Beyond the individual: Environmental approaches and prevention. *Prevention in Human Services, 4*(1–2), 11–33.

Winogrond, I.R. (1984). Sensory changes with age: Impact on psychological well-being. *Psychiatric Medicine, 2*(1), 1–26.

Winstanley, M.H., & Woodward, S.D. (1992). Tobacco in Australia: An overview. *Journal of Drug Issues, 22*(3), 733–742.

Winter, F.W. (1974). The effect of purchase characteristics on postdecision product evaluation. *Journal of Marketing Research, 11*(2), 164–171.

Wolfe, M. (1975). Room size, group size, and density: Behaviour patterns in a children's psychiatric facility., *Environment and Behaviour, 7*, 199–225.

Wollin, D.D., & Montagne, M. (1981). College classroom environment: Effects of sterility versus amiability on student and teacher performance. *Environment and Behaviour, 13*, 707–716.

Wright, G. (1947). Terrae Incognitae: The place of imagination in geography. *Annals of the American Association of Geographers, 37*, 1–15.

Wrong, D. (1979). *Power: Its forms, bases and uses*. Oxford: Blackwell.

Wysocki, C.J., & Gilbert, A.N. (1989). National Geographic Smell Survey: Effects of age are heterogeneous. *Annals of the New York Academy of Sciences, 561*, 12–28.

Yamamoto, T. (1984). *Current trends in Japanese psychology*. Paper presented to the annual conference of the American Psychological Association, Toronto.

Yerkes, R.M., & Dodson, J.D. (1908). The relation of strength of stimulus to rapidity of habit-formation. *Journal of Comparative Neurology and Psychology, 18*, 459–482.

Young, M., & Willmott, P. (1957). *Family and kinship in East London*. London: Routledge & Kegan Paul.

Zajonc, R.B. (1965). Social facilitation. *Science, 1429*, 269–274.

Zalesny, M.D., & Farace, R.V. (1988). Job function, sex and environment as correlates of work perceptions and attitudes. *Journal of Applied Social Psychology, 18*(3), 179–202.

Zalesny, M.D., Farace, R.V., & Kurcher-Hawkins, R. (1985). Determinants of employee work perceptions and attitudes: Perceived work environment and organisational level. *Environment and Behaviour, 17*(5), 567–592.

Zamkova, M.A., & Krivitskaya, E.R. (1990). The effect of middle and long wave ultraviolet erythema lamps on visual reception and performance of school-aged children. *International Journal of Biosocial and Medical Research, 12*(2), 125–129.

Zeisel, J. (1981). *Inquiry by design: Tools for environment–behavior research*. Monterey, CA: Brooks-Cole.

Zhang, T., & Pan, K. (1994). Crane drivers' depth perception thresholds. *Psychological Science, China, 17*(2), 93–98.

Zhong, Y., & Gao, D. (1992). An experimental study of ambient odours and memory performance. *Psychological Science, China, 1*, 16–20.

Zillman, D. (1979). *Hostility and aggression*. New York: Halsted Press.

Zimbardo, P.G. (1969). The human choice: Individuation, reason and order versus deindividuation, impulse and chaos. In W.J. Arnold & D. Levine (Eds.), *Nebraska Symposium on Motivation, No.17*. Lincoln, NE: University of Nebraska Press.

Author index

Subject index